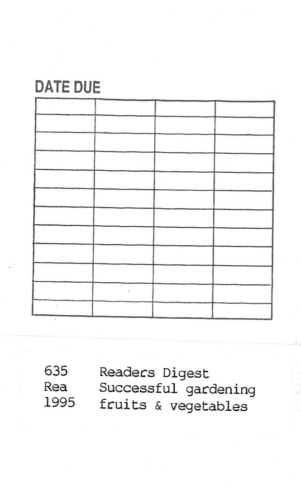

DATE DUE

Staff for Successful Gardening (U.S.A.)
Senior Associate Editor: Theresa Lane

Contributors
Editor: Thomas Christopher
Art Editor: Joan Gramatte, Diane Lemonides
Picture Researcher: James McInnis
Editorial Assistant: Claudia Kaplan
Consulting Editor: Lizzie Boyd (U.K.)
Consultant: Dora Galitzki
Copy Editor: Sue Heinemann
Art Assistant: Andrew Ploski

READER'S DIGEST GENERAL BOOKS
Editor in Chief: John A. Pope, Jr.
General Books Editor, U.S.: Susan Wernert Lewis
Affinity Directors: Will Bradbury, Jim Dwyer,
Kaari Ward
Art Director: Evelyn Bauer
Editorial Director: Jane Polley
Research Director: Laurel A. Gilbride
Group Art Editors: Robert M. Grant, Joel Musler
Copy Chief: Edward W. Atkinson
Picture Editor: Marion Bodine
Head Librarian: Jo Manning

Originally published in partwork form.
Copyright © 1990 Eaglemoss Publications Ltd.

Based on the edition copyright © 1994
The Reader's Digest Association Limited.

Copyright © 1995 The Reader's Digest Association, Inc.
Copyright © 1995 The Reader's Digest Association (Canada) Ltd.
Copyright © 1995 Reader's Digest Association Far East Ltd.
Philippine Copyright 1995 Reader's Digest Association Far East Ltd.

Library of Congress Cataloging in Publication Data

Fruits & vegetables
    p.   cm. — (Successful gardening)
    Includes index.
    ISBN 0-89577-824-6
    1. Vegetable gardening.   2. Fruit-culture.   3. Herb gardening.
4. Vegetables — Pictorial works.   5. Fruit — Pictorial works.
6. Herbs — Pictorial works.   I. Reader's Digest Association.
II. Series.
SB321.F865   1995
    635—dc20   95-12022

Printed in the United States of America

Opposite: Early summer in the vegetable garden arrives with sweet-tasting peas
and the first crop of juicy rhubarb.

Overleaf: A fall harvest that includes strings of firm, sun-ripened onions
more than repays the hours spent in the vegetable garden.

THE READER'S DIGEST ASSOCIATION, INC.
Pleasantville, New York / Montreal

SUCCESSFUL GARDENING

FRUITS
& VEGETABLES

CONTENTS

Orchard Fruits

Garden Fruits

Vegetables

Espalier-grown apples Wall-trained fruit trees are handsome, easy to maintain, and require little space.

Orchard fruits

Few gardeners have space for a fruit orchard, but a garden or yard can yield good crops of a variety of fruits if trees are chosen to suit its particular size and style. Fruit trees occupy the ground for several decades, and their roots and branches spread over a wide area; they cast too much shade to be grown in the vegetable garden. They can be grown as specimen trees near the lawn — even if they only produce blossoms, they are a cheerful sight in spring. If there is room in the garden for only one fruit tree, make sure you choose one of the self-pollinating varieties.

Many fruit trees, apples, pears, and plums for example, are grafted onto particular rootstocks which have predictable effects on the eventual size of the trees and how they will crop. Fruit trees come in different forms, the largest of which is the standard full-size tree; semidwarf and dwarf trees are suitable for more restricted areas. Cordons are the most economical in terms of space; these trees are grown obliquely against a wall and consist of one main stem, with short fruiting side spurs. Fan-trained trees, too, take up little ground space and are an ideal form for apricots and peaches.

Even the small garden can support fruit trees. Consider espaliers — you can train them against walls and fences, and they are attractive when grown as low screens on post and wire supports. Another option is to grow fruit trees grafted onto dwarf rootstock in patio containers. You can also buy family trees, which have been grafted with two, three, or four different varieties of apples or pears and which provide a long cropping season of different flavors and keeping qualities.

Most fruit trees are supplied by nurseries as two- or three-year-olds, with the initial training already completed. In the first few years after planting, establish a framework of main branches through hard pruning to achieve a proper balance between new growth and fruit production. Thereafter, only light pruning is necessary.

There are many cultivars to choose from beyond those included in this book. To help you determine if a particular tree will thrive in your area, we've given you zones that correspond to the plant hardiness map on page 176.

PRUNING FRUIT TREES

**Apples, pears, plums, cherries, and other
fruit trees need regular pruning to achieve a balance
between new growth and fruit production.**

The pruning of a fruit tree is carried out in two stages: training a young tree to the shape required, and regular pruning once the framework is established. The training methods are the same for most trees, such as apples, apricots, cherries, nectarines, peaches, pears, and plums; but after the initial years, the annual pruning varies from fruit to fruit.

One of the main aims of pruning is to regulate the crop and improve its quality on established trees; pruning will vary with a particular tree's growth habit.

Pruning apples and pears

Apple and pear trees are trained and pruned in much the same way, but pears tolerate more severe pruning. Also, pears produce

fruiting spurs more readily; they need thinning in early summer.

The method of pruning depends on the size of the trees. Apple trees may be grafted onto a number of different rootstocks, and the type of rootstock determines the size of the mature tree. Mature fruit trees range in height from 18-22 ft (5.5-6.7 m) or more for standard trees, 12-18 ft (3.7-5.5 m) for semidwarfs, and 4-12 ft (1.2-3.7 m) for dwarfs. Dwarfing rootstocks are best for espaliered trees. Pears are grafted on quince rootstock.

Late-winter pruning encourages growth by directing energy to vegetative buds rather than to flower buds. Pruning in mid- to late summer, however, promotes the formation of fruit spurs.

When pruning a fruit tree, you must be able to distinguish between a flower bud (which will produce a blossom and then fruit) and a vegetative bud (which will produce leaves and can eventually develop into a new shoot). Flower buds are large and round, while vegetative buds are smaller and lie flatter on the stem. Vegetative buds develop into flower buds on tip-bearing cultivars.

Spurs are short stems, often in groups of two or three, on which fruits are formed. A leader (the leading shoot of a branch) must be distinguished from a lateral (a side shoot from a branch or the main stem). You can train a lateral to form a new branch or prune it to develop fruiting spurs.

A tree should not be allowed to bear fruits in the first year after planting, although one or two fruits are permissible. A standard tree on a vigorous rootstock may take five years before it sets fruit.

The time a tree takes to reach its full bearing capacity will depend on the cultivar, rootstock, and method of pruning. Trees on dwarfing and semidwarfing rootstocks begin cropping in either the third or fourth year.

Trees bought from a nursery are usually partly trained and may be up to four years old. To continue a tree's training, find out its age when you buy it.

Training new trees Grow standard trees 20-30 ft (6-9 m) apart, semidwarf trees about 20 ft (6 m) apart, and dwarf trees 10-15 ft (3-4.5 m) apart. If you buy a one-year-old tree, cut the stem back to 1½-2 ft (45-60 cm) high, just above a bud, after planting it in late fall or winter.

The buds or small shoots just below the cut will grow out the

◄ **Pruning apple trees** On established standard trees, light pruning in late winter will ensure good crops of uniform fruits. Try to keep the center of the tree open by removing crossing and crowded branches or by shortening them to form fruiting spurs.

APPLE AND PEAR TREE SHAPES

Apple and pear trees are grafted on various rootstocks, depending on the size of tree desired and the local climatic and soil conditions. For general garden planting, semidwarfing rootstocks are an excellent choice; these trees will start to yield in the third or fourth year after planting. Most apples and pears need another cultivar — one that flowers at the same time — nearby as a pollinator. This need for two trees means that the cultivation of standard trees requires a lot of space. Dwarfs are suitable for smaller gardens and training on walls or fences as espaliers.

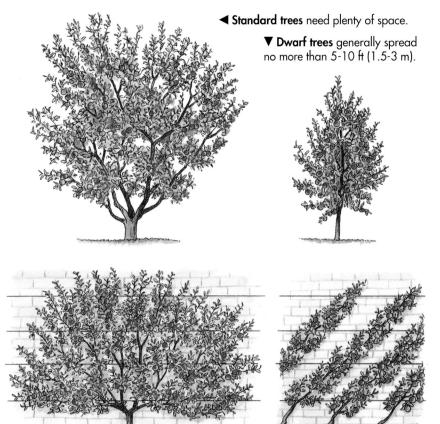

◀ **Standard trees** need plenty of space.

▼ **Dwarf trees** generally spread no more than 5-10 ft (1.5-3 m).

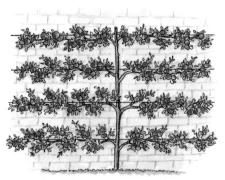

Formal espaliers are trained with an upright main stem and several horizontal tiers tied to strong wire supports.

Informal espaliers are also trained flat against a wall but with a shorter main stem and an irregular fan of branches and shoots.

For espaliered screens, you can train trees as cordons with stems at a 45° angle.

following summer. There may be only three or four, perhaps more. Choose three or four to form the first branches. They should be evenly spaced around the stem, with none pointing toward the supporting stake. Rub off any unwanted buds or young shoots with your thumb.

Though more expensive, it may be easier for the beginner to buy trees that are two to four years old from a nursery and thus avoid the initial training.

Second year Three or four branches will develop during the summer. In winter, cut back each branch of a two-year-old standard tree to an outward-pointing bud. If the branches are vigorous and

thick, cut them back by half. If they are weak and thin, cut them back by two-thirds. Rub off any inward-pointing buds below the cuts with your thumb.

Third year By the third winter a number of lateral shoots will have grown out from the branches. Choose some of these laterals to form, with the first branches, the tree's framework. They should all point outward, and their tips, after pruning, should be at least 1½ ft (45 cm) apart.

Cut all the main branches back to an outward-pointing bud, shortening new laterals on each branch by one-third if the branch is growing vigorously or by half if it is of average growth. If growth

is weak, shorten the new laterals by two-thirds.

Each of the laterals not chosen to form the main branches should be cut back to four buds from the base; these will form future fruiting spurs. Cut off any side shoots emerging from the main stem flush with the stem. After this third year of pruning, the shape of the tree is fully established.

Pruning established trees The subsequent pruning of a free-standing tree is based on whether it is spur bearing or tip bearing.

Spur-bearing cultivars bear their fruits on short spurs; apple cultivars include 'Baldwin,' 'York Imperial,' and 'Wealthy.' Prune these cultivars each winter by the

VEGETATIVE AND FLOWER BUDS ON APPLE AND PEAR TREES

Spurs are short lateral growths, often in twos or threes, on which fruits are produced.

Flower buds are large, plump, and rounded; they first produce blossoms and later fruits.

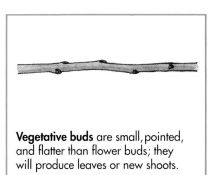

Vegetative buds are small, pointed, and flatter than flower buds; they will produce leaves or new shoots.

PRUNING AN ESTABLISHED SPUR-BEARING APPLE OR PEAR TREE

  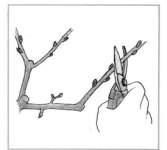 

Branch leaders should be cut back by half of their new growth in winter. Cut back strong ones by one-third and weaker ones by two-thirds.

One-year-old shoots from a main branch bear vegetative buds. Leave these unless they are extension shoots on older laterals in need of shortening.

Two-year-old shoots bear flower buds. Prune by cutting back hard to two flower buds on weak growth; leave more buds on stronger laterals.

Three-year-old shoots have spurs. Prune back to the lowest fruiting spur to encourage new replacements. The cycle of growth then starts again.

SPUR-BEARING TREE

TIP-BEARING TREE

PRUNING AN ESTABLISHED TIP-BEARING APPLE OR PEAR TREE

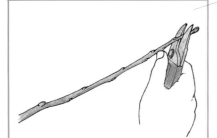 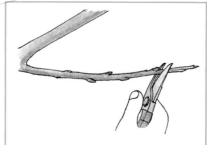 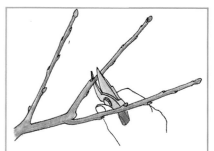

Branch leaders that are crowded require pruning in late winter. Cut the flower bud at the tip back to a lower vegetative bud, forcing new tip-bearing shoots to grow out.

If shoots have no flower buds at the tips, cut them back to just above the highest flower bud. Or prune back to four vegetative buds from the base.

Shoots with flower buds at the tips need no pruning unless they are crowded. To thin out the shoots, prune them back to two flower buds from the base.

PRUNING A NEGLECTED STANDARD APPLE OR PEAR TREE

An apple or pear tree that has been neglected for some years can sometimes be brought back to fruitfulness by a systematic program of pruning, fertilizing, and spraying against pests.

Neglected trees may be overgrown, producing fruits out of reach on lofty branches, or they may be run-down, bearing diminishing crops of undersized fruits. Tall trees can be pruned back gradually over three or four winters. Remove all dead, broken, and diseased branches entirely, as well as high branches from the center, cutting them cleanly back to the main trunk. Prune outer, tall-growing branches back to the lower ones, and thin out small laterals to 1½ ft (45 cm) apart.

Restore run-down trees to vigor by reducing the length of long spur systems in winter. Cut out the weakest spurs; leave the plumpest flower buds, which produce larger fruits. Feed the trees with a fruit tree fertilizer in late winter or early spring.

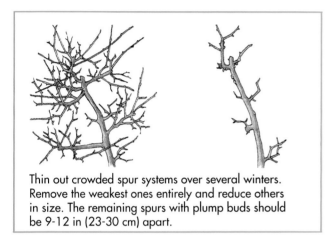

Thin out crowded spur systems over several winters. Remove the weakest ones entirely and reduce others in size. The remaining spurs with plump buds should be 9-12 in (23-30 cm) apart.

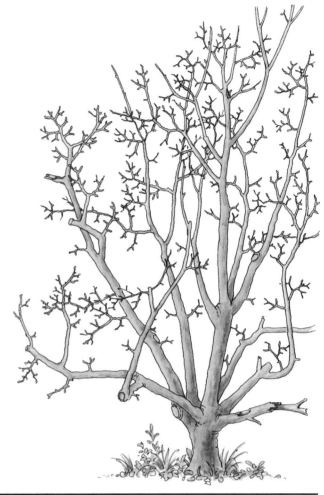

renewal system. This system produces new growth each season to replace old growth that has already borne fruits. It is based on a three-year cycle.

A vegetative bud sends out a shoot in its first summer. In the second summer this shoot produces flower buds. By the third summer the flower buds form spurs and bear fruits then and in following summers.

During its second summer, a shoot not only produces flower buds but also new growth from its tip; a two-year-old shoot has one-year-old extension growth. In the same way, a three-year-old shoot has two-year-old and one-year-old extension growth.

When practicing the renewal system, a number of two-year-old and three-year-old shoots are cut back in winter. This keeps the center of the tree open, allowing good air circulation. It also prevents overcropping and overcrowding, improves fruit quality, and makes way for new growth.

There is no rule governing how many shoots to prune off and how many to leave. Use your own judgment to maintain a balance between new growth and crops. Try to keep the tree from becoming overcrowded with branches, and entirely cut out any crossing branches and wood that is dead or diseased; but allow enough new fruit-bearing shoots to form.

Do not prune one-year-old shoots growing out from a main branch. However, when cutting back two- and three-year-old shoots, you cannot avoid cutting off some of the one-year-old extension growth they bear.

On trees with weak growth, cut selected two-year-old shoots back hard to two flower buds. The weak trees cannot support a big crop of fruits, and this treatment encourages stronger, more compact growth. On stronger trees leave more buds. Cut back selected three-year-old shoots to the lowest fruiting spur. Vegetative buds on the spur produce new shoots the following season, and the cycle of growth starts again.

In the early years, branch leaders should be shortened by one-third if the branch is growing vigorously, by half if it is of average growth, and by two-thirds if it is weak. When the branches are fully grown (8 ft/2.4 m long), prune them in late winter in exactly the same way as laterals.

Tip-bearing cultivars are fewer in number, but they include such common apples as 'McIntosh,' 'Golden Delicious,' and 'Rome Beauty.' They produce some of their flower buds on the tips of the shoots and some on spurs. The cycle of growth is the same as for spur-bearing trees, but many one-year-old shoots produce a flower bud at the tip.

Tip-bearing trees need comparatively little pruning. Once a year, in late winter, prune back shoots without a flower bud at the tip. Cut just above the highest flower bud, if there is one; or cut back to four or five vegetative buds from the base of the shoot.

Shoots that have a flower bud at the tip should not be pruned unless they are crowded — that is, if the tips are less than 1 ft (30 cm) apart. Thin them out by pruning some back to two buds from the base, preferably above a flower bud, if there is one.

Prune branch leaders by removing the flower bud at the tip, cutting back to a vegetative bud

PRUNING A TWO-YEAR-OLD DWARF PLUM

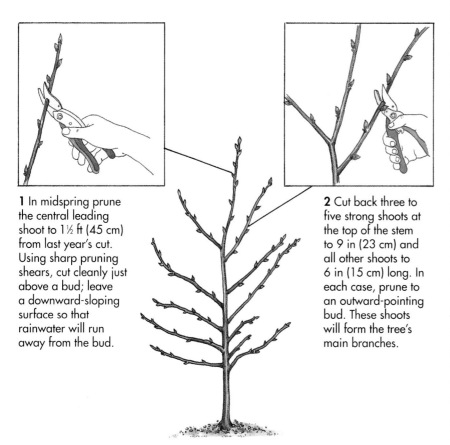

1 In midspring prune the central leading shoot to 1½ ft (45 cm) from last year's cut. Using sharp pruning shears, cut cleanly just above a bud; leave a downward-sloping surface so that rainwater will run away from the bud.

2 Cut back three to five strong shoots at the top of the stem to 9 in (23 cm) and all other shoots to 6 in (15 cm) long. In each case, prune to an outward-pointing bud. These shoots will form the tree's main branches.

PRUNING A THREE-YEAR-OLD DWARF PLUM

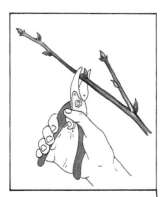

1 In midspring cut back new growth on the branch leaders by half if the leaders are of average vigor, by two-thirds if they are growing weakly, or by one-third if they are strong.

2 Prune back the strongest lateral shoots to 9 in (23 cm) and all others to 6 in (15 cm) long, cutting just above outward-pointing buds.

that is healthy. This induces some of the lower vegetative buds to break and produce more shoots with flower buds at their tips.

Pruning sweet cherries
Sweet cherries are very vigorous. Espaliered trees can span 15-20 ft (4.5-6 m), while standard cherry trees reach up to 30 ft (9 m) high. However, dwarfing rootstocks make it possible to restrict the growth of standard trees to 7 ft (2.1 m) high. Another bonus supplied by these dwarf trees is that they bear fruits several years sooner than standard ones.

Espaliered cherries Cherry trees often grow several competing trunks; you can train them by spreading them outward like the spokes of a fan. For the first three years after planting the young tree, develop this framework by tying shoots into place against the wall. In midspring rub out all the new shoots growing toward or away from the wall; leave the tips of the leading shoots unpruned.

Even after the framework of branches has been established, pruning is light; sweet cherries produce more spurs and fewer laterals than apples.

In early summer snip off any new shoots growing directly toward or away from the wall. Pinch back the tips of the remaining shoots when they have produced five to six leaves in early summer or midsummer.

When the branches reach the top of the wall or support system, cut them back to a weak lateral shoot, or bend the shoots horizontally and tie them in place along the wires. This will slow down growth and encourage new shoots to break.

In late summer cut back the shoots pinched back in early summer to three or four flower buds. Also cut out any deadwood.

On older trees, where room is available, tie new shoots into the fan shape in early summer or midsummer. Some may be needed to replace old shoots.

Freestanding cherry trees
Prune trees lightly in spring just before the bud-break stage. Once the tree has started to fruit (in the second or third year after planting), thin it to let in light and air. Cut back older shoots to just above one-year-old laterals. Thin the outer spread occasionally, where new growth develops.

PRUNING AN ESTABLISHED PYRAMID PLUM

1 In midsummer cut back the central leader of a pyramid-trained plum tree to a 9 ft (2.7 m) high lateral branch. Plum trees are quite vigorous growers and generally reach this height after about six years under good conditions.

2 Using finger and thumb, pinch back vigorous new side shoots to six or seven leaves each — the stems are very soft, so there is no need to use pruning shears. Take care not to damage the bud lying in the axil of the last remaining leaf.

Pruning sour cherries

As with sweet cherries, you can grow sour ("pie") cherries either as freestanding trees or as fans. Fan-trained sour cherries will grow against any wall, even a north-facing one.

Prune fan-trained sour cherries in the same way as fan peaches (see pp.14-15) in early spring. Sour cherries fruit on spurs borne the previous summer. Thin out the branches on established freestanding trees as for sweet cherries, cutting out nonproducing shoots to one-year-old laterals; leave those over three years old.

Pruning plums

Plum trees are classified as American plums, European plums, Japanese plums, and Japanese-American hybrids. The most popular types are European plums, such as 'Italian Prune' and 'Stanley.' Japanese cultivars are less winter hardy, but include 'Santa Rosa' and 'Shiro'; both are popular on the Pacific Coast.

European plums are upright trees that are often grown as semidwarfs in a pyramid shape; they reach a height of 9 ft (2.7 m) and spread to 8-10 ft (2.4-3 m).

Japanese plums, by contrast, are naturally open, spreading trees that are best trained to an open center. As with tip-bearing apple trees or peaches, several main limbs (or "scaffold branches") are developed that radiate outward from a short trunk.

Pyramid training To train a young semidwarf European plum into a pyramid shape, in midspring cut back the stem to 5 ft (1.5 m) above ground during the first season after planting; make the cut at an angle just above a bud. Cut off flush with the stem young branches that are lower than 1½ ft (45 cm) above ground.

If a newly planted tree is less than 5 ft (1.5 m) high, allow it to continue growing for at least another year before training it.

On a two-year-old plum tree, cut back the central leader in midspring to about 1½ ft (45 cm) from last year's cut. Again, make the cut just above a bud.

Cut back three to five of the strongest side shoots at the top of

MAINTAINING AN ESPALIERED PLUM

1 At the beginning of midsummer, pinch back the tips of all side shoots that are not needed as branches as soon as they have produced six or seven leaves.

Prevent shoots from growing toward or away from the wall by rubbing off the offending buds before they begin to develop in spring.

2 At the end of summer, after the crop of plums has been harvested, shorten by half those shoots that were pinched back earlier in the season.

ESTABLISHING A FAN-TRAINED PEACH

1 In late winter, before growth begins, cut back both side branches to 1-1½ ft (30-45 cm); make each slanting cut just | above a vegetative bud. Secure stakes to wires at 40°, then tie the branches to the stakes. (To secure wires, see p.35.)

2 During the summer after planting, tie in the shoots that have grown from each bud. Allow two well-spaced shoots to | grow upward from each branch and one from the lower side. Tie these to stakes and rub off any other buds.

side shoots to six or seven leaves from the parent stem.

Thin out overcrowded branches as necessary, cutting flush with the parent stem. Also cut away any deadwood. If branch leaders grow exceptionally long, cut them back to a strong main lateral shoot. Keep branches at a maximum length of 4-5 ft (1.2-1.5 m).

Espaliered plums are treated like fan-trained peaches (see facing page) until the third year from planting; delay pruning until early spring when growth begins. Unlike peaches, plums fruit on both old wood and on shoots produced the previous season.

After the third summer, when the framework is built up, rub off all buds pointing toward or away from the wall as soon as growth starts in spring. At the beginning of midsummer, when side shoots not needed as branches grow six leaves, pinch off their tips.

After the crop has been picked, shorten by half those shoots that were pinched back. Do not let any shoots grow strongly upward; they can rob lower branches of nourishment. If a shoot is needed to fill a space or replace an old branch, tie it to a support wire.

Cut out any unwanted shoots flush with the wood from which they sprout. Also remove any diseased, damaged, or dead wood.

Reclaim a neglected plum tree in the same way as a neglected apple, but work on it in summer.

Pruning apricots
Train espaliered and freestanding apricot trees like apples until the framework is built up, but prune in early spring as growth begins. Then prune espaliered apricots like plums and freestanding apricots like sour cherries.

Pruning peaches/nectarines
Cold-sensitive peach and nectarine trees may die if the temperature drops to -20°F (-29°C); even a drop to -10°F (-23°C) can kill flower buds, thus reducing the crop. Peaches are best adapted to temperate regions, such as the Atlantic Coast states from Florida to Massachusetts, the area south and east of the Great Lakes, and the Pacific Coast states. At the northern edge of their range, peaches and nectarines fruit best if grown as fan-trained espaliers against a sunny south- or southwest-facing wall.

the stem to 9 in (23 cm); prune to outward-pointing buds. Let these shoots grow on to form the first main branches. Cut back other side shoots to 6 in (15 cm). Lower growth tends to be weak; cut it back hard to prompt even growth.

From the third year onward, until the plum tree reaches full height, cut back the central leader in midspring to about 1½ ft (45 cm) above last year's cut. Cut back the branch leaders according to their vigor — by one-third of new growth if they are of average vigor or by two-thirds if weak.

Cut back the strongest laterals from the main branches to 9 in (23 cm) long and the remainder to 6 in (15 cm) long. Make the cut above an outward-pointing bud.

When a plum tree reaches 9 ft (2.7 m), in about six years, keep it at this height by cutting back the central leader to a strong lateral in summer. You may need to do this every second or third year, depending on the rate of growth.

The amount of pruning required by plum trees usually decreases with age. If a mature tree is fruiting regularly, prune as little as possible; fruits are borne on the previous season's shoots as well as on spurs on old wood. Merely pinch back vigorous new

Fan-trained peaches/nectarines are pruned in early spring. They grow side shoots off the current year's growth; pinch these side shoots off one bud from the base.

From the fourth spring after planting a year-old tree, when it has 24 to 32 rib branches, pruning is dictated by the tree's growth habit, as peaches and nectarines fruit on last year's shoots.

When growth starts in the fourth spring, rub or pinch off any buds or shoots that point toward or away from the wall. Then from the remaining buds, select only the good ones on each side of a rib spaced at about 6 in (15 cm) intervals, and rub off all others except the bud at the tip.

During the fourth summer these buds will produce laterals that will fruit the following summer, and the bud at the tip will grow on as a rib leader.

In the fifth spring at least two vegetative buds will emerge at the base of last year's laterals. Allow one to grow on as a replacement; remove any others when they are 2-3 in (5-7.5 cm) long.

Let the tips of fruit-bearing laterals grow on in order to draw the sap and help develop the fruits. If space is limited, pinch them back to four leaves when they have borne six leaves. Pinch off any side shoots that grow from them.

In fall or early winter, after picking the fruits, cut back each lateral that has borne fruits to its replacement, and tie in the replacement with soft string.

Repeat this process of disbudding, pinching back, cutting out old shoots, and tying in replacements every year.

Free-standing peach trees are pruned in late spring. On year-old trees cut back the central leader to 2 ft (60 cm) above the ground.

Leave the top three or four buds or side shoots below the cut to form the scaffold branches. Remove the side shoots lower down.

In the following years remove any crossing branches, cutting flush with the parent branch.

Remove any shoots from the main trunk below the lowest branch, flush with the trunk. Peaches are prone to dieback, so cut back any branch that is dying at the tip to a healthy side shoot.

On established trees cut out branches drooping to the ground, and cut older branches as their fruit-bearing capacity diminishes.

PRUNING A MATURE FAN-TRAINED PEACH

1 In midspring pinch back vegetative buds on last year's laterals (those with flowers) to one leaf, leaving one bud to provide a replacement shoot.

2 In late spring thin out new laterals on the upper and lower sides of the rib branches to 6 in (15 cm) apart. These will fruit the following year.

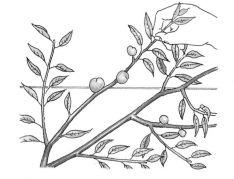

3 Also in late spring, if space is limited, pinch back fruit-bearing laterals to four leaves, unless they are needed as replacement shoots.

4 After harvesting cut out fruited laterals to the replacement shoots, unless they are needed as part of the framework. Tie in the replacements.

APPLES

**No supermarket apple can match the flavor
of homegrown fruits. Fortunately, there are cultivars adapted
to almost every garden and every taste.**

Apple trees are grafted onto rootstocks of varying performance, ranging from vigorous types for standard and semidwarf trees to dwarfing rootstocks, which produce compact trees that are suitable for the small garden or for espaliering. A tree's height and spread depend on the rootstock, the cultivar, and the type of soil. Standards — trees grafted onto seedling rootstocks that grow to a height of 18 ft (5.5 m) or more — are often too big for the average garden. Their size makes standards difficult to maintain and harvest, too.

Semidwarf trees reach a mature height and spread of 12-18 ft (3.7-5.5 m); they are good choices for gardens with plenty of space. They carry heavy yields; one well-grown tree can produce 80-100 lb (36-45 kg) of fruits annually.

If space is restricted, dwarf trees, planted 10-15 ft (3-4.5 m) apart, are better choices. They are especially compact if grown as espaliers. The yields from espaliered trees are smaller than those from freestanding ones, and espaliers require more attention.

If space is really limited, you may choose to grow a family tree; on this tree the nursery has grafted branches of several apple cultivars. These different branches will bloom simultaneously, but because the fruits are different, they will ripen at different times.

Apples are often divided into cooking and eating (or dessert) apples, but there is no real distinction. While some cultivars are used mainly for cooking, they can be enjoyed for their tart flavor if eaten raw. Similarly, some dessert apples can be used for cooking.

The first apples are ready for picking and eating in late summer. With careful storage of late-maturing fruits, you can enjoy homegrown apples until the end of the following spring.

Pollination

Most apple trees cannot pollinate themselves, so it is necessary to plant at least two cultivars that blossom at the same time for cross-pollination to take place. Catalogs often indicate whether specific apple cultivars bloom in early, middle, or late spring; if in doubt, ask your nursery if two cultivars will cross-pollinate successfully. Don't hesitate to call a mail-order nursery to make sure your choices are compatible before sending in an order. A few

▲ **Apple harvest** Established and well-tended trees yield heavy crops of dessert or cooking apples for up to 50 years.

cultivars, such as 'Baldwin,' 'Jonagold,' and 'Winesap,' are such poor pollinators that a third cultivar must be planted together with them and their mates if all the trees are to bear fruits.

Site and soil

Apples may be grown throughout the United States, except in the warmest regions, such as the Deep South and Southern California. The introduction of "low chill" cultivars, such as 'Anna' and 'Golden Dorsett,' is making apple growing possible even in the cooler parts of zone 9.

Consult your nursery or Cooperative Extension Service to select cultivars adapted to your soil and climate. An open, sunny, but sheltered site is best. Most soils, except those that are waterlogged or strongly alkaline, are suitable. Well-drained, moisture-retentive, slightly acid soil is the ideal.

In early fall to midfall, mix well-rotted manure or compost into the soil at the rate of a bucketful per sq yd/m. Apply 3 oz per sq yd (75 g per sq m) of a general fertilizer before planting.

Buying apple trees

Nurseries and garden centers offer one-, two-, or three-year-old trees. One-year-old apple trees are cheaper than older trees because they require training and pruning. But two- or three-year-

PLANTING

▲ Dig a hole large enough to hold the roots of the tree when they are well spread out. Drive in a stake and plant the tree close to it with the graft union 4 in (10 cm) above soil level.

old trees, while a little more costly, may be better buys; the nursery has done the initial pruning, and the trees bear fruits sooner.

Planting an apple tree

The best time for planting is during frost-free weather in late fall or in early spring.

If you have a bare-root tree, dig a hole big enough to take the roots of the tree when they are well spread out. Drive a supporting stake into the bottom of the hole and plant the tree against it. For a balled-and-burlapped tree, dig the hole equal in depth to the root ball and five times as wide; drive two stakes into the ground on opposite sides of the hole and guy them to the tree. For either type of tree, keep the graft union, where the rootstock and the scion (the grafted branch) join, at least 4 in (10 cm) above soil level.

To train cordons, espaliers, and fans, secure horizontal wires at 1 ft (30 cm) intervals along a wall. When planting trees against a wall for espaliering, set them 9 in (23 cm) away from the wall. Plant cordons 2½-3 ft (75-90 cm) apart, formal espaliers and fans 12 ft (3.7 m) apart. To grow espaliers as freestanding screens, make a supporting framework of sturdy posts and wires before planting.

Looking after the trees

Until the trees are established, water them during dry spells. In spring mulch them with manure or garden compost to help the soil retain moisture.

In late winter, the first year after planting, start an annual feeding routine. Perform a soil test (available through your Cooperative Extension Service) to set up the routine. It will usually call for the application of ¼ lb (115 g) of actual nitrogen per tree per year. In other words, if you apply the fertilizer calcium nitrate, which is 15 percent nitrogen (indicated by the first of the three numbers on its label; in this case, 15-0-0), you must apply 1⅔ lbs (750 g) of the fertilizer to give the tree the ¼ lb (115 g) of nitrogen it needs.

Reduce weeds by shallow hoeing or hand weeding. For training and pruning trees, see pages 8-12.

Apple trees are hosts to a number of pests and diseases. Control them with a spraying program based on the stage of flower bud development (see below) and with regular winter applications of horticultural oil to kill aphids, scale insects, and spider mites.

Thinning the crop

A heavy crop puts a strain on a tree, leading to poor-quality fruits. Thin the fruits in early summer to ensure that the remaining apples grow to full size.

Heavy thinning is rarely needed on espaliers and dwarf trees. On semidwarf or standard trees, the fruits will require space.

Start thinning the crop in early summer; remove badly shaped or damaged fruits and the central apple of each cluster. Use scissors to cut the stalk; or holding it with two fingers, press the apple away with your thumb. Never pull the fruit off; this damages the spur (a short, fruit-bearing side branch).

By midsummer there is a natural drop of fruits. If there is still a plentiful crop afterward, thin again to leave one apple on each spur for espaliered trees. On free-standing trees, the fruits should be 4-6 in (10-15 cm) apart or even more for large-fruited cultivars.

Harvesting

Early apples are ready for picking from late summer to early fall. Eat them right away because they won't keep. Pick midseason and

SPRAYING PROGRAM

1 Spray at bud burst and green cluster with dimethoate for aphids and with benomyl or thiophanate-methyl for scab.

2 Spray at pink bud stage with benomyl for scab and mildew and with permethrin for sawflies, aphids, and caterpillars.

3 From 80 percent petal fall, spray every two weeks with benomyl. Use permethrin for woolly aphids and sawflies.

4 Spray with phosmet or permethrin for codling moth in early summer and again three weeks later.

late cultivars as they ripen or even slightly before and let them ripen in storage. Apples are ready to pick when, with a gentle twist, they part easily from the spurs.

For reaching fruits high on a standard tree, use an apple picker (a net on a long pole). Push the frame of the net against the stalk, and if the apple is ready, it will drop into the net. Handle apples with care, as they bruise easily.

Place the apples in a cool, well-ventilated room or shed for a couple of days. Then sort them out for storing, putting any that are even slightly damaged (without a stalk, for instance) or diseased to one side for immediate use.

Storing

Store midseason cultivars separately from late cultivars. They are ready for eating at different times: midseason cultivars from midfall to early winter and late cultivars from midwinter to midspring. If stored together, the gases given off by early apples can hasten the ripening of later ones.

To store apples, wrap them in pieces of waxed paper or newspaper (to keep them dry and prevent them from touching each other). Wrap them loosely; don't make an airtight seal. Place two or three layers of wrapped apples in a well-ventilated box, and store in a dark, cool place.

You can keep apples in plastic bags, but make small punctures in the bag to let gases given off by the apples escape.

In cool climates wrap apples in waxed paper, store in a plastic trash can with a loose-fitting lid, and set in a cool but frost-free location, such as a basement.

Pests and diseases

Common pests of apples are aphids, codling moths, apple tree borers, apple maggots, plum curculios, green fruitworms, red spider mites, and woolly aphids. Use traps, biological controls, and recommended pesticides as needed.

The main diseases are fire blight, apple canker, powdery mildew, cedar-apple rust, and scab. Good cultural practices and correct pruning are essential.

▶ **Thinning apples** By reducing the number of apples from each spur, you help the remainder grow to uniform size. Heavy crops put a strain on fruit trees.

THINNING

◀ In early summer remove badly shaped and damaged fruits and the central apple of each cluster, using scissors. After the natural drop by mid-summer, thin the apples to one per spur.

HARVESTING

▶ Pick early apples from late summer to early fall. Pick midseason and late cultivars in early fall to midfall. Holding the apple in the palm of your hand, lift and twist simultaneously. If the apple is ready for picking, it will come away easily.

CULTIVARS TO CHOOSE

Cultivars in the same pollination group (A, B, C) blossom at the same time — which is essential for cross-pollination. Cultivars are grouped according to harvest time.

Early

'Gravenstein': dessert and cooking apples; red-and-yellow fruits; sweet, tart flavor; do not store well; A.

'Jersey Mac': dessert apples; red fruits; crisp, sweet, juicy flesh; do not store well; A.

'Prima': good dessert and cooking apples; red-and-yellow fruits; scab resistant; B.

Midseason

'Cortland': dessert and cooking apples; green-streaked red fruits; tart, juicy, flesh; store until late winter; moderately cold-hardy tree; B.

'Gala': dessert and cooking apples; red-stippled yellow fruits; crisp flesh, sweet flavor; scab resistant; B.

'Macoun': dessert and cooking apples; red fruits; juicy flesh; C.

'McIntosh': cooking apples; yellow-streaked red fruits; crisp, tender flesh, moderately acid flavor; do not store well; cold-hardy tree; A.

Late

'Golden Delicious': dessert apples; crisp, sweet, juicy fruits; eat early winter to spring; C.

'Idared': dessert and cooking apples; crisp, juicy, red fruits; eat early winter to midspring; A.

'Liberty': dessert and cooking apples; red-and-yellow fruits; crisp, juicy; resists cedar-apple rust, powdery mildew, scab; store well; A.

'Mutsu': dessert apples; yellow-and-orange fruits; sweet, juicy, crisp flesh and hint of acidity; store well; moderately cold-hardy tree; B.

'Spigold': dessert and cooking apples; crisp flesh; store well; C.

Low chill (for southern regions)

'Braeburn': dessert and cooking apples; sweet and tart, crisp flesh; ripen early fall to midfall.

'Granny Smith': dessert and cooking apples; green fruits; sweet and tart flesh; store well; ripen midfall.

Apple 'Cortland'

Apple 'Mutsu'

Apple 'Braeburn'

APRICOTS

**An unusually versatile tree, the apricot bears
well in regions too warm for most apples and yet is also
winter hardy, producing good crops into zone 5.**

Delicious home-grown apricots surpass the ones found in stores. While apricot trees are suited to the temperate but almost frost-free parts of the Pacific Coast, they can survive temperatures as cold as -20°F (-29°C). The flower buds are susceptible to winter winds and in the North they are vulnerable to late frosts. If you grow apricots in the North, set them in a spot sheltered from the wind on the north side of a house; hopefully, a shaded site will delay the opening of the flowers until after the last frost.

Apricot 'Moorpark'

Cultivation

Apricots need a well-drained, moisture-retentive, and neutral loam. If the soil is heavy, plant the trees high, setting the tops of their root balls slightly higher

▼ **Fan-trained apricot** Given sun, shelter, and hand pollination, a fan-trained apricot tree will produce a reasonable harvest into zone 5.

than the adjacent ground level; mound the surrounding soil so that the graft union will be 1-2 in (2.5-5 cm) above ground level. Mix the soil used to refill the hole with half as much again of bulky organic matter and coarse builder's sand.

Buy two- or three-year-old trees; they will begin fruiting at four years old. Choose cultivars that are naturally dwarf, such as 'Stark Golden Glo,' or hybrids that have been grafted onto a dwarfing rootstock such as 'Pixy.'

PLANTING

A layer of rubble at the base of the planting hole can benefit trees in less than perfectly drained soil. Plant trees up on a mound if the soil is truly heavy.

Apricot 'Goldbar'

Although these trees are compact, they are productive. Make sure that the rootstock is appropriate to your climate; 'Pixy,' for example, is sensitive to drought and thus is a poor choice for the Southwest. Most apricots are self-fertile, but their fruits set better when they are cross-pollinated by another cultivar.

Plant in late fall in areas with mild winters and in early spring elsewhere. Set the tree to the same depth as the soil mark on the stem and, for an espaliered tree, 6 in (15 cm) away from the wall or fence. Mulch with compost, and water in well. Keep the ground clear of weeds.

A soil test will determine the apricot's need for fertilizer. Generally, ¼ lb (115 g) of actual nitrogen per tree (see p.17) applied in late winter or early spring is good; in regions where the soil is deficient in phosphorus or potassium, you should use a fertilizer that includes those nutrients too. Spread the fertilizer as a top-dressing over the entire rooting area, which is equivalent to the spread of the branches.

When the flowers open fully, use a camel-hair brush to transfer pollen from one flower to another to ensure fruits will set.

In mid- to late spring thin the small fruits to 4 in (10 cm) apart; this helps the remaining fruits to develop. If thinning is neglected, some trees may become biennial bearing, yielding fruits only every other year. Water the tree in dry spells to ensure that the swelling of the fruits is not checked.

CULTIVARS TO CHOOSE

'Alfred': juicy fruits ripen mid- to late summer; cold hardy.

'Farmingdale': moderate vigor; somewhat resistant to dieback; fruits ripen in midsummer.

'Goldbar': very large yellow to orange fruits; vigorous tree, crops light; adapted to Pacific Coast.

'Goldcot': good harvest; cold hardy; adapted to Northeast and Great Lakes region.

'Moorpark': old favorite; good harvest; large fruits ripen in late summer; adapted to South.

'Tomcot': vigorous tree; blooms early; adapted to Pacific Coast.

Espaliering

Where late frost or winter cold is a problem, plant apricots against a warm, south-facing wall.

Before planting, attach horizontal wood supports or training wires securely to the wall or fence at 9 in (23 cm) intervals.

After planting the tree, tie in the young branches in a fan shape to stakes secured to the supports. For a three-year-old tree, tie in four leading branches on each side of the main trunk. In late winter shorten each leader by one-third; prune to a downward-pointing bud with 1½ ft (45 cm) of stem remaining.

In mid- or late summer tie in three extra shoots from each pruned leader to stakes fixed on the supports, training them to face outward to fill the space on the wall. Pinch off remaining shoots. Allow these laterals to grow to 1½ ft (45 cm), then pinch off the growing point; they will bear fruits the following summer.

The following spring rub off any buds pointing toward or away from the wall; prune the leaders by one-quarter. Early in midsummer pinch off the tips of side shoots six leaves from the base. After cropping, cut back these laterals by half.

Apricots carry the best fruits on short spurs on two- and three-year-old wood. Every four to six years cut out old shoots that have fruited. You will need to cut back some lateral fan-trained branches. Tie in replacement shoots, and don't cut them back until the second season.

Ripe apricots have a good color and part easily from the spurs. Depending on the cultivar, they are ready for harvesting from mid- to late summer. They will keep for up to a month if stored in a cool, well-ventilated place.

Pests and diseases

The major pests are aphids, peach tree borers, and red spider mites; spray with a recommended insecticide. Diseases include brown rot and cytospora canker; prune off affected shoots.

CHERRIES

Cherry trees bear beautiful spring flowers and juicy sweet or sour fruits in summer. Grow them as freestanding trees or espaliered against a wall.

There are two basic kinds of cherries: sour, or "pie," cherries are used for cooking, canning, and making preserves; delectable sweet cherries are eaten fresh as a dessert fruit.

Both kinds of cherry require very deep, preferably alkaline, well-drained soil, although sour cherries will thrive on less fertile soil than sweet cherries do. Sour and sweet cherries are usually ready for harvesting from mid- to late June, although this will often vary somewhat, depending on the local climate.

Birds are delighted to devour ripe sweet cherries and will even occasionally eat sour cherries. To ensure that you have fruits to harvest for yourself, drape the cherry trees with netting (which is obtainable at most garden centers) as the fruits start to ripen.

Sour cherries can be grown as freestanding trees or espaliers. They are naturally less vigorous than sweet cherries. As each tree is self-fertile, only a single tree is needed, although the fruit crops are better if a second tree of a different cultivar is grown nearby. A sour cherry cultivar will pollinate a sweet cherry cultivar if the two trees' seasons of bloom overlap — but often they miss each other.

Sweet cherries are very vigorous and, as standard trees, can grow up to 30 ft (9 m) high or more. However, the appearance of dwarfing rootstocks, such as 'Colt' and 'GM-61,' has made the backyard cultivation of sweet cherries more practical, especially when the tree's natural vigor is further contained by espaliering.

Older cultivars of sweet cherries require cross-pollination, and at least two cultivars must be grown for pollination to take place. It takes several years for newly planted trees to fruit.

Some of the newer sweet cherry cultivars, such as 'Lapins' and 'Stella,' are self-fertile and do not need a pollinating partner. When grafted onto dwarfing rootstocks, they often begin bearing fruits in the second year after planting.

Sweet cherry

Planting a cherry tree
A fan-trained tree grown against a wall will reach a span of 15-20 ft (4.5-6 m), unless grafted onto a dwarfing rootstock, in which case the spread may reach as little as 6-8 ft (1.8-2.4 m). In either case, set trees far enough apart so that their branches and roots don't crowd each other; an interval of 20-25 ft (6-7.5 m) will work for standard trees. Make sure you consult the nursery about a cultivar's need for cross-pollination to ensure that you plant it with a compatible cultivar.

Plant in early spring, and stake new trees in the same way as apple trees (see p.17).

Cultivation
Use a soil test (available through your county Cooperative Extension Service) to establish a fertilizer program. In general, cherries benefit from a program similar to that of other fruit trees: $\frac{1}{4}$ lb (115 g) actual nitrogen applied over the spread of the roots in early spring (see p.17). Feeding with phosphorus and potassium may also be indicated by the soil test. Follow the fertilization by covering the root area with a mulch of well-rotted manure or garden compost. Water cherries deeply during dry spells.

Pruning cherries
In the first spring after planting sweet cherry trees grown on dwarfing rootstock, select three

Sour cherry 'Morello'

▲ **Sweet and sour cherries** Birds are the greatest threat to cherry crops, sweet cherries being the favored fruit. Protect both espaliered and freestanding trees by draping them with plastic netting.

or four well-spaced side shoots for the framework. Use spring-type clothespins to spread these young branches outward from the trunk to an angle of at least 45°; wedge a clothespin down into the valley between the leader and the branch, clipping the clothespin's jaws around the leader to hold it in place. Then cut the framework branches (these are also called scaffold branches) back by half to outward-facing buds. By the following spring there should be between six and nine well-spaced laterals. Prune these laterals lightly; you can leave them unpruned if there is enough room. Cut out upright sublaterals in the center, and cut any sublaterals that compete with the main laterals back to three buds.

When training young sour cherry trees, do not head back the central leader, as this may stunt growth. Allow side branches to develop in a spiral of four or five scaffold branches radiating out from the trunk. Leave one branch every 6 in (15 cm), with the lowest one about 2½ ft (75 cm) above the ground. After the scaffold branches are established, you can cut the central leader back to an outward-growing lateral. Take care not to prune the young tree more than is necessary; too much pruning can delay fruiting for several years.

Espaliered cherry trees are usually trained to a fan shape; training for these trees is similar to that recommended for peach trees (see pp.12-13 and p.14).

Harvesting and storing
Use scissors to cut off the fruit clusters of cherries. Avoid pulling on the cherries, because this can wound their spurs, allowing diseases to enter the fruits. Sweet cherries do not store well; they are best eaten soon after harvesting. However, sour cherries can be frozen, made into preserves, or used in wines.

Pests and diseases
Apart from birds, the pests likely to attack cherries are aphids and cherry fruit flies; spray with a recommended insecticide if necessary. The more troublesome diseases are bacterial canker, black knot, brown rot, and fungal leaf spot. These diseases are more likely to occur on neglected and badly pruned trees.

PRUNING FAN-TRAINED SWEET CHERRIES

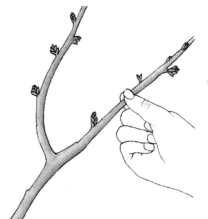

1 In midspring rub off with your finger and thumb any side shoots that grow toward or away from the wall; leave the leading shoots to grow on unpruned.

2 Within a few weeks, when the remaining shoots have five or six leaves, carefully pinch off the growing tips of all laterals other than branch leaders.

3 When leaders reach the top of the wall, prune them back close to a side shoot, or bend them over horizontally and fasten them to the top wire.

4 In late summer cut back shoots that were pinched back earlier; reduce them to three or four fruit buds. Also cut away dead, damaged, or diseased shoots.

CULTIVARS TO CHOOSE

Sour cherries

'Meteor': fruits with light red flesh; ripen just after 'Montmorency'; very cold hardy.

'Montmorency': red-skin fruits with yellow flesh; late June to late July.

'Morello': bittersweet, dark red fruits; late summer to early fall.

'North Star': a naturally dwarf tree; late-ripening red-fleshed fruits; exceptionally cold hardy.

Sweet cherries

'Bing': large fruits; almost black when ripe; firm, juicy, and sweet.

'Hedelfingen': dark red fruits; good pollinator; moderately cold hardy.

'Lambert': heart-shaped dark red fruits; flavorful; late blooming, so may escape late frosts.

'Lapins': large dark red fruits with rich flavor; self-fertile cultivar; high yields, resistant to skin splitting; late summer.

'Rainier': yellow fruits with red blush; early bearing, very productive tree; cold hardy.

'Stella': large dark red fruits, almost black; good pollinator for other sweet cherries; self-fertile; excellent cropper; midsummer.

'Van': fruits resemble that of 'Bing'; excellent pollinator; high yields; exceptionally cold hardy.

CITRUS FRUITS

**Easy to grow, productive, and offering a wide range
of flavors, citrus trees provide one of the most rewarding crops
for warm-weather gardeners.**

A symbol of the sunny South, citrus fruits grow best in regions with consistent heat and brilliant sunshine. Indeed, in the warmest and driest parts of the United States, the members of this family — lemons, oranges, grapefruits, and others — are almost the only practical fruits to cultivate in home gardens. Because they are outstandingly productive and the quality of their fruits is so good, citrus trees are also well worth growing in areas of humid warmth, such as southern Florida, where the full range of tropical fruits may be grown.

Citrus trees are grafted onto a variety of rootstocks. Depending on the types of rootstock, citrus trees range in size from dwarfs just 5 ft (1.5 m) tall to standards that grow up to 22 ft (6.7 m) high. A single standard tree will produce all the lemons, oranges, or grapefruits that the average family can eat.

Citrus for cold hardiness

The most familiar citrus fruits, such as grapefruits and oranges, thrive only in virtually frost-free regions, which can be found in the hardy zones 9-11 (see p.176). There are, however, a number of related fruits that flourish in the warmer parts of zone 8.

In general, the least cold-hardy citrus trees are limes, whose foliage is often damaged if the temperature drops below 32°F (0°C), and grapefruits, which bear fruits satisfactorily only in the warmest regions. Oranges are hardier, particularly when grafted onto trifoliate orange rootstock. In this situation, hardier cultivars, such as the blood orange 'Moro,' will usually weather temperatures of 25°F (-4°C) without harm.

Even hardier are some of the less familiar citrus fruits. The kumquat *(Fortunella),* which may be recognized by those who have enjoyed Chinese cuisine, bears small, tart orange fruits. The calamondin (× *Citrofortunella mitis)* bears fruits that resemble small tangerines, but they are

▲ **Citrus tree** With proper care, this tree will produce plenty of refreshingly tart lemons — enough to have your fill of fresh lemonade and lemon custard pie.

tarter in flavor. Both of these fruits are hardy to 18°F (-8°C).

Hardiest of all is the trifoliate orange *(Poncirus trifoliata),* which will grow as far north as zone 6. This is often grown purely as an ornamental shrub or tree, but the sour yellow fruits, 1½ in (3.75 cm) in diameter, can be used as a substitute for lemons or made into a marmalade.

Citrus for dry or wet climates

Another issue that gardeners must consider before selecting citrus trees for their plots is the humidity in their climate. In general, the dry air and cooler nights of Southern California and the desert Southwest produce strongly colored, thick-skinned fruits high in both sugar and acidity; whereas the eastern regions, such as Florida and the Gulf Coast, produce thin-skinned fruits that are paler and sweeter than their western counterparts.

Lemons and limes, fruits valued for their tartness, taste better when grown in the Southwest. By contrast, such naturally acidic fruits as grapefruits and tangelos benefit from the extra sweetness

Orange 'Valencia'

Kumquat 'Nagami'

they develop in the Southeast. Blood oranges, named for their blood-red flesh and red-blotched skin, color less well in Florida — though they still retain their delicious raspberry-like flavor.

Soil and site
A moist but well-drained soil is best for citrus trees. Very sandy and heavy clay soils should both be enriched with generous quantities of organic matter, such as well-rotted manure or compost. Citrus trees do not tolerate saline soil and prefer a pH of 6.0-6.5.

Because of their need for heat, citrus trees are best planted in a sunny, sheltered spot. In the Southeast place the trees so that they will receive the maximum heat and sun — for example, next to a south-facing wall that has been painted a light-reflective color, such as white. In the desert Southwest some protection from midday sun is beneficial.

Plant container-grown trees at any time of the year, but a late-winter or spring planting is best. Set the trees at the same height in the soil as they were in the nursery (look for the soil lines left from the nursery plantings). Set standard-size orange and grape-fruit trees 20-25 ft (6-7.5 m) apart, and standard-size lime and lemon trees 12-15 ft (3.7-4.5 m) apart; plant dwarf trees 6-10 ft (1.8-3 m) apart.

Cultivation
The bark of citrus trees is thin, and that of young trees can sunburn easily. Paint the lower part of the trunks with a diluted latex-base white paint (one part water to one part paint), or wrap them with newspaper for the first year.

In dry areas or during rainless periods, water trees weekly, wetting the soil slowly and deeply with a drip irrigation system or with a bubbler (available at garden centers) attached to the end of a hose.

Cover the roots of the tree with some organic mulch, such as shredded bark, but you should take care to keep the mulch at least 6 in (15 cm) away from the base of the trunk.

Feed mature trees with 1-1½ lb (450-680 g) of actual nitrogen annually (e.g., 10-15 lb/4.5-6.8 kg of 10-10-10; see p.17). Apply it in four installments each year, one every three months.

Pruning
Excessively vigorous branches may emerge on young trees; prune them back to maintain a balanced crown. Otherwise, you should prune only to remove diseased or damaged branches.

Harvesting
Citrus fruits color long before they ripen. To check for ripeness, sample fruits periodically after they reach full size.

Snip ripe fruits from the branches with pruning shears; pulling fruits off the branches may injure the tree.

Do not harvest fruits until they are needed; ripe fruits keep well on the tree up to three months.

Pests and diseases
In dry climates, scale insects, whiteflies, mealybugs, and mites may attack trees. Knock them off with a strong jet of water or spray with insecticidal soap or horticultural oil. Gophers may gnaw the bark; eliminate them promptly.

CULTIVARS TO CHOOSE

Grapefruit
'Ruby Red': very sweet and juicy fruits; pink flesh.

Kumquat
'Nagami': small, oval, bright orange fruits; thick, tender, sweet rind; moderately sour flesh; hardy to 18°F (-8°C).

Lemon
'Eureka': medium-size, yellow fruits; sour flesh; few seeds; year-round bloom; very productive.

'Meyer': rounder, thin-skinned orangish fruits; juicy, tart flesh that is slightly sweet when ripe; hardy to 17°F (-8.5°C).

Lime
'Bearss': large, almost seedless fruits; sour, yellow-green flesh; very productive; hardy to 28°F (-2°C).

Mandarin
'Owari Satsuma': medium to large fruits with loose, orange rind and mild, almost seedless flesh; ripen in winter; hardy to 20°F (-6.5°C).

Orange
'Moro': medium-size fruits with blood-red to purplish flesh; productive, vigorous tree; hardy to 25°F (-4°C).

'Valencia': medium to large fruits with sweet, slightly tart flesh; excellent for making juice; vigorous, prolific tree.

'Washington Navel': medium to large fruits; very sweet, juicy, seedless flesh; heavy-bearing tree; hardy to 24°F (-4.5°C).

FIGS

Figs are a rare delicacy and delicious as fresh dessert fruit. They flourish in the South and in sheltered spots north through zone 7.

Figs flourish throughout the lower South and are grown commercially in Texas and Southern California. In the middle South, figs flourish in sheltered, sunny spots, and they may be cultivated as far north as zone 7 if given some winter protection, such as bundling the branches in burlap. Even in the South, figs do best in a south-facing site that enjoys maximum sun and warmth.

Figs harvested in summer are formed during the previous year. They are present on the trees during the winter as embryo fruits next to the terminal growth buds on young shoots. It is these shoots and the tiny fruits that require protection in cold weather, and they are easily killed off by a harsh winter.

Site and soil preparation
Fig trees are generally supplied as two- or three-year-olds. Only one tree is necessary, as most cultivated figs bear fruits without pollination and fertilization.

The root system must always be restricted to stop the tree from producing excessive, unfruitful wood. Dig a hole 3 ft (90 cm) square and 3 ft (90 cm) deep, and

◄ **Fresh figs** Picked straight from the tree, figs are at their sweetest and juiciest. They take two years to reach harvesting size, surviving most winters outdoors in zone 7 if given protection. The most common cultivars are 'Brown Turkey' and 'Celeste.'

line the sides with bricks, concrete, or stone slabs.

To prevent the development of long taproots, spread a layer of rubble 1 ft (30 cm) deep in the bottom of the hole. Fill the hole with two parts of good, but not rich, garden soil mixed with one

part of coarse builder's sand and 2 lb (900 g) of bonemeal.

In the North, you can grow fig trees in 15 in (38 cm) pots of potting soil. Plunge (or sink) the pot in the ground, with the rim just above ground level to reduce loss of moisture. In midfall dig around the pot with a sharp spade to sever protruding roots; lift the pot out of the soil and store the fig indoors in a cool but frost-free spot.

Cultivation
Plant in early spring. Make a hole in the prepared bed big enough to take the spread-out roots; cover with soil and firm the ground. Mulch lightly with well-rotted manure or garden compost.

In spring, after new growth has begun, start training the tree. It can be grown as a freestanding tree but it will also adapt well to

Fan-trained fig Even in the mid-South, fig trees do best against sheltered, south-facing walls, which will soak up all available sunlight. The "ribs" and immature fruits need winter protection, so cover them with burlap, suspending the sheets from the training wires.

espaliering. Train the fig tree in a fan shape against a sunny, sheltered wall. Cut the main central stem back hard to leave two strong lateral branches — one to the left and one to the right. Attach lengths of wire to the wall before tying each lateral branch to a stake and attaching these to the wire at an angle of about 45°.

When all danger of frost has passed, cut the stems back to 16 in (41 cm). If the stem has side shoots, reduce these by about a quarter to stimulate the growth of more laterals. During the summer tie in the new shoots.

In subsequent years, by early summer, pinch the side shoots back to five leaves from their base. Early in the season, rub off crossing shoots and any growing toward the wall.

Once the framework is established, cut two or three branches back by half in fall or early winter to encourage new, young shoots; otherwise the lower branches will become bare. Fruiting occurs on two-year-old shoots, with one-year-olds continuously coming along to replace them.

By early fall thin the fruits and protect the remainder by piling straw or evergreen branches over the shoots or by loosening the branches from their supports, bunching them together and wrapping them with straw or burlap. Gradually remove the protection in spring.

Feeding is unnecessary during the three years the framework is being built up. In subsequent years mulch with manure or garden compost at the rate of a bucketful per sq yd/m in spring.

Harvesting
Figs must ripen while on the tree, usually between late summer and midfall. The fruits are ripe when they hang down, the stalks soften, and the skins show signs of splitting; a drop of moisture (nectar) may appear in the "eye."

Pests and diseases
Figs are generally free of pests. Diseases liable to attack are canker on the shoots and botrytis on ripening fruits.

Fig canker sometimes occurs when a fungus enters through wounds or cut twigs, particularly during the growing season. Prune diseased branches, cutting back into clean and healthy wood.

TRAINING AND PRUNING

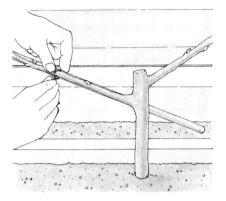

1 In spring, after growth has begun, cut back the main stem to leave two strong lateral branches, which will form the first two ribs of the fan. Secure wires across the wall or fence. Tie each lateral branch to a stake, and attach the stakes to the wires at an angle of about 45°.

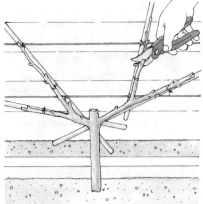

2 When all danger of frost has passed, prune the two main laterals back to 16 in (41 cm). Cut any side shoots on the laterals back by a quarter. This stimulates the growth of yet more side shoots. Train them fanwise along additional stakes as they grow out.

3 In subsequent years pinch side shoots back to at least five leaves before midsummer. This encourages new fruit-bearing shoots to form. Train them into the fan shape where there is room. Also entirely pinch off any shoots growing toward or away from the support.

4 Before fall remove all immature figs that have grown larger than peas during the summer, as they will not survive the winter. The smallest fruitlets that are left near the end of the shoots, and which survive the winter, will mature for harvesting the following year.

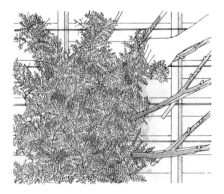

5 Protect the fig tree in winter by tying evergreen branches loosely over the shoots. Alternatively, detach the fig branches from their supports, bunch them together, and wrap them in either straw or burlap, afterward tying the bundle to the training wires.

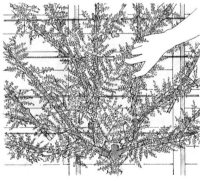

6 In mid- to late spring gradually expose the fig tree to normal weather conditions. Remove the protective covering of straw, burlap, or evergreen branches in several stages, freeing the shoot tips and young fruits only after all danger of frost has entirely passed.

PEACHES AND NECTARINES

**Luscious and juicy, peaches and nectarines
are among the most popular fruits. Outdoors they
need sunny and sheltered conditions.**

Peaches and nectarines thrive in
the Pacific Coast states and on
the Atlantic Coast from Florida to
Massachusetts. They also flourish on the southwestern slopes of
the Rocky Mountains in Colorado
and along the southern shore of
the Great Lakes. They prefer a
sunny, sheltered site and are un-
likely to fruit if the temperature
drops below -10°F (-23°C); they
are hardy into zone 6. At the
northern edge of their range they
do best as espaliers grown against
a south-facing wall. Nectarines, a
smooth-skinned variety of peach,
are slightly less hardy.

These trees are self-fertile
(each flower can fertilize another
on the same tree); a second pollinating tree is not needed.

Peaches and nectarines require
well-drained soil. If the soil is
heavy, plant the trees on a slight
mound as suggested for apricots
(see p.20). When ordering peaches, make sure the rootstock is
adapted to your soil and climate.
'Bailey' is a rootstock adapted to
northern conditions. 'Lovell' is
disease resistant, but 'Nema-
guard' is a better choice in warm-
weather areas where nematodes
are a serious pest. 'Citation' is a
dwarfing rootstock that performs
well in warm-weather regions.

Peach 'Loring'

Nectarine 'Fantasia'

▲ **Peaches and nectarines** These sweet
and delicious fruits flourish in temperate
sunny regions and perform well in the
North as espaliers trained against a
sheltered wall. They should begin to bear
fruits the fifth summer after planting.

Cultivation
Plant peaches and nectarines in
fall in mild-winter regions and in
early spring in more northerly areas. Set trained espaliers 12-15 ft
(3.7-4.5 m) apart, but plant freestanding trees 15 ft (4.5 m) apart.

Dig a hole that is deep and wide
enough to hold the spread-out
roots; plant the trees to the same
depth as at the nursery. Set the
stems of fan-trained trees about
9 in (23 cm) from the wall, and
angle the trunks slightly inward.

Peaches and nectarines vary in
their needs for nitrogen. Perform
a soil test to determine the needs
of your trees. In general, for fast-
growing young trees apply ¼ lb
(115 g) of actual nitrogen in early
spring (see p.17). Older trees will
require less nitrogen.

Pollination is needed to ensure
fruits. In the North the flowers
may open before insects are active, so artificial pollination is
necessary. Dab each flower with a

THINNING AND HARVESTING

1 Thin fruits when they are the size of
marbles. Reduce clusters to one fruit; on
espaliers remove fruits growing toward
the wall. Thin later to 9 in (23 cm) apart.

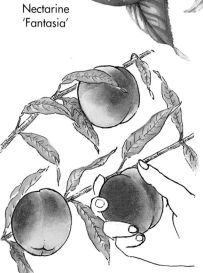

2 Fruits are ready for harvesting when
they yield to gentle pressure. To pick the
fruits, carefully grip them in the palm of
your hand and twist them off the spurs.

camel-hair brush daily at midday. If frost is predicted, cover blooming trees at night with sheets; remove the sheets in the day to keep flowers accessible to insects.

Water trees well during hot, dry weather. Espaliers have a special need for irrigation — the soil near walls dries out very quickly.

Thin peach fruits when they are the size of marbles. Reduce clusters to single fruits. On espaliered trees remove fruits growing toward a wall or lacking space to grow. Thin peaches to a final spacing of 9 in (23 cm) when they are the size of golf balls. Thin nectarines to 6 in (15 cm) apart.

Pruning

Prune peaches and nectarines to an open-center shape. At planting time pick three strong, spreading branches evenly spaced around the trunk; remove all others. Cut the three scaffold branches back to two to three buds each. During the next two to three years, limit pruning to the removal of shoots that emerge from the trunk and compete with the scaffold branches. When the scaffold branches reach 3 ft (1 m) long, head them back. Once the trees mature (at about 12 ft/3.7 m high), remove annually 20 to 40 percent of the wood that has borne fruits; this encourages the growth of new branches for the next year's crop.

Harvesting and storing

The fruits are ready for picking when the flesh around the stalks yields to gentle pressure.

Pests and diseases

Pests likely to attack peaches and nectarines are aphids, peach tree borers, scale insects, and plum curculios. Common diseases include bacterial canker, brown rot, peach leaf curl, powdery mildew, shot-hole fungus, and silver leaf; copper fungicide is often effective.

CULTIVARS TO CHOOSE

Peaches

'Belle of Georgia': white-fleshed fruits; cold-hardy tree with cold-hardy flower buds; reliable harvest.

'Flamecrest': large red-and-yellow fruits; vigorous tree; bears well in low-chill areas (very mild winter).

'Loring': round, medium to large freestone fruits; red blush on yellow skin; yellow flesh; resists leaf curl.

'Redhaven': early-season fruits; red skin, yellow flesh; sets fruits heavily; needs early and thorough thinning.

Nectarines

'Fantasia': large, yellow-fleshed, firm fruits; bears well in low-chill areas (very mild winter).

'Sun Red': Delicious early-season fruits; good choice for Deep South.

PRUNING PEACH TREES

1 Mature peach trees need regular pruning. In late spring cut out older branches from the center and remove any branch that crosses another, cutting it flush with the parent branch.

2 Damaged and diseased branches should also be removed in late spring. Cut them back to just above a healthy side shoot to encourage new growth.

Nectarine 'Sun Red'

Peach 'Redhaven'

PEARS

Pears require less spraying than peaches, plums, and apples and are easily trained to fit into small spaces in compact or crowded gardens.

Pears grow wherever you find apples, but they are less resistant to extremes of heat and cold. Because pears blossom early, they need a protected site in areas with late frosts. They also need frequent watering in droughts.

Few pears are self-fertile, so plant two different cultivars that flower at the same time. Pear cultivars are not grown on their own roots but are grafted onto rootstocks; to grow dwarf pear trees, use quinces as the rootstocks.

Asian pear trees bear fruits at a younger age than Western pears and produce exceptionally heavy crops, as much as 400 lbs (180 kg) of fruits per mature tree.

Pears naturally form upright, sturdy trees and adapt well to espaliering. Espaliered pears strike an elegant note against a wall and make fine freestanding screens when supported by a framework of strong poles and wires. Freestanding trees yield heavier crops but need plenty of room; espaliers yield less fruits but are better suited to small gardens.

The crop from your pear trees will vary each year, depending on the severity of spring frosts and the amount of rainfall. As a guide, expect 40-50 lb (18-23 kg) from a standard tree, 20-25 lb (9-11 kg) from an espalier with three tiers of branches, and 7-11 lb (3-5 kg) from a dwarf tree.

Site and soil

Plant pears in a sunny, sheltered spot. They grow well inland but dislike the salt-laden winds of coastal areas. Spring frosts in the North can destroy the blossoms of early cultivars. While they will grow and fruit satisfactorily in the upper South, the hot and humid weather of that region makes pears prone to the disease fire blight. Regions with dry climates,

▶ **Dessert pears** By choosing a selection of early, midseason, and late cultivars, you can have pears ready for picking and eating from late summer through New Year's and into early spring.

▲ **Living screen** Fan-trained pears make a handsome screen grown against a fence, wall, or post-and-wire supports. Before planting the trees, calculate their mature spread; crowding will stunt them.

such as eastern Washington or the Rocky Mountain states, are best for pears; in the Northeast, Midwest, and the upper South, plant disease-resistant cultivars.

The soil should be deep and loamy and retain moisture well in summer, but avoid waterlogged sites. On quick-draining, shallow, sandy soils, increase the water-holding capacity by incorporating well-rotted strawy or garden compost into the soil at planting time. A week before planting, fork in a light dressing of an all-purpose fertilizer, such as 10-10-10.

Buying pear trees

Most garden centers offer some pear trees, but mail-order nurseries offer a greater choice of cultivars. Buy larger, older stock; the one-year-old trees are cheaper, but they need training — a job best left to the nursery. You can buy espaliered trees whose basic training is complete; they are expensive, but they save gardeners years of pinching and tying.

A three-year-old tree should fruit within two or three years of

▶ **Pear espaliers** Ideal where space is restricted, espaliers grow several tiers, or horizontal branches. Prune the main stem when it reaches the top of its support.

planting, depending on its position and your climate.

Specialized nurseries will advise on suitable rootstocks and cultivars for your garden.

Planting a pear tree

Plant pear trees in late fall or early spring. A late-fall planting gives the best start in areas with mild winters and hot summers.

Space standard and semidwarf trees 12-15 ft (3.7-4.5 m) apart; set dwarf trees 4-5 ft (1.2-1.5 m) apart. If you have room to place espaliers or fan-trained trees side by side on a wall or fence, calculate their eventual width before planting; in general, set espaliers and fans 12-15 ft (3.7-4.5 m) apart. Leave 9 in (23 cm) between

the wall and the planting hole to give the roots room to spread.

Mail-order trees arrive bare-rooted. Dig a hole big enough to hold the tree's roots when they spread out. For a standard tree, drive a stake at least 2 ft (60 cm) deep into the soil and plant the tree against it, securing it with strong plastic strap ties.

Plant to the same depth as the tree was set in the nursery, judging by the soil mark on the stem. Make sure the graft union between the rootstock and the scion is 4 in (10 cm) above soil level. Spread the roots out evenly to balance the tree; return the soil over the roots, firming it in well. Water thoroughly after planting.

Set a balled-and-burlapped tree from a garden center so that the soil mark on the trunk is even with the surface of the soil. Secure balled-and-burlapped trees to stakes driven into the soil on either side of the planting hole.

Cultivation

Water well during dry spells, especially during the first growing season. Mature pear trees are intolerant of drought; water well during prolonged dry weather.

Mulch the root area in early spring with well-rotted garden compost or manure.

Fertilize in late winter or early spring with a nitrogen fertilizer; pears should receive somewhat less than the ¼ lb (115 g) actual nitrogen given annually to apple trees, since excessive nitrogen promotes susceptibility to fire blight. Base fertilization on the

results of a soil test; include phosphorus, potassium, and micronutrients as indicated.

Spraying

A number of pests and diseases affect pear trees, attacking either the foliage or the fruits. Where damage is known to be problematic, institute a spraying program tailored to bud development. Begin spraying at bud burst and continue until the blossoms are fully open. Do not spray when the blossoms are open, or you may harm pollinating insects.

Don't spray on windy days. Overspraying will do more harm than good; follow the instructions on the product label carefully.

Spray with a horticultural oil at the bud-burst stage to kill the eggs of overwintering insects. At the green-cluster stage use a recommended fungicide to control scab. Follow with a second application of fungicide when the buds begin to show white. This is also the time to begin watching for plum curculios, which lay eggs in the forming fruits.

Watch for a sudden blackening of leaves on new shoots; this is a symptom of fire blight. Prune off infected twigs; use bleach to disinfect the shears between cuts.

After 80 percent of the petals fall, spray every two weeks with a fungicide for scab. Set out pheromone traps for codling moths; if necessary spray in early summer and again three weeks later with a recommended pesticide.

A fall application of horticultural oil helps control pear psyllas, which suck out the tree's sap and spread fire blight.

Pruning and training

Pear trees, both standards and dwarfs, are trained and pruned in the same way as apples (see pp.8-12). Established standard pear trees can be cut back harder than apple trees, so always remove overcrowded branches, particularly in the center of the tree, during winter pruning.

Summer pruning of espaliers and dwarf trees is earlier than for apples. Start when the summer growth matures and begins to harden, which may happen in early summer to midsummer or even later, depending on your local climate. Cut back the lateral shoots made during the current season, not the leading branches.

PRUNING AND THINNING

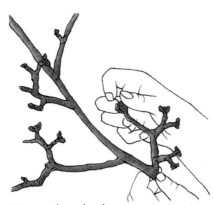

1 To avoid overloading a tree's cropping capacity, rub fruit buds off the spurs in spring; leave a bud or two on each spur.

2 Prune laterals on espaliered trees as soon as the summer growth matures (by midsummer). Cut back to three leaves.

3 Thin fruits after the natural midsummer drop, when immature fruits start to turn downward. Aim for two fruits per spur.

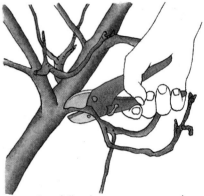

4 From late fall to late winter cut weak and crowded branches flush with main branches. Keep the center of tree open.

As a pear tree matures, it will produce fruiting spurs (short fruit-bearing side branches) more freely than apple trees do. Thin these out in winter.

Thinning the crop

Pears need less thinning than apples do, but a heavy crop strains any tree's resources, leading to poor-quality fruits. Pears on full-size trees do better if spaced out. Espaliers, fans, and dwarfs rarely need thinning; the fruits on these trees are naturally spaced out by the fruit drop in midsummer.

After the natural fruit drop is complete, remove badly shaped or damaged fruits, and the central pear in a crowded cluster.

Never pull the fruit off; this may damage the spur. Hold the fruit firmly but lightly and cut the stalk with a pair of scissors.

Harvesting and storing

Most pears ripen off the tree. To harvest early cultivars, cut the stalk close to the spur when the fruit is mature in size but hard.

Pick midseason fruits (for eating in mid- or late fall) and late cultivars (for eating from early winter) when you can easily twist the stalks away from the branch without tearing the spurs.

Store pears in a cool room at 36°-40°F (2°-4.5°C). Lay them on trays in a single layer, making sure they don't touch each other. Check the pears often. When they begin to soften slightly and the color changes near the stalk, bring the pears into the warmth at 61°F (16°C) for a few days to finish ripening. Don't store damaged or diseased fruits; even a slightly bruised pear can cause the others to go bad.

Pests and diseases

Pears are affected by the same pests and diseases as apples. Besides the pests found in the spraying section, watch for red spider mites and pear leaf blister mites.

The main diseases and disorders are boron deficiency, brown rot, fire blight, scab, splitting, and stony pit.

Pear 'Seckel'

Asian pear 'Shinseiki'

Pear 'Bosc'

Pear 'Bartlett'

CULTIVARS TO CHOOSE

Cultivars are grouped according to when pears are ready to eat. Dessert pears can also be used for cooking if firm and not fully ripe.

Early
'Bartlett': eat fresh; large, juicy fruits; self-fertile in arid West, elsewhere pollinated by 'Bosc.'

'Clapp's Favorite': eat fresh; large, juicy fruits; ripen late August; susceptible to fire blight; pollinated by 'Bartlett,' 'Bosc,' 'Moonglow,' 'Seckel,' 'Comice,' or 'D'Anjou.'

Midseason
'Moonglow': bear young; medium-size, mild-flavored fruits;

resist fire blight; pollinated by 'Clapp's Favorite,' 'Bosc,' 'Bartlett,' 'Seckel,' 'Comice,' or 'D'Anjou.'

'Seckel': eat fresh; hardy tree; small, sweet fruits; some resistance to fire blight; pollinated by 'Clapp's Favorite,' 'Bosc,' 'Moonglow,' 'D'Anjou,' and 'Comice.'

Late
'Bosc': eat fresh: dark yellow fruits with brownish skin; juicy, white flesh; susceptible to fire blight; pollinated by 'Bartlett.'

'D'Anjou': large tree; green fruits; cold hardy; resistant to fire blight; 'Bartlett' is the best pollinator; can

be pollinated by 'Bosc,' 'Clapp's Favorite,' 'Seckel,' and 'Comice.'

Asian pears
'Shinko': small tree; bears young; late-ripening fruits; resistant to fire blight; cold hardy but flower buds susceptible to late frosts; may be pollinated by Western pears.

'Shinseiki': yellow fruits with crisp flesh; moderately resistant to fire blight; pollinated by 'Bartlett,' 'Chojuro,' 'Hosui,' or 'Nijiseiki.'

'Ya Li': sweet fruits; tolerant of fire blight; ideal for warm-weather areas; pollinated by other Asian pears, such as 'Tsu Li' or 'Seuri.'

PLUMS

**Compact, fruitful, and less demanding than
most orchard fruits, plum trees are beautiful as well —
a desirable addition to any home landscape.**

Asian gardeners recognize the grace of the long-lived plum tree, planting it in their gardens for its ornamental properties. Westerners value plums for their delicious fruits, which need less spraying than apples or peaches do.

Select a plum cultivar adapted to your climate. The European types, such as 'Italian Prune,' bear the tastiest fruits but thrive only where the climate is neither too hot nor too cold. Japanese plums, which are sensitive to late frosts, thrive where peaches do; their fruits are juicier but less sweet. American hybrids (crosses of native American species with Japanese plums) are disease resistant and cold hardy — the best choice for northern gardens.

Plum trees are often grafted onto dwarfing rootstocks, such as 'St. Julian A' or 'Pixy,' which ensure early fruits and small trees. Standard rootstocks, such as 'Myrobalan,' will produce long-lived trees; standard plums are easy to keep compact through pruning. Plums take well to espaliering (especially fan training); this is a good choice for a small garden.

Some plums are self-fertile, but others need a nearby pollinator.

Site and soil
Plums grow best in sunny, sheltered sites. Because the trees flower early in spring, avoid frost

Plum

▲ **Dessert plums** Excellent as fresh fruits, most types of dessert plums are also good for cooking and preserving.

Gage

pockets — this is especially important with Japanese plums.

Plum trees succeed in most well-drained soils; the ideal is a fairly heavy clay loam with a pH between 6.0 and 6.5. Top-dress very acid soils after planting with enough lime to raise the soil pH.

A single self-fertile tree will bear enough plums for a family. A mature dwarf will yield 30-75 lb (13.5-34 kg) per season, depending on the cultivar and rootstock. If planting more than one tree, set them 8-12 ft (2.4-3.7 m) apart.

A fan-trained espalier will produce 15-25 lb (7-11 kg) of plums

when it is fully grown. Plant fans 15-18 ft (4.5-5.5 m) apart.

Mature standard trees produce 50-100 lb (23-45 kg) of fruits. Set them 12-15 ft (3.7-4.5 m) apart.

Planting and pruning
Plant plums in late fall or early spring. Prepare a 3 ft (90 cm)

SUPPORTING, THINNING, AND HARVESTING PLUMS

1 Plum tree branches are often brittle and may snap under a heavy weight of fruits. Support them with props (using cloth to prevent chafing of the bark) or tie them to stakes.

2 Thin a heavy crop at the beginning of early summer. After the natural early-summer drop, do a final thinning with fruits 2-3 in (5-7.5 cm) apart or remove all but one plum from each cluster.

3 Plums ripen from midsummer to late fall, depending on the cultivar and the locality. Pick cooking varieties before they are fully ripe, but leave dessert plums to ripen on the trees.

▲ **Fan-trained plum** These trees may bloom before insects are active. If so, pollinate by hand, transferring pollen from one flower to another with a brush.

square area a few weeks ahead. Remove all weeds. Fork in well-rotted garden compost or manure; use one bucketful per tree or two bucketfuls on light soil.

For a bare-root tree, dig a hole just wider than the spread of the roots. Plant the tree at the same depth as in the nursery (look for a soil mark on the stem). Drive a stake into the bottom of the hole; fill the hole. Attach the tree trunk to the stake with plastic ties.

With a balled-and-burlapped tree, set the root ball high enough so that the old soil mark on the trunk rests even with the surface of the surrounding soil. Guy the tree to stakes driven into the ground on either side of the hole.

Before planting a tree for fan training, secure horizontal wires 6 in (15 cm) apart to screw eyes along the fence or wall; place the lowest one 15 in (38 cm) above the ground. Allow for a final height of 6-8 ft (1.8-2.4 m). Position the stem 9 in (23 cm) from

the wall; slope it slightly toward the wall as you replace the soil.

Spread out the ribs of the fan evenly, and tie them to the support wires with soft string.

Base the fertilization program on a soil test. The needs of plum trees are similar to those of other fruit trees: ¼ lb (115 g) actual nitrogen per year (see p.17) for a young and rapidly growing tree but less for a mature tree. Apply a topdressing in early spring, covering the entire root area. Apply potassium, phosphorus, and trace elements as indicated by the soil test. Also mulch with well-rotted garden compost or manure in early spring to midspring at the rate of a bucketful per sq yd/m.

Avoid disturbing the roots as you weed, or the tree will throw up suckers. If suckers do appear, pull them out; don't cut them off.

Training plum trees
Most plums are supplied as two-year-old trees, on dwarfing or standard rootstocks. For training and pruning into fan, pyramid, or standard shapes, see pages 12-14.

Plum trees follow one of two patterns of growth. The European cultivars have upright trees,

which adapt to a modified leader system of pruning (see p.12). Japanese plums and most of the Japanese-American hybrids are better adapted to an open-center system of pruning, as shown for peaches (see p.29). In either case, after the framework is established, plums need little structural pruning. Cut out deadwood and crowded and crossing shoots in late winter or early spring; cut a few of the side shoots back to encourage younger fruiting growth.

Thinning
Plum tree branches are brittle and may snap under a heavy crop of fruits. To guard against this, thin a heavy crop at the beginning of early summer. After the natural early-summer drop, do the final thinning with fruits spaced 2-3 in (5-7.5 cm) apart or pick all but one from each cluster.

Support and protection
If the branches are still overladen after thinning, support them with wooden props or forked branches, or tie them to sturdy stakes driven into the ground.

Protect dwarf trees grown in the open and espaliered trees

from frost at blossom time by draping them with burlap or old bedsheets. To protect the buds and fruits from birds, cover the trees with plastic netting (available at most garden centers).

Harvesting and storing

Plums ripen from midsummer to late fall. Leave dessert plums on the tree as long as possible; for cooking, canning, or freezing, pick them before they ripen. Pick the stalks along with the fruits. If the weather is very wet, pick the plums before they are very ripe; otherwise their skins may split.

Pests and diseases

Plums may be attacked by aphids, peach tree borers, plum curculios, apple maggots, cherry fruit flies, mites, and scale insects. Plum curculios are the most common pests; control them by spraying with a recommended insecticide when crescent-shaped scars first appear on the fruits and again two weeks later. Plums are vulnerable to bacterial canker, black knot, and brown rot. The last two are fungal diseases, which may be controlled by removing the infected branches.

AMERICAN PLUMS

Also known as sand cherries, beach plums, Chickasaw plums, and Canada plums, this is a group of several species of plums native to North America. Though their fruits are smaller than those of traditional garden plums and are generally too tart for eating raw, American plums make excellent jams and preserves. These hardy plants grow better than European or Japanese plums in areas of extreme winter cold. In areas such as the upper Midwest, where late-spring frosts are common, American plums are often welcome, as the other plums rarely set fruits successfully.

Prunus americana is a wild shrub that is common from Manitoba south to Georgia and west to Utah and New Mexico. In the wild the shrub spreads by suckers to form large colonies. It may be maintained as a single-stem tree by pruning. This shrub bears 1 in (2.5 cm) diameter, yellow to red fruits that ripen in June or July. Superior cultivars include 'DeSoto' and 'Hawkeye.'

Prunus angustifolia (Chickasaw plum) is another suckering,

spreading shrub. Native from Maryland to Florida and west to Texas, it bears ½ in (1.25 cm) wide red fruits and resists disease better than other plums in hot, humid climates.

Prunus besseyi, the sand cherry, thrives from Manitoba to Wyoming and south to Kansas and Colorado. It bears purplish-black sweet fruits, ¾ in (2 cm) long, in July and August. This species is particularly well adapted to areas with hot, dry summers and frigid winters. It has been crossed with cultivated plums to yield a number of "cherry plum" cultivars, such as 'Compass,' 'Opata,' and 'Sapa.'

Prunus maritima, the beach plum, is another shrubby plum that makes a dense, suckering mound 6 ft (1.8 m) tall. Tolerant of salt and sandy soil, it is a fine plum for seaside gardens. It produces ½-1 in (1.25-2.5 cm) fruits of dull purple or crimson color, and they ripen in August. Superior cultivars include 'Eastham,' 'Hancock,' and 'Premier.'

Planting and cultivation

Plant in early spring in a sunny spot in well-drained soil. *Prunus besseyi* and *P. maritima* thrive on poor, sandy soils.

As the American plums commonly form suckering shrubs rather than trees, the gardener must contain these plants to stop them from crowding other plants. Avoid overfeeding; this spurs excess growth, which will be prone to disease and insect damage. These plums thrive on neglect.

▲ **Prunes** Many of these European plums, including the 'Italian Prune,' are suitable for drying, either in the sun in dry climates or in a dehydrator. They are excellent for eating fresh and are a good choice for canning.

▼ **A fruitful ornament** Delicate blossoms that often appear before the leaves, and a graceful profile, have made plums a traditional favorite of Asian gardeners, who value the plants as ornamental trees.

PLUM CULTIVARS

European plums

'Early Laxton': dessert or cooking plums; medium yellow-red fruits; early, end of midsummer; requires cross-pollination by European plums.

'Green Gage': round, sweet, greenish-yellow fruits; best adapted to warm, sunny climate; plant with other European cultivars for cross-pollination.

'Italian Prune': large to medium, dark purple fruits with yellow flesh that turns a wine-color when cooked; self-fertile but not a good pollinator.

'Stanley': large dark blue fruits with sweet greenish-yellow flesh; cold hardy, thrives in the Northeast; does not require a pollinator.

'Yellow Egg': good for canning; small, sweet yellow fruits; requires cross-pollination by other European plums.

Japanese plums

'Black Amber': large, dark purple to black fruits with amber-colored flesh; self-fertile, but you can increase the harvest by cross-pollination with other Japanese cultivars.

'Santa Rosa': excellent dessert plums; large, attractive dark purple fruits with red flesh; self-fertile, but you can increase the harvest by cross-pollination with other Japanese cultivars.

'Shiro': medium, yellow fruits with mild, sweet flavor; dependable, heavy harvest; self-fertile; increase the harvest by cross-pollination with other Japanese cultivars.

Japanese-American hybrids

'Superior': red fruits with yellow flesh; cold hardy; bears younger than European plums; requires cross-pollination by another Japanese-American hybrid or Japanese plum.

'Toka': small apricot-colored fruits with spicy flavor; vigorous, cold-hardy tree, but less resistance to insects and disease than other hybrids; excellent pollinator for other hybrids; requires pollination by another Japanese-American hybrid or Japanese plum.

'Underwood': medium to large yellow-and-red fruits; sweet and juicy yellow flesh; early-blooming, reliable harvest; vigorous, large tree; requires pollination by another Japanese-American hybrid or Japanese plum.

European plum 'Stanley'

Japanese plum 'Santa Rosa'

European plum 'Green Gage'

Harvest basket Homegrown garden fruits offer flavor, freshness, and tremendous variety.

Garden fruits

Garden fruits (sometimes called small fruits) are produced on bushes, canes, and low-growing plants. They include blackberries, blueberries, currants, raspberries, and strawberries. This section also covers grapes and melons, as well as rhubarb, which is usually grown as a perennial crop in the vegetable plot. Garden fruits can be incorporated into a vegetable garden. As permanent plantings, they do not interfere with crop rotation, and they make attractive screens between the vegetable garden and ornamental plantings near it.

Berry fruits start cropping sooner after planting than fruit trees and generally give a better return for the space they occupy. On the other hand, they have a shorter life span; under good growing conditions, bush fruits can be expected to crop for 10 to 15 years and cane fruits for 10 years. The yield and vigor of strawberries decrease rapidly, and the plants should be renewed at least every four or five years.

No store-bought produce can compare in flavor and freshness with homegrown garden fruits, but the plants demand regular attention in order to ensure healthy and heavy crops. Pruning and feeding are mandatory chores every year, and the gardener must keep an eye out for hungry birds and other wildlife. If you have only a few canes or bushes, protect them with a temporary cover of fine-mesh plastic netting supported on stakes. Put the covering in place before the birds begin to gorge on the ripening fruits. Wall-trained espaliers can be protected in the same way, with netting fixed to the training wires or to battens attached to the wall. The ideal, though more expensive, way of protecting fruits is with a permanent fruit cage. You can construct one from a sturdy wooden frame clad with wire netting or plastic mesh.

To help you determine if a particular plant will thrive in your area, we've given hardy zones that correspond to the plant hardiness map on page 176.

PRUNING BERRY BUSHES

Pruning cane fruits, such as raspberries, involves only cutting out stems that bore this year and tying in replacement shoots. Bush fruits need more careful treatment.

PRUNING CANE FRUITS

Cane fruits are slender deciduous shrubs with sturdy fruit-bearing stems. They include raspberries, blackberries, loganberries, and the lesser-known hybrid berries, such as boysenberries, tayberries, youngberries, and wineberries.

Their flexible stems are too weak to support themselves and must be either trained to wires stretched between posts or tied to wires against a wall or fence. Every year after fruiting, cut out the canes at ground level to make room for the new shoots that will carry the following year's crop. Cane fruits will crop for 10 years.

Pruning raspberries

Some raspberry cultivars bear fruits in midsummer on the previous year's shoots; others fruit in early or midfall on the current season's shoots. In both cases, canes that have borne fruits must be replaced annually by new ones.

To make training and harvesting easy, raspberry canes are best grown in straight rows and supported on wires stretched between wooden stakes or posts. The height of the posts and wires depends on the type of raspberry.

If there is not enough space to train rows of raspberries on wires, you can train these canes up single posts. Train four or five canes up a post, such as a sturdy fence post standing 6 ft (1.8 m) above the ground. Tie the canes to the post with strings or wire loops. Several posts will be necessary to crop enough raspberries for the average family, but these can be dotted around the garden wherever space permits.

First-year pruning Immediately after planting raspberry canes, cut each stem down to just above a healthy growth bud 1 ft (30 cm) above ground level. Prevent fruiting in the first year so that the plant can build up its strength for subsequent years.

As the canes grow, tie them in with garden twine to the support wires. Rub off any flowers.

Subsequent years Allow the canes to bear fruits in the second year after planting. In early fall, when summer-fruiting types have been picked, untie all the canes that have fruited and cut them down to just above ground level.

Select up to eight of the strongest new canes on each plant, and tie them to the wires or other supports. Cut out all unwanted new canes at soil level in the same way as for old canes.

Vigorous raspberries tend to produce sucker canes directly from their roots, and these spring up between the rows, getting in the way of weeding, training, and harvesting. Eliminate suckers by pulling them away from the roots, using a tearing action. Protect your hands from the scaly, often prickly, stems by wearing gardening gloves. Do not sever sucker canes with pruning shears, as any buds left intact at the base will soon start growing.

In late winter cut back any summer-fruiting canes extending above the top wire to a bud that is just above it. This reduces wind

◄ **Raspberry canes** The best crops are borne on stems produced the previous season. They need full sun and good air circulation. Space the canes evenly along the rows, and tie them to wires.

PRUNING AND TRAINING RASPBERRIES

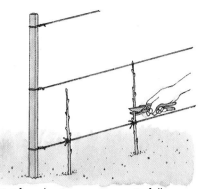

1 After planting new canes in fall to early spring, cut down each cane to 1 ft (30 cm) above ground. Cut cleanly just above a healthy bud with pruning shears. Tie the cane to the bottom wire.

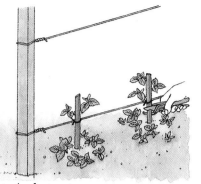

2 In the first spring, new canes appear from ground level. Let them grow on, but cut out the original cane at ground level. No fruits grow in the first year, but the plants grow strong canes and roots.

3 During summer and early fall, tie new canes to the wires as they develop, using garden twine or plastic ties. Keep the canes apart in the row; allow an interval of 4 in (10 cm) between each one.

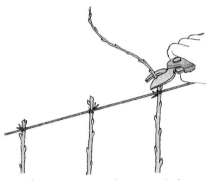

4 In late winter or early spring, before new growth begins, cut off the tips of all canes above a healthy bud to encourage vigor in the lower buds. Trim the tallest canes to just above the top wire.

5 In subsequent years cut down to the ground all canes that have borne fruits. Do so right after the harvest. Remove spindly new growth at ground level; leave up to eight new canes per plant.

6 Tie the selected new canes to the horizontal wire supports. Remove any sucker shoots growing directly from the roots in the pathways between rows; to do this, pull away with a tearing action.

---

damage and encourages stronger growth from the lower buds.

With fall-fruiting raspberries pruning is easy. Cut all canes to the ground in late winter. The new stems, which will bear fruits in fall, appear from ground level soon afterward. Tie them to the wires as they grow in summer.

Pruning blackberries
In the wild, blackberries scramble through other bushes, using their profuse thorns to gain support. Cultivated blackberries, including thornless cultivars, are best grown on a support system of posts and wires. The best fruits are borne on shoots produced in the previous season, so prune out canes that have already borne fruits at the end of each growing season and allow one-year-old shoots to replace them.

Blackberry canes are very long, and it is difficult to separate them from other stems without getting yourself entangled in the thorns and without breaking them. They are best trained in a fan shape on wires against a fence or a wall in such a way that the new growing shoots are kept away from last year's growth. This setup makes replacement training and harvesting easier and also helps to prevent the spread of disease.

Immediately after planting, cut back the canes about 9-15 in (23-38 cm) above ground level; prune just above a healthy bud. In subsequent years cut out all the old canes as soon as possible after they bear the year's crop. Sever them at ground level with either pruning shears or long-handled loppers (see the illustrations on p.42).

Wear gardening gloves to protect your hands from prickly thorns. Thornless cultivars are easier to handle.

On fan-trained blackberries untie the current year's shoots, reposition them, and tie them in once again. In their new position they should replace the old shoots that you have removed.

Loganberries and other hybrid cane berries are trained and pruned like blackberries.

PRUNING BUSH FRUITS
Bush fruits, such as currants and gooseberries, differ from cane fruits in forming compact bushes with a mixture of old and new shoots. However, they also differ from each other in the way the fruits are borne. Black currants, for example, produce their best fruits on young wood of the previous season, while red and white currants, whether grown as bushes or espaliered, bear the finest crops on spurs on old wood. Gooseberries fruit on new wood as well as on spurs on older wood. Pruning in each case is aimed at encouraging the healthy growth of fruit-bearing shoots.

TRAINING BLACKBERRIES

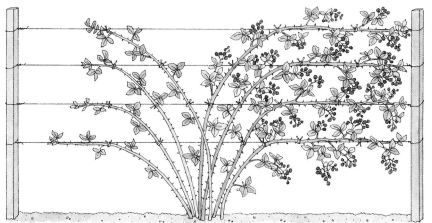

1 The main requirement of any training system for blackberries, loganberries, and hybrid berries is to keep the current year's stems clear of the fruiting canes. Once they get entangled, it is difficult to harvest the crop and carry out the correct replacement pruning later on.

Given enough space, blackberries are best grown against strong galvanized wires stretched tautly between posts. Tie fruiting canes in one direction and canes of the current season in the opposite direction. Attach one cane only to each wire, using twine or plastic ties. Fruits will be borne on alternate halves of the support system each year.

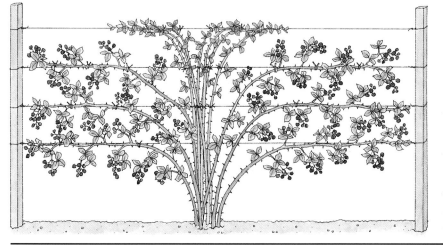

2 Fan-trained blackberries, with fruiting canes spread evenly along the wires in both directions, give the flower and fruit clusters the maximum amount of space and light available. The berries are also much easier to pick.

The new canes, which will carry next year's blackberry crop, are trained upward between the fan-trained fruiting canes and tied in temporarily to the top wire. After harvesting is completed in late fall, cut out the fruited canes at ground level and untie the new canes. Tie them into position along the wires, and repeat this replacement system on an annual basis.

In addition, prune fruit bushes to prevent overcrowding of the branches, especially those in the center of the bush. Sunlight must reach as many of the fruiting branches as possible, and air must circulate freely between them. Fruit clusters that are shaded by surrounding foliage, and thus do not dry out thoroughly after rain or morning dew, are more liable to contract diseases. Most fruits ripen faster and more uniformly in sunlight than in shade, although black currants are more tolerant of poor light than other fruit crops.

The particular growth habit of a bush influences the method of pruning. For example, gooseberry cultivars range from spreading bushes, in which the branches usually droop, to upright bushes. Prune the spreading cultivars to upward-pointing buds, but prune the upright cultivars to outward-pointing buds. For cultivars with an intermediate habit, always prune to outward-pointing buds.

Birds not only steal fruits but may also do a lot of damage to fruit bushes in winter by nibbling the dormant growth and fruit buds. Where this is a problem, delay winter pruning until the buds begin to swell in late winter. Prune back to undamaged buds.

Use sharp pruning shears for making pruning cuts to small, young branches, and use long-handled loppers or a small pruning saw for thicker, older wood.

Pruning black currants
Cut newly planted black currant bushes down to 1 in (2.5 cm) above ground level, making the cuts just above a bud. As a result, the bushes will not yield fruits in the first summer; instead, their energy will go into producing vigorous new growth that will provide a crop in the second summer after planting.

In the fall of the first growing season, cut any weak shoots back to one bud within 2 in (5 cm) of ground level. By the second fall after planting, the bush should have developed considerable new growth. Remove a few of the two-year-old shoots entirely (you may

have to sacrifice new growth), but remove no more than a quarter of the shoots. This will stimulate the development of new shoots.

Black currant bushes produce the majority of their fruits on the previous season's new growth, so the actual aim of pruning is to remove some older, darker wood each year to encourage the new shoots to emerge.

The desirable new growth takes the form of either extension shoots from the older branches or new shoots springing from or near the base. Keep a good balance between old and new wood; retain some older wood to support further extension growth.

Prune an established bush after picking the fruits or during the fall months. Remove enough of the older wood to make way for younger shoots. On regularly pruned bushes, no wood should be older than four years.

A neglected bush with congested growth needs hard pruning to induce new shoots. First cut out entirely any shoots drooping to the ground or so low that the fruits will get muddy. Next, cut out older wood from the center of the bush to let in light and air.

Cut out the oldest of the remaining wood, which can be distinguished by its dark color. Clear away all debris from the base of the bush.

Pruning red or white currants

After planting a one-year-old bush, cut each branch back to four buds from the main stem, above an outward-facing bud.

In the second winter cut out flush with the stem any branches that spoil the shape. Shorten branch leaders by two-thirds of the new growth if growth is weak or by half if growth is strong, cutting to outward-pointing buds. Prune side shoots to one bud to promote spurs.

In the third and fourth years leave some laterals to grow into branches, where there is room, so that the established bush has eight to ten main branches on a 6-9 in (15-23 cm) leg. Otherwise, prune the laterals back to spurs each year. Cut branch leaders back by half the new growth in the third winter. In the fourth winter remove a quarter of new growth. After that, prune by about 1 in (2.5 cm) yearly. Keep the center of the bush open, and as the oldest branches become too spreading or unproductive, cut them out entirely; they will be replaced by strong new shoots.

On bushes to be espaliered on a trellis of wires and posts, select the strongest shoots and cut the remainder back to the base.

PRUNING A ONE-YEAR-OLD GOOSEBERRY BUSH

Shorten three or four well-spaced shoots by three-fourths in winter. They form the main framework.

Thereafter, winter pruning consists of shortening the leading shoots by one-third and cutting all laterals back to one bud. Head back any upward-growing shoots when they reach 6 ft (1.8 m) high.

Bush and espaliered red and white currants need pruning in summer as well as winter, beginning when they are two years old. In each case, prune by midsummer; reduce all lateral shoots to three to five leaves, cutting just above a leaf base.

Pruning gooseberries

After planting, prune a one-year-old bush in fall or winter or as late as bud burst in late winter if birds are likely to eat the buds. Choose the best three or four shoots, and cut them back above a bud to about a quarter of their length. Cut out all other shoots flush with the main stem.

When pruning, firm in with the heel of your foot any plants that have been heaved up from the soil by frosts.

During the first summer after planting, concentrate on establishing the basic framework of branches. In midsummer shorten any unwanted lateral shoots to about five leaves. Do not prune the leaders.

In the second winter choose six to eight of the strongest shoots. Cut the new growth on these shoots back by half if they are growing strongly or by two-thirds if growth is weak. Remove all dead, damaged, or diseased wood. Cut back all other shoots to one bud from their base.

Aim to produce a vase-shaped bush with an open center. This not only encourages the highest yields, but also makes picking the fruits much easier — the sharply spined branches are difficult and painful to deal with once they have become congested and contorted by inadequate pruning.

On established bushes cut back the branch leaders by half their new growth in winter. To encourage spur formation, shorten the strongest side shoots to 3 in (7.5 cm) of new growth and the weaker ones to 1 in (2.5 cm). Remove weak shoots entirely, cutting them flush with the branch.

If a branch has drooped to the ground, pick a new shoot as a replacement and cut the drooping branch back to the new shoot. Prune the replacement branch by

at least half. Keep the center of the bush open.

In summer shorten all side shoots to five leaves, cutting just above a leaf joint. Do not shorten the branch leaders.

PRUNING A TWO-YEAR-OLD GOOSEBERRY BUSH

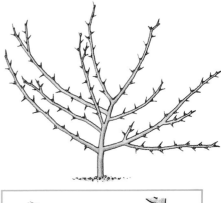

Reduce new growth by half on six to eight of the strongest shoots.

PRUNING AN ESTABLISHED GOOSEBERRY BUSH

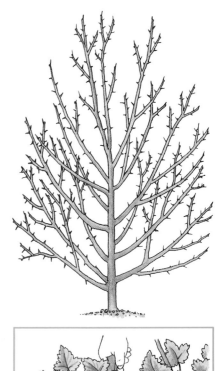

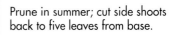

Prune in summer; cut side shoots back to five leaves from base.

BLACKBERRIES

**Prolific and easy to grow,
blackberries are the ideal fruits for training
against a wall or fence.**

Cultivated blackberries are larger and juicier than the wild kind. They flourish in any moisture-retentive, well-drained soil and will tolerate slightly impeded drainage. However, soil preparation and some training are necessary for really good yields.

Blackberries are self-fertile, so you can grow just a single plant if space is limited. Ideally, train them against a trellis of wires and posts. Three plants will provide more than enough berries for the average family.

Site and soil
Grow blackberries where they will be in the sun for at least part of the day. Blackberries do best in a slightly acid soil. Enrich alkaline soil with garden compost, well-rotted manure, or other organic matter a few months before planting; this will help to retain moisture during dry weather. Sandy, dry soil should be improved in the same manner.

Cultivation
Late fall (in the South) or early spring (in the North) are the best

▼ **Fruit trellis** Trained up a trellis arbor, a thornless blackberry is decorative as well as productive, though picking the topmost berries can be a stretch.

Cultivated
blackberries

times for planting. Blackberries arrive from the nursery bare-rooted; dig a hole wide and deep enough to hold well-spread-out roots. After planting, firm the soil with your feet; cut back each cane to 9 in (23 cm) from ground level, just above a bud.

You can train blackberries up posts but they are easier to manage if you train them on wires. Secure the wires to a sunny fence with screw eyes, or stretch them between strong end posts. Use 10- to 12-gauge wires; set them 1 ft (30 cm) apart with the first wire 3 ft (90 cm) above ground and the top wire at 6 ft (1.8 m).

Space the blackberry clumps 8 ft (2.4 m) apart; vigorous cultivars need 12-15 ft (3.7-4.5 m) of space between each plant.

Blackberry 'Ebony King'

TRAINING BLACKBERRIES

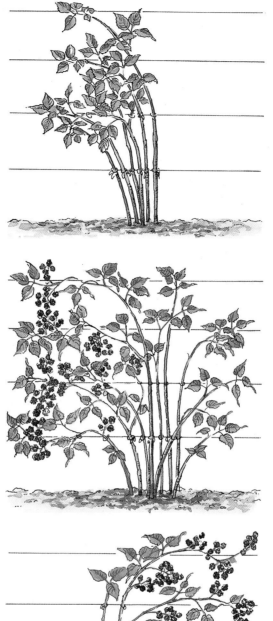

1 Blackberries can be trained along wires or up posts, but the wire system exposes more canes to sun and air and makes harvesting easier. The one-way system is simpler than fan training. In the first year, train all fruiting branches in one direction along the wires. Train the longest cane straight up until it reaches the top wire.

2 Train the current season's canes in the other direction along the wires, in the same way as before. Separating the current season's wood from that of the previous year helps to prevent disease from spreading. It also helps to keep the canes tidy and easier to manage. Tie the branches firmly to the wires, using plastic ties or ordinary garden twine.

3 After gathering the season's fruits, cut the fruiting canes down to soil level. The new canes are then ready to fruit the following year; afterward cut them down to the ground in their turn. Keep training the branches to alternate sides for healthy stock.

The one-way system of training is simple. Young branches are all trained in one direction along the wires, to one side of the plant, and the following year's growth is trained in the opposite direction (also see pp.41-42).

Feed the canes with ½-¾ cup (120-180 ml) of a balanced fertilizer, such as 5-10-10, on a regular basis in spring; sprinkle it in a band 1 ft (30 cm) from the canes. Water well in dry spells. Mulch around the bushes' bases with shredded bark, leaves, or hay.

After the harvest cut the canes that fruited during the current season down to soil level, and tie in the replacement canes.

Propagation
To increase the canes, layer the tips of new (current-season) branches from midsummer to early fall. Dig a hole 4 in (10 cm) deep near the plant. Bend down a shoot; plant its tip in the hole.

The tip should root by late fall. The following spring, sever the young plant from its parent, taking about 10 in (25 cm) of stem. Cut just above a bud, remove the new plant, and plant it in its permanent site.

Harvesting and storing
Pick fruits when they are ripe (black), even if you don't need them; this helps later fruits to reach a good size. The fruits deteriorate quickly after picking.

Pests and diseases
Blackberry plants are attacked by raspberry cane borers, blackberry leaf miners, and spider mites. They may suffer from cane blight, botrytis fruit rot, crown gall, and mosaic virus disease.

BLUEBERRIES

A native American plant, the fruitful blueberry thrives in almost every region of the United States, with little care.

Blueberry 'Berkeley'

Several species within the genus *Vaccinium* are referred to as blueberries; they have similar fruits. The diversity of species is important, because it is the secret of the blueberry's adaptability to different climates and soils. Highbush blueberries thrive in the northern and central regions of the country. Southerners have equal success with rabbit-eye blueberries. Lowbush blueberries and hybrids of lowbush and highbush plants thrive in the coldest regions. All supply excellent fruits for a minimal investment of time and resources.

Depending on the species and cultivar, the sweet blue fruits measure $1/4$-$3/4$ in (6-18 mm) wide. Good when fresh, the berries also preserve and freeze well.

Site and soil preparation

Although they tolerate many kinds of conditions, blueberries grow best in a sunny spot on well-drained soil rich in organic matter. An acid pH of 5.0 is essential.

Alkaline soils must be treated with powdered sulfur to lower the pH — a soil test will reveal the exact amount of sulfur needed.

A few weeks before planting, prepare the site by digging a hole $1\frac{1}{2}$ ft (45 cm) square for each bush. Break up the subsoil, and mix sphagnum peat or garden compost with the topsoil in equal amounts. Fill the hole with the mixture and give it time to settle.

A mulch of sawdust will help to maintain soil pH at the proper level, in particular, helping to acidify naturally alkaline soils.

Planting

Yields depend on the weather and soil conditions, as well as the type of blueberry cultivated. One highbush blueberry provides 5-10 lb (2.3-4.5 kg) of fruits, while lowbush blueberries yield 10-15 lbs (4.5-7 kg) of fruits per 100 sq ft (9 sq m) of plants. Because cross-pollination is essential with some kinds of blueberries and improves yields with all kinds, plant at least two bushes of different cultivars together.

Plant two- or three-year-old bushes in the late fall or early spring; set highbush blueberries 6 ft (1.8 m) apart and rabbit-eyes 7-8 ft (2.1-2.4 m) apart. Plant lowbush plants 2 ft (60 cm) apart in beds 2-3 ft (60-90 cm) wide.

Cultivation

Do not fertilize blueberries during their first season in your garden. In early spring of the second year, feed a highbush or rabbit-eye bush with 4 oz (115 g) of aluminum sulfate, increasing this amount by 1 oz (28 g) annually until the sixth year; then raise the dosage to 8 oz (230 g), an adequate annual feed for a mature bush. For lowbush blueberries use similar amounts aluminum sulfate (1 oz/28 g the first year, 8 oz/230 g by the sixth year) over 100 sq ft (9 sq m) of bed.

During the first two winters after planting, prune out damaged or prostrate stems on highbush or rabbit-eye bushes. In the third winter and annually thereafter, cut out weak stems; cut back old wood to the base or to vigorous new side shoots. To encourage

◀ **Highbush blueberries** As they begin to crop in their third year, blueberries bear fruits at the shoot tips. The berries are green at first but turn slate-blue. They are ready for picking when they are soft and covered with a waxy bloom.

new growth, prune annually. Blueberries bear fruits on the tips of the previous season's growth.

Lowbush blueberries need no pruning for the first four years. Thereafter cut them back to 1 in (2.5 cm) high every second year. By pruning half of the bed each year, you ensure there will be another half bearing fruits.

Blueberries are surface rooting; weed by hand to avoid disturbing the roots. An annual mulch in spring prevents weeds and conserves soil moisture.

Harvesting

Pick blueberries from midsummer to early fall. They do not all ripen at once; harvest them several times. Ripe berries are light to dark blue with a waxy bloom.

Pests and diseases

Blueberries are free of pests and diseases. Use netting to protect flower buds and fruits from birds.

CULTIVARS TO CHOOSE

'Berkeley': vigorous highbush; large, sweet fruits; ripen in midseason.

'Bluecrop': highbush; good cropper; large, sweet fruits; ripen at start of season in mid-July.

'Bright Blue': vigorous rabbit-eye; large, light blue fruits.

'Coville': vigorous highbush; large, light blue fruits; ripen late, around mid-August; good yields.

'Herbert': highbush; 4 ft (1.2 m) high and wide; large medium-blue fruits; ripen late summer.

'North Blue': highbush-lowbush hybrid; 2 ft (60 cm) high; dark blue, flavorful, tart fruits; cold hardy.

'North Country': highbush-lowbush hybrid ; 2 ft (60 cm) high; sky-blue fruits with mild flavor; cold hardy.

'Tifblue': rabbit-eye; light blue, sweet fruits; ripen in late midseason; tolerates heat and drought.

LAYERING

1 In early fall select a long shoot; cut a tongue slightly into the heartwood where it can be bent to reach the ground.

2 Peg down the shoot with wire staples; if needed, tie the tip to a stake. After a year or two sever the rooted branch tip and plant it in a permanent site.

TAKING CUTTINGS

1 Take semihard shoots with heels in midsummer. Remove the soft growing tip; dip the heel in hormone rooting powder.

2 Insert the cuttings in a peat-based potting mix in a cold frame. Spray them frequently with water until they are well rooted. Then plant them out.

PRUNING

Highbush and rabbit-eye blueberries need no pruning for the first two years after planting. After that, prune each winter to encourage new growth — fruits are borne on the previous year's shoots. Remove wood that is weak, damaged, or dead, and cut back old wood to the base or to vigorous new side shoots.

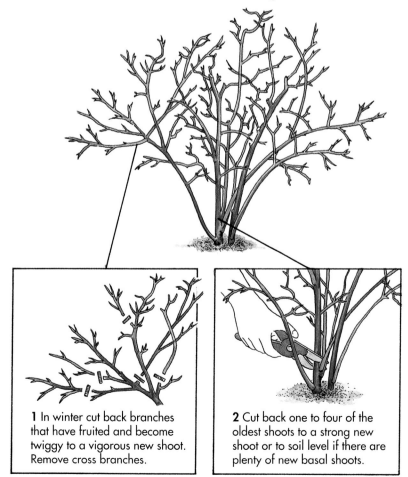

1 In winter cut back branches that have fruited and become twiggy to a vigorous new shoot. Remove cross branches.

2 Cut back one to four of the oldest shoots to a strong new shoot or to soil level if there are plenty of new basal shoots.

CRANBERRIES

Traditionally used as a garnish for turkey, cranberries are wetland shrubs that will flourish only on acid, boggy soil.

Cranberries commonly appear on dining tables at Thanksgiving and Christmas. These berries are versatile, adding zest to breads and muffins and furnishing a flavorful ingredient for jellies and sherbets. They are not only tasty but also healthful. Cranberries are rich in vitamin C; New England sea captains used to take them on their voyages to keep the crew free from scurvy. Best of all, cranberries are easy to grow, as long as you meet the plant's handful of special requirements.

True cranberries belong to the same genus as blueberries *(Vaccinium)*. The species commonly cultivated for its fruits is *V. macrocarpon*, a native of bogs and swamps from Newfoundland west to Minnesota and south to North Carolina. Several species of viburnums (a group of ornamental shrubs) produce tart red fruits and are sometimes called cranberries. *Viburnum trilobum* is known as the highbush cranberry, and *V. opulus* is referred to as the European cranberry. The fruits of these shrubs are not of the same quality as *Vaccinium macrocarpon*, but they make a good jelly or sauce. Viburnums are less exacting in their cultural requirements than the true cranberry, and flourish in any moist garden soil in a sunny or semi-shaded spot from zones 3-8.

The true cranberry (hardy in zones 2-6) is a mat-forming 3 ft (90 cm) wide shrub with small, elliptical evergreen leaves. The red berries, which ripen in September and October, measure ½-¾ in (12-18 mm) in diameter. High-yielding, cultivated strains of cranberries yield up to 1-1½ lb (450-680 g) per sq yd/m.

▲ **Cranberries** Growing wild in bogs and wetlands throughout the Northeast, the true cranberries offer a handsome as well as appetizing spectacle when they fruit in early fall.

Preparing for planting

Cranberries need a constantly moist, cool, acid soil; because they grow naturally in sphagnum bogs, these berries grow particularly well in wet peat. Other types of organically rich soils may retain enough moisture, but they still lack the strongly acidic pH of 3.2-4.5 that cranberries require.

While few gardens naturally include soils that are suitable for

CREATING A BOG BED

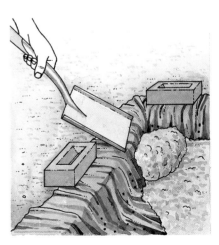

1 Dig a 2 ft (60 cm) deep trench 1½ ft (45 cm) wide for one row, 2 ft (60 cm) wide for two rows. Layer the bottom with crushed rock 4 in (10 cm) deep.

2 Perforate a sheet of 2 ml thick polyethylene with a skewer. Lay it in the trench; make sure it covers the side walls to stop water from leaking too quickly.

3 Keep the plastic in place with bricks; fill the trench with a mixture of two parts peat to one part loam or three parts peat to one part coarse sand.

cranberry cultivation, you can create a special planting area that satisfies this plant's needs. One solution is to grow cranberries in tubs of potting soil heavily enriched with peat; a mixture of half soil and half peat is ideal. Set the tubs in a sunny spot.

If you wish to grow more than a few cranberry bushes, create a bed in the ground in a sunny spot. Dig a trench 2 ft (60 cm) deep and 1½ ft (45 cm) wide for one row of plants or 2 ft (60 cm) wide for two. Fill the bottom with a layer of drainage material 4 in (10 cm) deep, and cover this with a sheet of perforated plastic (use a skewer to puncture holes in the plastic). Fill in the rest of the trench with a mixture of two parts peat to one part loam or three parts peat to one part coarse sand (parts by volume).

Planting

Plant container-grown plants in spring or fall and bare-root plants in early spring. Space them 1 ft (30 cm) apart in rows spaced at the same distance. If you peg down long shoots, cranberries root at the leaf joints, increasing the shrubs' sturdiness and size.

Immediately after planting, water the bed until the peat mixture is thoroughly soaked. To prevent the peat surface from drying out, cover it after watering with a 1 in (2.5 cm) layer of coarse, lime-free sand; this will also help the stems root.

The following spring, feed the plants with a balanced complete fertilizer at the rate recommended for evergreen shrubs on the product label. If it doesn't rain soon after application, water the bed lightly so that the fertilizer doesn't sit on the leaves and branches of the plants.

In early spring, prune any creeping stems to confine the plants to the peat bed. Remove

CULTIVARS TO CHOOSE

'Ben Lear': large to medium, deep red fruits; ripen early; bear well.

'Cropper': large, deep red fruits; ripen midseason; adapted to Pacific Northwest.

'McFarlin': large fruits with especially good flavor.

PLANTING AND PRUNING

1 Plant bare-root bushes in early spring, container-grown plants in spring or fall. Peg down any straggly growth, and water the bed until thoroughly soaked. Cover with a layer of coarse, clean sand.

2 In early spring, prune creeping stems to confine the plants to the bed. Remove tall, upright stems along with any deadwood. Keep the bed saturated throughout the year.

any upright fruiting shoots that are old, weak, or crowding the center. If frost threatens in spring, when the cranberries are in bloom, temporarily protect the flowers with a floating row cover. Simply spread spunbonded polypropylene fabric (available from garden centers) loosely over the bushes and bury its edges in the soil to hold in place.

Water is vital throughout the year; keep the bed saturated.

Propagation

Raise new plants by layering shoots in early fall; they are ready for severing and planting out in one or two years. Divide strong plants, and replant them between fall and winter.

Harvesting

Harvest when the berries turn deep red in early fall and midfall. The berries keep for 3 weeks in a cool, dry place, 8 to 12 weeks in a refrigerator, and several months in a freezer. Use any leftover berries to make jelly.

Pests and diseases

Cranberry bushes are generally disease and pest free.

Cranberry bog

CURRANTS

**Currants are not only hardy and long-lived,
but easy to grow. With good management these bushes
will yield heavy crops for many years.**

Though not grown very often in the United States, currants are actually one of the most versatile fruits in the kitchen. These tart berries are delicious when used for making jellies, jams, and pies, and they can even be used for producing wine.

Site and soil preparation
Currants grow best in an open, sunny spot, although they will tolerate light shade. Red currants are the most shade tolerant, fruiting well even when grown in semishade. The commonly cultivated currants — red, white, and black — are mostly of northern European origin and prefer cool, moist climates. They perform best in zones 3 through 5 or 6, though cold tolerance can vary with the cultivar. Those gardeners who live in areas of greater summer heat and drought or in areas of extreme winter cold should try two native American species: the clove currant *(Ribes odoratum)* and the American black currant *(R. americanum)*. The clove currant is well adapted to the climate of the Midwest, and the American black currant is hardy as far north as zone 2 and as far south as New Mexico.

In general, any well-drained, moisture-retentive soil is suitable for currants. Black currants thrive in organic, slightly acidic soils. Before planting the bushes, work in a generous amount of well-rotted manure or good garden compost.

Planting
Because currants can serve as hosts for a fatal disease of the white pine, the planting of these bushes was once banned in many parts of the United States where the white pine is an important timber tree. However, disease-resistant strains of currants have been introduced to the market and the ban has been relaxed in some states. Before you order and plant any currant bushes in your garden, first consult your county Cooperative Extension Service or state agricultural department to

▲ **Black currants** The best crops are produced on spurs on shoots of the previous season, although older stems continue to bear fruits.

determine what, if any, regulations exist in your locality.

Always transplant currant bushes while they are dormant. Because they leaf out early, plant these bushes in fall or very early in spring, as soon as the soil can be worked. Excavate holes that are large enough to accommodate the roots comfortably when they are well spread out. Plant the black currant plants about 1-2 in (2.5-5 cm) deeper than they were growing at the nursery; look for the soil mark left on the stem as a guide. Plant red and white currants to the same depth at which they were grown in the nursery; again, use the soil mark as a guide. Plant the bushes 5-6 ft (1.5-1.8 m) apart.

No matter the type of bush, cut back the top growth immediately after planting. Cut back black currant stems to just above the second bud from soil level. For red and white currant bushes, cut back the shoots to an outward-facing bud, ideally the fourth one up from the base of the shoot. Although this severe pruning will prevent the bearing of fruits in the first year, it will also ensure stronger bushes. You should mulch with a 2 in (5 cm) layer of well-rotted manure, garden compost, or leaf mold.

Looking after the crop
To help retain moisture in the soil, replace the mulch of rotted manure, garden compost, or leaf

mold every year in early spring; two buckets per sq yd/sq m should be adequate.

In late winter, broadcast (sprinkle evenly) a 10-10-10 fertilizer over the roots at a rate of $^{1}/_{4}$-$^{1}/_{2}$ lb (115-230 g) per plant. Avoid overfeeding the bushes, especially with nitrogen, since this makes the plants more susceptible to diseases.

When weeding around currant bushes with a fork or hoe, make sure you avoid disturbing their shallow roots. After hard frosts, check that the bushes have not heaved up from the soil. If they have, simply press them back in the ground with your feet. Water the plants regularly during any dry periods.

Pruning currants

While black currants are closely related to red and white currants, their growth habits are not the same. Black currants bear fruits on stems produced in the previous season, while red and white currants fruit on new shoots that develop in the current year. Because of this difference, pruning methods will also differ.

Black currants bear the most fruits on one-year-old wood — that is, on shoots or side branches produced in the previous season of growth. Older stems will continue to produce some fruits, though not as abundantly as new shoots do. The objective of pruning is to keep a supply of the fruitful, one-year-old twigs going into the new season of growth and to retain some older growth, while also stimulating new shoot production on the older growth.

In winter after the first growing season, cut any weak shoots back to 2 in (5 cm) above ground; this encourages stronger growth from the base.

Once a bush is established (in the second winter after planting), each winter remove entirely up to a quarter of all the two-year-old or older shoots, and cut all other tall old growth back to a vigorous, one-year-old side branch. Aim to keep the center of the bush open so that air can circulate freely.

In addition to this annual winter pruning, black currant bushes may need rejuvenation as they age. If you notice that the fruit production on an older bush has dropped, cut all the shoots back to ground level in wintertime.

You can resume regular pruning the winter after next.

Red or white currants should be pruned right after planting; cut all the shoots back just above an outward-pointing bud, the fourth from the base. In the second winter after planting, cut back all the main branches by a half; make the cuts just above an outward-facing bud. If necessary, thin out branches at the center of the bush to produce an open, spreading pattern of growth.

In succeeding winters cut back new leaders (upward-reaching shoots) by a half, and shorten laterals (side branches) to two buds each. Continue to maintain the open pattern of growth, gradually removing woody branches and allowing new growth to fill in.

Propagating currants

Currants root easily from cuttings of one-year-old wood taken in the fall. Cut pieces 8-10 in (20-25 cm) long, and dust the bases with a hormone rooting powder. Then stick the cuttings in a sheltered, well-drained nursery bed of loam emended with sphagnum peat and sand. For cuttings from a red or white currant bush, remove all but the top three buds; set the cuttings with all the remaining buds above ground.

After rooting, allow the cuttings to grow on in place until the following fall, at which time transplant them to the garden.

Harvesting and storing

Pick currants when they are fully ripe; with black currants this comes a week or two after the fruits have turned black. Cook or freeze fruits as soon as possible after picking.

Pests and diseases

Black currants are attacked by aphids and currant borer; spray in spring with a recommended insecticide, before flowering, and again afterwards. Imported currantworms — green, caterpillar-like larvae — may feed on leaves; you can control them by hand-picking. Botrytis and leaf spot may attack the foliage; bright orange spots on the leaves in midsummer are a symptom of white pine blister rust.

Red and white currants are attacked by the same pests and diseases as those that attack black currants; treatment is the same.

Red currant 'Red Lake'

White currant 'White Imperial'

51

GOOSEBERRIES

This easy-to-grow fruit is delicious fresh or cooked, and though not common, it thrives even in most northern states.

Gooseberries make an excellent sauce for a roast goose — hence their name. These berries are delicious in pies, jellies, and preserves. When fully ripe, sweet, aromatic gooseberries are delightful right off the bush.

Hardy through zone 3, gooseberries prefer the cool climate of the northern half of the country. They were banned as a host for the white pine blister rust, but in many places the ban has been lifted. Check with your county Cooperative Extension Service before placing an order at the nursery.

Plants may be grown as cordons (specimens maintained as single- or double-stemmed plants by means of pruning) but are more commonly cultivated as bushes. These bushes are grown on a "leg," an 8 in (20 cm) length of clear main stem below the branches. This prevents suckers from growing out and keeps the fruits clear of the soil. A mature,

▲ **Gooseberries** Ranging widely in color from green to white, yellow, or red, gooseberries also vary in flavor from tart to very sweet. They are in season from late spring until the end of summer.

well-tended bush will yield up to 8-10 lb (3.6-4.5 kg) of fruits and a cordon about 2-4 lb (0.9-1.8 kg).

Site and soil preparation

Gooseberries do equally well in semishade and full sun. Choose a site protected from cold winds and late frosts, which could damage the flowers.

Any moist, well-drained soil is suitable, but the best results are obtained on deep, fertile loam free of perennial weeds.

Before planting, work large quantities of compost into the soil: a bucketful per sq yd/m. Apply potassium sulfate at the rate of 1 oz (28 g) per sq yd/m.

Planting

Plant out bare-root bushes in very early spring while still dormant. Set bushes 5 ft (1.5 m) apart; but plant cordons at intervals of 15 in (38 cm). Leave 5 ft (1.5 m) between rows.

Grow cordons against a fence or wall. Staple or nail three horizontal support wires to the fence or wall 1 ft (30 cm) apart. Tie a

TAKING GOOSEBERRY CUTTINGS

In midfall, cut off hardened shoots of the current year's growth above a bud. Trim the top above a bud, the base below a bud. Root 6 in (15 cm) apart in a V-shaped trench 8 in (20 cm) deep, with four buds above the soil.

Midseason 'Whinham's Industry'

Late 'Whitesmith'

stake to the wires at a 45° angle; tie the cordon to the stake with string. Remove the stake when the cordon reaches the top wire.

Looking after the crop

At winter's end (but not the first year after planting), feed the plants with wood ashes, sprinkled around the bushes at a rate of ½ lb (230 g) per sq yd/m. Then apply a mulch of well-rotted manure or compost. In early spring apply 1 tablespoon of ammonium sulfate per sq yd/sq m. In every third year apply 2 tablespoons of superphosphate to each sq yd/m. You should kill any weeds with a contact herbicide or by hand-weeding with a fork.

THINNING

Start thinning gooseberries on heavy-bearing branches in late spring. Thinning can be carried out in several stages until the fruits are spaced 3 in (7.5 cm) apart. You can use any unripe fruits in cooking.

CULTIVARS TO CHOOSE

'Broom Girl': greenish-yellow fruits; ripen very early; good flavor; productive.

'Clark': very large red fruits; ripen in midseason; excellent flavor; mildew resistant.

'Leveller': large, pear-shaped yellow fruits; ripen in midseason;

excellent flavor; susceptible to mildew.

'Whinham's Industry': very sweet red fruits; ripen in midseason; productive bush.

'Whitesmith': pale green fruits ripen late; excellent flavor; disease-resistant shrub; tolerates shade.

If frost threatens in the flowering season in spring, cover the plants with floating row covers of spunbonded polypropylene at night. Remove the cover in the day to let pollinating insects in.

Remove any suckers that appear from the stem or roots. Water during hot weather.

Pruning

Cut the bushes back in winter (see p.43) or when the buds start to swell. Prune mature plants in early summer; cut side shoots to five leaves from the base.

On cordons allow the leaders to grow unpruned; cut back new growth at the tips in late spring once they reach the top wire.

Prune back mature laterals to three leaves in midsummer and side shoots to one leaf. Cut back any secondary growth produced thereafter to one bud in fall.

Raising new plants

In midfall take cuttings 12-15 in (30-38 cm) long from hardened, mature shoots of the current year's wood; cut just above a bud. If the top 1-3 in (2.5-7.5 cm) of the cutting is soft and not ripe,

cut it off just above a bud; if it is brown to the tip, leave it. Trim the lower end just below a bud.

In a sheltered, sunny site root the cuttings 6 in (15 cm) apart in an 8 in (20 cm) deep trench.

Transplant cuttings to the garden early in spring. Lift them from the ground with a fork. Cut off flush with the stem any shoots growing below ground and on the bottom 4-5 in (10-13 cm) of stem.

Harvesting

Pick gooseberries for cooking when ½ in (12 mm) in diameter. Do not pick fruits for eating raw until they are soft and fully ripe.

Pests and diseases

Gooseberry mildew appears as powdery white patches on new leaves; it can stunt foliage and destroy fruits. Spray with lime sulfur; avoid overfertilization.

Leaf spot causes foliage to yellow and drop prematurely; rake up and remove affected leaves.

Currantworms may attack foliage, and gooseberry fruitworms tunnel into the fruits; apply a recommended insecticide at the first signs of damage.

GRAPES

**South or North, East or West, wherever
you garden in the United States there are grapes
adapted to your climate and soil.**

Many species of grapes are native to North America, and Old World grapes of the species *Vitis vinifera* thrive in some parts of the country (especially along the Pacific Coast, but also in temperate parts of the Northeast). Even where European grapes do not thrive, gardeners grow grapes of excellent quality, with fruits that are good for eating fresh, as well as for cooking and making wine.

Grapes can be found growing wild throughout the country. Though these wild plants do not produce palatable fruits, they have provided materials for nurseries to breed an abundance of hybrids and improved cultivars. The fruits of these offer a range of flavors — and the plants are adapted to local soils and climates, as well as resistant to local diseases and pests. Success in growing grapes depends not only on careful cultivation, but even more on knowing which types of grapes flourish in your region.

Grapes for different regions

With the following species you will find the regions in which they flourish. Additional cultivars and hybrids are listed on page 57.
Vitis labrusca is the species whose fruits have become synonymous with grape flavor. Its flavor is the dominant one found in grape jellies and juices. Labrusca grapes are generally hardy in zones 5-7. Tolerant of hot summers and cold winters, they are well adapted to the Northeastern, middle Atlantic, and Midwestern states.
Vitis rotundifolia is the premier grape of the South, flourishing in zones 7-9. Well adapted to the lower Midwest and to the south Atlantic and Gulf states, it flourishes in conditions of heat and humidity and is resistant to Pierce's disease and other grape diseases indigenous to the South. Rotundifolia vines bear small clusters of marble-size grapes; they tend to ripen unevenly and drop off the stem when mature. The tangy, foxy (sharp, brisk flavor) fruits are good for eating

▶ **Grape varieties**
Modern white, red, and black cultivars have been bred to succeed in American climates. Some have highly ornamental fall foliage.

fresh and are prized for jams, jellies, and wines. Wild vines require cross-pollination by another plant to set fruits, but many cultivated types are self-fertile.
Vitis vinifera, the European wine grape, is best adapted to warm, dry regions. It grows well along much of the Pacific Coast, as well as in the more temperate areas of the Northeastern coast, the Finger Lakes region of New York, the western part of Texas, and the upland regions of Virginia, North Carolina, and Arkansas. Despite the species' wine-making heritage, the most famous vinifera grape in the United States is undoubtedly 'Thompson Seedless,' whose pale green fruits are eaten fresh or dried as raisins.

Compared with other types, vinifera grapes prove more susceptible to diseases and pests in the United States and are often less hardy. Better suited to most home gardens are the "French-American hybrids" — grapes bred by crossing vinifera grapes with native American species.

Cold-hardy grapes

In recent years a number of exceptionally cold-tolerant grapes have been bred, and these extend this fruit's range to areas with short growing seasons and harsh winters, such as the northern Midwest and the Rocky Mountain states (zones 3-4). The following two outstanding cultivars are well worth planting.

'Edelweiss,' a disease-resistant labrusca hybrid, is cold hardy to zone 3 without protection. Its vigorous and productive vines bear medium-size greenish-gold fruits that have a sweet but mild flavor. The fruits are delicious fresh and make a good wine.
'Swenson Red' is a labrusca hybrid that is hardy to zone 4 with winter protection. The large, red to bluish grapes are sweet, excellent to eat fresh, and make an acceptable white wine.

TRELLISING AND TRAINING

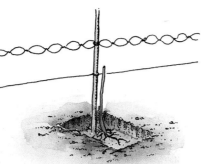

1 Staple a wire to posts 1½ ft (45 cm) from ground and two loosely twisted wires 2½ ft (75 cm) and 4 ft (1.2 m) from ground.

2 Drive a stake into planting hole; leave 6 ft (1.8 m) above ground to support replacement shoots. Tie stake to wires.

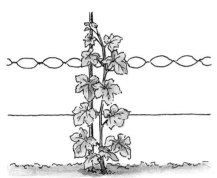

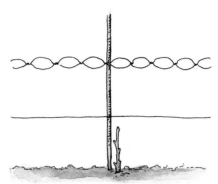

3 In the first summer after planting, tie the strongest shoot to the stake. Pinch back other shoots to one or two leaves.

4 After leaf drop, cut vine to about four buds. If winter will be severe, untie and bury weak vines in mulch until spring.

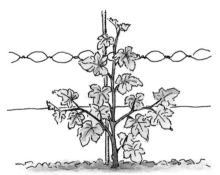

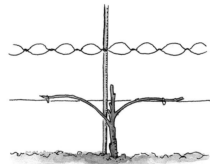

5 In the following summer allow the three strongest shoots to grow; tie them to the support stake. Pinch off other shoots.

6 In late fall tie two shoots to the bottom wire. (Stop growth when space is filled.) Cut center shoot back to three buds.

Preparing the site

Choose a sheltered spot in full sun with good drainage. A south- or southwest-facing slope is ideal. Avoid frost pockets and sites in even partial shade. In northern regions train grapes on a south-facing wall or fence.

Poorly drained soil is fatal for grapes, and soil that is too rich promotes soft, disease- and pest-susceptible growth. An ideal pH is 5.0-6.0; adjust more acidic or alkaline soils with lime or sulfur. If you do not know your soil's pH, have it tested by your county Cooperative Extension Service. Test results will include recommendations for amendment.

Prepare the soil for planting in fall. Carefully remove all weeds, especially perennial types. Then double-dig an area 3 ft (90 cm) in diameter for each vine, turning the soil to a depth of about 2 ft (60 cm). Fork in well-rotted manure or garden compost at the rate of a bucketful per sq yd/m. Vines grow best in a sandy, gravelly soil that warms up quickly in the sun, but they will succeed in any type of soil if the drainage is good. Heavy soil on a sloping site is acceptable but amend it with a liberal dose of coarse sand, one bucketful to each planting hole.

This is also the time to install supports. Grapevines need a trellis on which to climb; a wooden arbor is an attractive solution for a planting of one or two vines, but if you intend to grow grapes in quantity, you will probably need to erect a row of posts and wires.

To create a trellis, set support posts 6 ft (1.8 m) high at 8-10 ft (2.4-3 m) intervals. The end posts should be at least 4 in (10 cm) in

7 Next summer train the fruiting laterals from the two horizontal stems through the twisted wires. In late summer cut the tips of the laterals back to two or three leaves above the top wire. Remove the sublaterals. Tie in the replacement stems.

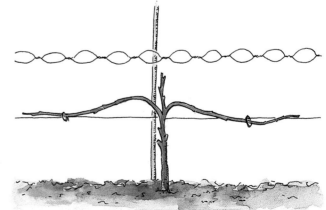

8 In late fall completely cut back the horizontal stems that have carried fruits. Tie two replacement shoots to the bottom wire, and prune the remaining center shoot back to three buds. These buds will provide the following year's shoots.

diameter and intermediate posts about 2 in (5 cm) in diameter. Allow 5 ft (1.5 m) between rows.

Staple a strand of 12-gauge galvanized wire to the posts about 1½ft (45 cm) from the ground.

Loosely twist two strands of wire together, and staple them to the posts 2½ft (75 cm) from the ground, with another length of twisted wires 1½ft (45 cm) above this. Train the fruiting shoots through the twisted double wires to save tying in individual shoots.

The length of the trellis will depend on the numbers of vines you intend to plant; plan on 6-10 ft (1.8-3 m) of trellis for each vine. An established vine in the open produces at least 10 bunches of grapes, or about 5 lb (2.3 kg), in a good year. A vine trained on a wall produces 15-20 lb (7-9 kg) or more, depending on the amount of wall covered. Start with just two or three vines, and add more later if you have space.

Planting

Vines are usually sold as one-year-old plants. More often than not, the cultivar is grafted as a scion onto a vigorous pest- and disease-resistant rootstock. Mail-ordered plants generally arrive as bare-root vines; plant them in early spring before the buds begin to swell and open. Garden centers may have container-grown vines; plant these in spring or fall.

Dig a hole wide enough for the roots to spread evenly and deep enough for the vine to be at the same level as in the nursery; look for the soil mark left on the stem. On grafted vines the graft union (the point at which the named cultivar joins the rootstock) is visible as a swollen area; this must be set above ground level.

Set the vines 6-10 ft (1.8-3 m) apart. Just before planting, drive a sturdy stake into the soil, leaving 6 ft (1.8 m) of the stake above the soil level. This will provide a support for tying in replacement shoots in subsequent years.

Allow only one strong shoot to grow in the first year. Tie this to the support stake; pinch off all other shoots at one or two leaves.

Training

In late fall after planting, the vine will be ready for training. Use the double Guyot system, the easiest way of growing vines in the open.

With this method grapes grow on lateral stems produced the previous year; at the same time replacement stems are trained for fruiting the following year.

After the leaves drop, cut the vine down to three or four buds. The following summer, allow the three strongest shoots to grow, pinching off all others.

In late fall tie two of the shoots along the bottom wire, one to the left and one to the right. Cut the third (center) shoot back to three buds. When the two sideway-reaching shoots fill the space available on the wires, stop their growth by pinching off their tips.

The following summer train the fruiting laterals from the two horizontal stems through the double wires. In late summer cut the tips of the laterals back to two or three leaves above the top wire; then remove all sublaterals completely, cutting them back to the point of origin.

Tie three replacement shoots to the support stake as they grow; pinch back laterals growing from them to one leaf in late summer.

In late fall completely remove the two horizontal stems carrying the laterals that have fruited. Tie two replacement shoots to the bottom wire (one to the left and one to the right, as before), and cut back the third to three buds.

Repeat this horizontal training each year. Restrict the crop to four bunches per vine in the first fruiting year (the third year after planting) and six in the second, then allow full cropping.

General cultivation

Water the soil near the roots well, especially in the first year after planting. Mulch lightly with compost in late winter or early spring.

With average soil begin fertilization the spring after planting a vine. Spread about ¼ lb (115 g) of 10-10-10 fertilizer in a circle 4 ft (1.2 m) from the the base of the vine. In following springs increase the dosage to 1 lb (450 g) spread in a circle 8 ft (2.4 m) from the vine's base. Take care to fertilize when the buds first swell. Late applications may encourage late-summer growth that won't mature properly before going dormant; this growth will be extra-vulnerable to winter cold.

If you plant the vines in rich soil, however, base your fertilization on the results of a professional soil test. Overfertilization will damage not only the health of your grapevines but also the quality of the harvest.

Wall-grown grapes

Train grapes on a wall or fence on a single cordon, or shoot. Secure support wires to the wall 1 ft (30 cm) apart, and hold them 5 in (13 cm) from the wall with vine eyes. Prepare the soil and plant the vines as in the open; set the vines 4 ft (1.2 m) apart and 9 in (23 cm) away from the wall.

Plant in late fall or early spring, then cut the cordon back to two buds from ground level. In the following growing season leave the strongest shoot untouched; pinch off the growing tips on other shoots when 4 in (10 cm) long. Pinch back subsequent sublaterals to one leaf and all flowers as they appear.

Grape 'Thompson Seedless'

Grape 'Concord'

In early winter, as soon as the leaves have fallen, cut back the vine by two-thirds. As growth develops in spring, let the topmost bud grow on as the new leader. Thin laterals, if necessary, pinching them back when 1 in (2.5 cm) long. The aim is to produce alternate fruit-bearing laterals on opposite sides of the stem.

If the vine is growing strongly, allow two laterals on each side to fruit. Pinch off these laterals at two leaves beyond the embryo bunch of grapes. Pinch back unfruited laterals when 2 ft (60 cm). In early winter shorten the leader by one-half. Cut back each lateral to 1 in (2.5 cm), leaving two buds. Repeat this training of the single-stem cordon annually.

Winter protection

The best guarantee against cold is to plant only cultivars reliably hardy in your area. If you garden in a particularly severe climate or are determined to grow cultivars of marginal hardiness, untie the vines from the trellis or arbor after they go dormant in late fall; bury them under a thick mulch of straw until early spring. Or keep the vines under 1 ft (30 cm) tall, training the arms on a single wire, and bury the whole vine in straw over the winter.

Pests and diseases

Caterpillars and Japanese beetles feed on grape leaves; spray with a recommended insecticide.

Black rot disfigures leaves with rusty brown spots and turns fruits into hard, black mummies. Botrytis fruit rot turns fruits brown and soft and covers large areas with powdery brown mold. Powdery mildew appears as a gray mold on canes; it spreads to the leaves and fruits, causing fruits to split. Downy mildew lightly blotches leaves; it may cover young shoots and fruit clusters with a white powdery mold. To control these problems, apply the recommended fungicides. Pierce's disease, a bacteria, causes the decline and death of *Vitis vinifera* and *labrusca* grapes in the South; the best preventive is to plant resistant strains of muscadine grapes *(Vitis rotundifolia)*. Grapevine root borers, another southern pest, are thick white worms that tunnel into roots and the base of the vine. Hill up soil around the base in midsummer to prevent the pest from completing its life cycle.

CULTIVARS TO CHOOSE

Vitis labrusca
'Canadice': good to eat fresh and for juice, jelly, and wine; large clusters of spicy-flavored, seedless red fruits; hardy to -15°F (-26°C); resistant to black rot; susceptible to mildew.

'Catawba': good for jams, jellies, and wines; vigorous vine; medium-size clusters of medium-size red fruits; suceptible to mildew.

'Concord': good to eat fresh and for wine; large crops of medium to large blue-black fruits; hardy to lower zone 4; disease resistant.

'Interlaken': good to eat fresh and for raisins; large crops of tangy, golden yellow seedless fruits; cold hardy to -15°F (-26°C).

'Niagara': good to eat fresh and for wine; tangy greenish-white fruits.

'Steuben': good to eat fresh and for wine; large clusters of spicy-flavored blue to purplish-black fruits.

Vitis rotundifolia
'Carlos': good to eat fresh and for wine; small to medium-size bronze fruits; self-fertile; holds fruit well; disease resistant.

'Magnolia': good for wine; sweet, bronze-colored fruits; self-fertile.

'Noble': good to eat fresh and for preserves and wine; small to medium-size blue-black fruit; productive; self-fertile.

'Scuppernong': sweet yet tart and foxy in flavor; large, thick-skinned reddish-bronze fruits; requires cross-pollination by another cultivar.

French-American Hybrids

'Aurore': good to eat fresh and for juice and wine; sweet, white fruits with a slight pink blush; hardy through zone 6; mildew resistant.

'Baco Noir': good for wine; small clusters of bluish-black fruits; very vigorous and productive; mildew resistant.

'Foch': good for wines, jellies, and juice; bluish-black fruits; vigorous.

'Seyval Blanc': syn. 'Seyve-Villard 5-276; good for wine; large crops of white fruits; compact, vigorous, disease-resistant vine.

LOGANBERRIES

A hybrid between the raspberry and the blackberry, loganberries produce ample harvests of large, sharp-tasting fruits.

▲ **Loganberries** While similar in shape to raspberries, loganberries are larger and wine-red when ripe. These berries have smaller thorns than their other parent, the blackberry, which makes them easier to handle.

The loganberry was first bred from the blackberry and the raspberry in 1881. It is less vigorous than the blackberry, and the canes are not as thorny. A further advantage is that the fruits are larger than those of either of its parents. The conical berries are wine-red and very juicy, with an excellent tart flavor.

The loganberry's success has prompted the introduction of other hybrid berries, such as the wineberry, tayberry, and boysenberry — some of which deserve the attention of home gardeners. These hybrids are similar to the loganberry, but each has its own characteristics, such as larger fruits or greater tolerance of drought. Grow them in the same way as the loganberry. Other hybrid berries, like jostaberry, are crosses between black currants and gooseberries. Grow them like other bush fruits.

Planning the crop

Loganberries give high yields in moisture-retentive, fertile soil but dislike alkaline soil. They prefer a sunny site, ideally a wall or fence with a southern exposure.

Like most hybrids, they are heavy bearers, so one to three plants are sufficient for the average family. These plants are self-fertile, and each needs a space of about 8-10 ft (2.4-3 m).

Planting

Dig up the soil in late summer, and remove all weeds. On shallow or sandy soil, work in at least one bucketful of organic matter, such as strong manure, to each planting site.

Loganberries ordered from the nursery arrive as bare-root plants in early spring; plant them immediately. Upon planting, cut the canes back to a bud 9 in (23 cm) above ground level; mulch with well-rotted manure or compost.

Training

Loganberries and similar hybrids produce their finest fruits on canes developed during the previous season. Train them so that fruiting shoots are kept well away from replacement shoots. This makes management easier and reduces the spread of fungal diseases. Train them by the fan system or a "one-way" system; both methods require a support framework of posts and wires.

Stretch a 10- to 12-gauge wire horizontally 5-6 ft (1.5-1.8 m)

FAN TRAINING

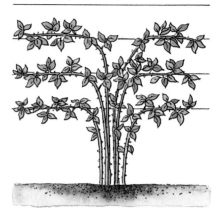

1 Stretch strong wires horizontally between posts set 8 ft (2.4 m) apart; allow 1 ft (30 cm) between each wire and 2 ft (60 cm) from the ground to the first wire. Train the first year's growth upward and then along the horizontals. Leave the top wire free.

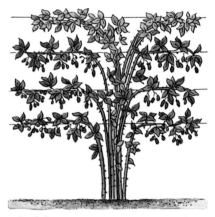

2 The following year train new growth upward through the middle of the fan. When the new canes reach the top wire, train them horizontally along it. Leave last year's stems in place — fruits will be produced on laterals from these canes.

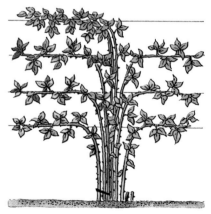

3 In midfall, when all the berries have been picked, cut off at ground level canes that previously bore fruits. Untie the current year's shoots from the top wire, and tie them onto lower wires to replace the cut-down shoots. Repeat steps 2 and 3 annually.

Boysenberry

Japanese wineberry

high and staple it to two posts. Or secure the wire to a sunny wall or fence with screw eyes. Continue stretching wires horizontally 1 ft (30 cm) apart, with the lowest wire 2 ft (60 cm) from the ground.

With the fan method, fan out the fruiting canes to the left and the right, and train replacement stems vertically up the middle and tie them to the top wire. With the one-way system, train and tie in the fruiting canes to one side of the center of the plant, and tie in

the new stems to the other side of the plant (see p.41).

In midfall, when all the fruits have been picked, cut the canes that bore berries down to ground level. Untie the current year's shoots from their temporary positions, and tie them in to replace the old cut-down shoots. Fruits grow on the laterals of the previous year's canes.

Watering and feeding
Water the plants only during dry spells in the growing season. These berry bushes are easily damaged by overfeeding. Feed them in early spring, before the bushes flower. Apply no more than 5 lb (2.3 kg) of 10-10-10 fertilizer per 100 ft (30 m) of bushes the first year; in following springs no more than 10 lb (4.5 kg).

Harvesting
Pick loganberries when they turn wine-red, starting around late summer and continuing for several weeks. Other hybrid berries turn different colors, such as black or purple, when ripe. Always pick loganberry fruits with its plug (unlike raspberries). Any surplus fruits are suitable for making jam or freezing.

HYBRID BERRIES

Boysenberry
This hybrid has thornless canes, making it easy to handle and pick fruits. Large and sweet purplish-black fruits ripen in mid- to late summer. Hardy in zones 5-9; requires winter protection at temperatures below -5°F (-20°C).

Japanese wineberry
The small scarlet fruits are best used for jam and wines; they have little flavor and consist of only a few drupelets. Attractive crimson canes are covered with red hairs in fall and winter. Grow the smallish plants 6 ft (1.8 m) apart; they are hardy in zones 6-8.

Loganberry
This plant originated in the wild as a cross of a red raspberry and a blackberry. Thornless clones are offered in nursery catalogs; these produce slightly smaller yields but offer easier picking and pruning. Hardy in zones 5-9, loganberries suffer cold damage in northern areas unless given winter protection.

Marionberry
The fruits are excellent for canning, freezing, making pies, jam, and wine. Developed in Marion County, Oregon, this blackberry hybrid bears large 3 in (7.5 cm) long, shiny black fruits with a sweet blackberrylike flavor in midsummer. This bush, hardy in zones 8-9, thrives only in a temperate climate like that of the Pacific Northwest.

Tayberry
This loganberry and black raspberry cross produces heavy crops of large, long and narrow, reddish or reddish-black fruits in mid- to late summer. The berries are sweet, with a hint of tartness. The bushes, hardy in zones 5-8, grow well even on poor soil.

Pests and diseases
The raspberry fruitworm appears as a yellow larva in small, soft patches on ripe fruits. To prevent attacks, spray with rotenone or pyrethrin when blossom buds appear and again as they open.

Plants may also suffer from anthracnose, which causes small purplish spots to appear on canes in the spring. Cut out and dispose of affected canes, and spray bushes with an approved fungicide in early spring.

MELONS

**With a sunny site and the right
cultivar, delicious melons can be grown
successfully from Maine to Arizona.**

Sweet, juicy melons, which are related to cucumbers and squashes, share similar needs. Like their cousins, they thrive in a sunny, well-drained corner of the vegetable garden.

In the past, melons were primarily grown in the South, since most of the old-fashioned types of muskmelons and watermelons demanded long, hot summers to ripen properly. Many of these melons required considerable acreage, too, for a single vining watermelon plant can sprawl over 100 sq ft (9 sq m). Compact modern cultivars, however, are making melons a more practical crop for the small garden, and types that mature early are making melons a good choice for planting even in the northern reaches of the United States.

Most of the melons grown in American gardens belong to one of two groups. Those that are often mistakenly called cantaloupes are actually muskmelons; this group also includes the so-called winter melons, such as honeydews, crenshaws, and casabas. The other major group of melons is the watermelons. It includes not only the well-known cultivars with sweet red flesh but also yellow- and orange-fleshed types. Watermelons range in size from 6-60 lb (2.7-27 kg).

Soil preparation

Melons need a sunny, sheltered spot, and they also require a site with good drainage and good air circulation; this will allow the foliage and fruits to dry quickly after irrigation and rain, thus helping to prevent disease. Melons do best in alkaline soil, so if a test shows the soil to be acid, enrich it with lime at least six weeks before preparing the site.

▶ **Muskmelons** Cantaloupe-type melons, such as 'Earlisweet,' perform well in northern climates; these are short-season melons. Casabas, while delicious, need a growing season of up to 115 days of warm weather.

In midspring dig an area for each plant that is approximately 1 ft × 2 ft (30 cm × 60 cm) and a spade-length deep (10 in/ 25 cm). Spread a bucketful of well-rotted manure or compost and ½ cup (120 ml) bonemeal over the bottom of the hole, then refill it with the topsoil. On sandy soil, topdress with a fertilizer that is high in potassium.

The spacing at which you set these prepared planting areas depends on the type of melon you intend to grow. For most muskmelons the planting areas should be set 4-6 ft (1.2-1.8 m) apart, but watermelons require a spacing of 6-12 ft (1.8-3.7 m). The spacing you select, however, should be based on a careful reading of your melon seed packets, since each

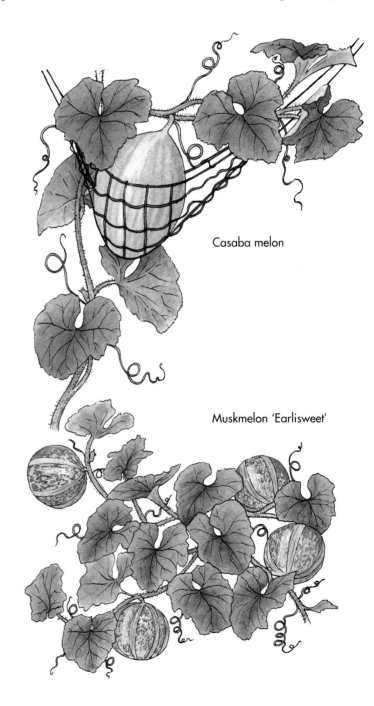

Casaba melon

Muskmelon 'Earlisweet'

MELONS IN THE NORTH

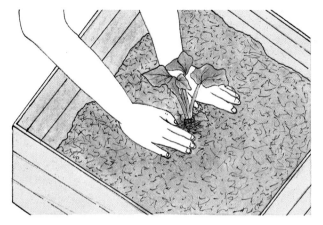

1 Set wooden frames over the well-dug and enriched patches of soil chosen for planting. Two weeks later plant out one seedling in the center of each frame, then water in.

2 When the plant has developed four or five additional leaves, pinch back the growing point immediately above the fifth leaf. This will encourage side shoots to form.

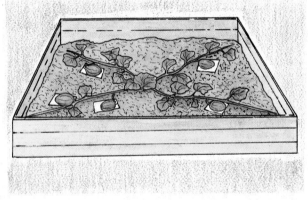

3 To hasten fruit set and ripening, allow only four side shoots to develop; pinch off all others. Direct side shoots toward the corners of the frame.

4 Pinch back shoot tips to two leaves beyond the fruits, and after midsummer pinch off all new flowers. Rest the fruits on pieces of cardboard or on inverted plastic pots to keep them clean.

cultivar has its own needs for space. Some modern bush-type melons may thrive at a spacing of just 2 ft (60 cm).

Melons require warm, well-drained soil if they are to flourish. In northern gardens these conditions may be obtained by heaping the soil in the planting area into a slightly raised bed and covering it with black plastic several weeks before planting time. Plant the melon seedlings through slits cut in the plastic. A less common but effective trick is to place a square wooden frame (2½ ft/75 cm wide and long, 10 in/25 cm deep) over each melon's planting place a couple of weeks before planting

▶ **Melon props** Ripening melon fruits need protection from damp soil, slugs, and snails. Set each fruit on a layer of straw or, for maximum protection, place each one on an overturned plastic flower pot. This will also keep it free of soil.

Watermelon 'Sweet Favorite'

(1.25 cm) deep in each pot. Moisten the soil and peat pots thoroughly, and set them in a covered propagating unit or underneath a clear plastic bag on a warm, sunny windowsill. Keep the soil temperature of the seed-starting mix at approximately 75°F (24°C); this is most easily accomplished in a heated propagating unit. When the seeds sprout, remove the plastic bag or propagating unit cover at once.

As soon as the seedlings reach a height of 2 in (5 cm), thin them to one seedling per pot by cutting all the others off at ground level. A couple of days before transplanting, begin hardening off the melon seedlings by setting them outdoors in a sunny area during the day and then bringing them back indoors at night.

Transplant seedlings outdoors by planting them through slits in the black plastic mulch or by planting them in the center of each wooden frame. Take care to disturb the seedling roots as little as possible during transplanting, and afterward water them in with a soluble fertilizer rich in root-strengthening phosphorus (the phosphorus content is represented by the second number on the fertilizer label, as in 5-10-5).

If nights are cool at transplanting time, cover the frames as the temperature drops during late

time. Cover the frame with an old storm window or a square of clear plastic, turning it into a solar heater. Leave the frame in place for several weeks after you plant the melons. Uncover the frame during the day but recover it each night to shelter the new seedlings. In this way you'll protect the seedlings from chilly nights, which can damage the plants and prevent mature vines from setting fruit.

Sowing seed
Melons need 80 to 100 days of warm soil and frost-free weather from the time the seeds are sown to reach maturity. Those needs can be satisfied from zone 8 and southward by sowing seeds outdoors as soon as soil temperatures reach 70°-80°F (21°-26.5°C). This should be at least two weeks after the last frost date for your area. When sown directly into the garden, melons are generally planted in "hills" — that is, as many as six seeds are planted together in a circle so that they rest 1 in (2.5 cm) deep and about 4 in (10 cm) apart. Once the seeds germinate, thin the seedlings to two to three plants per hill.

In more northerly gardens it is generally better to start melon seeds indoors by planting them in 4 in (10 cm) peat pots. Let them grow for two to four weeks before

transplanting them into the garden. Again, it is important that this transplanting time does not occur until two weeks after the last frost date for your area and after the soil has warmed to at least 70°F (21°C).

To sow the seeds, fill the pots with a sterilized seed-starting mix, and plant several seeds ½ in

ASSISTING POLLINATION

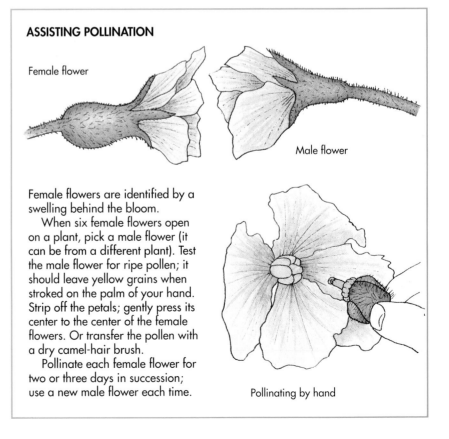

Female flower

Male flower

Pollinating by hand

Female flowers are identified by a swelling behind the bloom.

When six female flowers open on a plant, pick a male flower (it can be from a different plant). Test the male flower for ripe pollen; it should leave yellow grains when stroked on the palm of your hand. Strip off the petals; gently press its center to the center of the female flowers. Or transfer the pollen with a dry camel-hair brush.

Pollinate each female flower for two or three days in succession; use a new male flower each time.

CULTIVARS TO CHOOSE

Muskmelons

'Earlisweet': borne in 68 days; 5-6½ in (13-16 cm) fruits; bears well in northern climates.

'Musketeer': 90 days; 5-6 in (13-15 cm) fruits; 2-3 ft (60-90 cm) wide plants good for small gardens.

'Ogen': 80 days; dark green and yellow-striped, 5½-6 in (14-15 cm) fruits with pear-flavored flesh.

Watermelons

'Bush Baby II': 80 days; dark green, 10 lb (4.5 kg) fruits with red flesh; dwarf plant; ideal for small gardens.

'Charleston Gray': 85 days; pale green, 20-30 lb (9-13.5 kg) fruits; disease resistant.

'Sweet Favorite': 79 days; striped 10-12 lb (4.5-5.4 kg) fruits; sweet red flesh; good for northern regions.

'Yellow Baby': 70 days; striped, 7 in (18 cm) fruits with yellow flesh.

Casaba

'Casaba Golden Beauty': 115 days; 7-8 lb (3.2-3.6 kg) golden-skin fruits.

afternoon. Be sure to remove the frame covers the next morning, otherwise the melon seedlings may overheat. Seedlings planted through black plastic can be protected by covering them with hot caps made of 1 gal (4 L) plastic milk jugs. After cutting the bottoms off the jugs with a sharp knife, set the jugs (with caps on) down over the seedlings with the bottom ends toward the ground.

Fast-ripening melon cultivars, such as 'Earlisweet' (a muskmelon that bears fruits approximately 68 days after sowing) and 'Yellow Baby' (a watermelon that bears in 70 days), are the best bets for areas with short, cool growing seasons. You can also hasten fruiting by restricting the melon vine's growth. When a plant has developed four or five leaves, pinch back the growing point immediately above the fifth leaf; this will encourage lower side shoots to form.

Only four side shoots should be allowed to form on each plant grown in a frame — pinch off any others that grow. Direct the side shoots singly toward each corner of the frame.

When the main shoots on each plant reach the limit of the frame, stop them by pinching back the growing point just above a leaf; do the same for side shoots. If growth becomes very crowded, remove some side shoots completely, but leave those bearing fruits.

Another problem of growing melons in the North is that cool, cloudy weather may prevent insects from pollinating the female flowers. In this case, you may have to pollinate flowers by hand.

To accomplish this, first identify both the female and male flowers. These are easy to distinguish, for the male flowers have a narrow base and the female ones are swollen and round where they join the stem.

Check that the male flowers are shedding pollen. Brush the tip of the center of the blossom with a finger or stroke it on the palm of your hand, then look for deposits of the fine pollen.

If the male flowers are shedding pollen, pick one, remove the petals, and press the center of the male flower to the center of a female flower. Or transfer the pollen with a camel-hair brush, touching the tip of the brush first to the center of the male flower and afterward to the center of a female one. Repeat this process until you have pollinated all the female flowers. To ensure that fertilization occurs, repollinate the female flowers daily for two or three days in a row, using fresh male flowers each time.

When the fruits are the size of a walnut, thin them out until there is only one on each shoot.

Remove all new flowers and small fruits that form after midsummer; these will not have enough time to ripen before frost. Pinch off the tip of the shoot two leaves beyond the fruits.

Place a mulch of straw, a piece of cardboard, or an inverted plastic pot under each growing fruit to keep it clear of the soil, which can rot the fruit in damp weather. This also reduces the chances of slug damage.

Harvesting

The flavor of a melon depends on how ripe it is when picked. Muskmelons develop a strong fragrance when they are ripe, and the skin turns from green to tan. If a crack forms at the base of the stem right where it attaches to the fruit, the muskmelon is ready to pick.

A watermelon signals ripeness when its skin turns dull and tough, becoming difficult to break with a fingernail. The tendrils on the stem near the melon turn brown and dry, and the bottom of the melon commonly turns yellow (rather than green).

Pests and diseases

Striped and spotted cucumber beetles may attack the foliage, spreading bacterial wilt; squash vine borers may tunnel into vines. Both can be defeated with floating row covers of spunbonded polypropylene.

Bacterial wilts cause the wilting of leaves and stems; remove and destroy affected plants. Powdery mildew may attack foliage in rainy weather.

Muskmelon 'Ogen'

RASPBERRIES

Raspberries are one of the most delicious summer fruits, and they consistently produce large crops, even in cool, wet summers.

Raspberries yield more fruits for the space they occupy than other canes do. The berries freeze well, keeping their flavor better than strawberries. The canes thrive from zones 3-4 through zone 9 under a variety of conditions, and they do well in northern gardens, where summer days are long and not too hot.

There are two types of raspberry plants: summer-bearing cultivars, which fruit on the previous season's shoots between mid- and late summer, and fall-bearing cultivars, which begin to fruit on the current season's growth in late summer. Fall-bearing types often yield smaller crops than summer-bearing raspberries do. Gourmets claim that yellow-fruited fall raspberries are superior in flavor to the red summer berries.

Soil and site
Select a sunny site with moisture-retentive but well-drained soil. For the best results use a slightly acid soil. Raspberries will also grow in dry, sandy, and alkaline soil if the plot is given plenty of water in dry spells and receives extra fertilization, as nutrients quickly wash out of sandy soil.

Prepare the bed a few months before planting the canes. Dig a

PLANTING

Plant canes 1-2 ft (30-60 cm) apart in trenches 9 in (23 cm) wide and 3 in (7.5 cm) deep. Ensure that the roots are well spread out. Use your heel to firm the soil. Set rows 6 ft (1.8 m) apart.

trench about 10 in (25 cm) deep, break up the soil in the bottom with a fork, and mix in a thick layer of well-rotted manure or compost with the topsoil. This is very important if the soil is alkaline. Rake in a surface dressing of a balanced and complete fertilizer: 5 lb (2.3 kg) of 10-10-10 is good for 100 ft (30 m) of trench. A 12 ft × 9 ft (3.7 m × 2.7 m) plot will support two rows of four bushes each; they should produce an annual yield of 20 lb (9 kg).

Consider planting a row of raspberries by the vegetable garden. They are an attractive summer screen and cast little shade.

Cultivation
Raspberries are very susceptible to viral diseases. Always buy one-year-old canes, certified as free of disease, from a reputable nursery. Plant out the canes in midfall, if possible, or in early spring.

Before planting, set posts, 8 ft (2.4 m) tall, at the ends of each row; sink them 2 ft (60 cm) into the ground. Make sure the posts are sturdy and pressure-treated with a wood preservative. Staple three 12- to 13-gauge galvanized wires to the posts, spacing them 2½ ft (75 cm), 3½ ft (1.1 m), and 5½ ft (1.7 m) from the ground for summer-bearing cultivars.

▲ **Raspberries** Vying in popularity with strawberries, raspberry plants have a much longer productive life. They can bear fruits for up to 10 years, yielding deliciously juicy crops in summer or fall.

As the canes grow, tie them to the wires with garden twine. Alternatively, attach short horizontal arms of wood to the posts; stretch wires from the ends of the arms, parallel to the wires already stapled to the posts. As the canes grow up between the wires, they will be supported by the wires and won't need tying up.

Fall-bearing cultivars do not grow as tall as summer-bearing ones. Space pairs of horizontal support wires 2½ ft (75 cm) and 5 ft (1.5 m) from the ground, then stretch cross ties of wire or string between the horizontal wires every 1 ft (30 cm) to support the canes without tying them up.

For each row dig a trench 9 in (23 cm) wide and 3 in (7.5 cm) deep. Plant the canes about 1-2 ft (30-60 cm) apart with the roots spread out. Cover the roots with soil; firm it down with your heel. Space rows 6 ft (1.8 m) apart.

After planting, cut each cane down to 1 ft (30 cm) above soil level. This will stop fruits from being borne the following summer but will make the plants more vigorous in the following years. Each year apply a mulch of shredded bark or garden compost in early spring to feed the canes and improve moisture retention. In early spring, before the bushes flower, apply a 10-10-10 fertilizer at the rate of 10 lb (4.5 kg) per 100 linear ft (30 m) of bushes.

If the applied mulch does not control weeds, eliminate them by scuffle-hoeing the surface of the soil. Give the plants plenty of water in summer.

To keep birds away from ripening fruits, cover the bushes with plastic netting (available at garden centers). Ideally, raspberries

CULTIVARS TO CHOOSE

Summer-bearing
'Amber': large, conical amber-colored fruits; very sweet and highly flavored; ripen very late; vigorous, productive plant.

'Canby': large to very large red berries of delicious flavor; ripen early; thornless plant is resistant to virus and immune to aphids; prefers cool summers.

'Festival': medium to large red fruits of good quality; ripen midseason; short, high-yielding canes tolerate spur blight and are immune to mosaic virus.

Fall-bearing
'Fall Gold': sweet, mild-flavored yellow-fruited cultivar; not hardy in extreme North.

'Heritage': large, dark red fruits of superior quality; tall, productive canes; bears moderately in summer, more heavily in fall.

should be grown in cages of wire netting stapled onto wooden frames. Such structures offer full protection from birds, which like to eat not only fruits but also immature flowers and leaf buds.

Raspberries throw out numerous suckers from the parent bush. Unless they are needed for new plantings, remove them by pulling them out of the soil — cutting them off encourages the formation of more suckers.

Training and pruning
In the first spring after planting, cut out the original stems at ground level and allow the new canes to grow up. Tie them to the wires with garden twine, spacing them evenly, with 4 in (10 cm) between them. These canes will carry the following season's crop. Rub off flower buds as they appear to prevent fruiting in the first year. After the leaves fall, or in late winter, cut back the tips of the canes to promote growth in the lower buds; trim the tallest canes to just above the top wire (see pp.40-41).

In subsequent years, after harvesting summer-bearing cultivars, remove canes that produced berries; cut them off just above ground level. Select the strongest of the current year's canes (a maximum of eight per plant), and tie them to the wires; space them 3-4 in (7.5-10 cm) apart. Cut out the remaining new shoots.

In late winter cut off the top of each cane to a healthy bud a little way above the top wire.

Fall-bearing raspberries set fruits on canes of the current year's growth. Cut canes that have borne fruits down to the ground in late winter; new ones, which will carry that fall's crop, will appear soon afterward. Tie the canes in place as they grow.

Raising new plants
If the canes are healthy and free of disease, dig up suckers in late fall and replant them to create new bushes, thus increasing the harvest. Generally, raspberry canes begin to deteriorate after 10 years; at this time replace them with new, virus-free stock. Plant the canes in a fresh site.

Harvesting and storing
Pick raspberries when they have colored well all over. They will come away easily from their

Summer raspberry 'Festival'

Fall raspberry 'Fall Gold'

stalks, leaving the cores behind. Raspberries do not keep well, so eat or freeze them at once.

Pests and diseases
The most common raspberry pests are aphids, leafhoppers, spider mites, raspberry cane borers, and raspberry fruitworms.

Diseases include cane spot and cane and spur blight, which appear as discolored and splitting canes. Cut out badly affected canes; spray new ones with a copper fungicide. Botrytis can ruin the fruits; to reduce the incidence of this disease, maintain good air circulation through the planting. Viral diseases may show as yellow discoloration on the leaves. There is no cure; dig up and destroy all affected plants. Replant, in a different site, with new canes that are certified as free of viruses.

RHUBARB

While classified as a vegetable, rhubarb's tender, tart stems are traditionally used as a fruit in pies, jams, and jellies.

Rhubarb is a prolific plant and easy to grow; once established, it grows well with little attention. Though it is usually grown in the vegetable garden, rhubarb does well in a flower border or other sunny corner. Rhubarb can grow in the same spot for 10 years. Select a spot in the vegetable garden that does not interfere with the annual rotation plan.

Three or four plants should be enough for a family garden, but do not pull stalks for the first two years after planting, while the plants build up strength. You can force mature plants indoors or outside in late winter or early spring; this technique will yield more delicately flavored stalks.

Rhubarb thrives throughout most of the United States except in the extreme South.

Planting
You can raise rhubarb from seeds, but it is much easier and quicker to buy crowns (mature roots) from a nursery or to lift established plants and divide the roots. Each piece of root must have at least one strong new growth bud.

Plant in early spring while the buds are still dormant, or in fall. Rhubarb requires a sunny site and fertile, well-drained but moisture-retentive soil that is free of perennial weeds.

Forced stems

Set plants 3 ft (90 cm) apart. Dig holes deep enough to accommodate the woody part of the rootstock, and leave the buds just showing above the surface. Firm the soil in around the roots, and water well.

To start from seeds, sow them outdoors in midspring in drills ½ in (1.25 cm) deep and 1 ft (30 cm) apart. Thin seedlings 6 in (15 cm) apart; transplant them to their permanent sites the following year.

Looking after the crop
Mulch the plants deeply in early spring with well-rotted manure or compost. After the spring harvest, use a spading fork to turn

Maincrop stems

▲ **Rhubarb** These hardy perennials offer long-term dividends — not only do they last several years, but you can harvest the stalks in spring and in early summer.

the mulch into the topsoil. Topdress around the plants in midsummer, using a slow-release general-purpose fertilizer at the rate given on the product label.

Harvesting
Do not harvest stems in the first two years after planting. Once the plants are established, pull the stalks freely, but do not remove all the stalks from one plant at one time; leave a couple to feed the roots. Harvest rhubarb from midspring to early summer.

Only the rhubarb stalks are edible; the leaves are poisonous and must be cut off and discarded before cooking. Remove at ground level any flower stalks that may spring up, since these only divert strength from the roots.

Forcing
Rhubarb can be forced indoors or outside. Choose strong clumps of

PLANTING AND HARVESTING RHUBARB

1 Plant the crowns with the roots covered but the growth buds above ground.

2 To harvest, twist the stalks from the crown. Leave some stalks on the plant.

FORCING INDOORS

1 Lift one or two plants in mid- to late fall; turn them over to expose the roots to frost. This will encourage early dormancy and faster growth during forcing. Use plants that are at least three years old.

2 In early winter set the crowns the right way up in boxes. Cover them lightly with moist soil or compost; water thoroughly. Place the boxes in a dark shed. Maintain a temperature of 45°-64°F (7°-18°C).

3 Keep out the light by covering the boxes with black plastic. The stalks should be ready for pulling in five to six weeks. After all the stalks have been pulled, discard the crowns; they will be too depleted to be replanted outdoors.

plants that are at least three years old. For outdoor forcing, invert a garbage can or bucket over the crowns in mid- or late winter; bank plenty of straw around it. The plants will be ready to harvest three weeks early. Or to hasten the harvest by a few weeks in early spring, cover the crowns just with straw. Do not force the same crown two years in a row.

To force rhubarb indoors, dig the plants up in mid- or late fall, after the leaves die back; turn them over to expose the roots to the cool air. The plants should go dormant early. You can coax them back into growth, as if it were spring, when you bring them into warmth and darkness indoors.

FORCING OUTDOORS

1 In late winter invert a garbage can or bucket over a mature crown; bank straw or leaves around it for insulation. To guard against wind, weight or rope the cover down and secure the insulation.

CULTIVARS TO CHOOSE

Growing from seeds
'Glaskin's Perpetual': green stems; can be pulled in first year; least acid of cultivars.

'Victoria': green stalks shaded red; late spring harvest.

Growing from crowns
'MacDonald': bright red stalks with tender skin and excellent flavor.

'Strawberry Rhubarb': deep red stalks stay red when cooked; late maturing; harvest into early fall.

'Valentine': broad, deep red stalks; retain rosy color when cooked; outstanding flavor.

As winter sets in outdoors, move the dug-up crowns indoors. Plant their roots (right way up) in boxes and cover them thinly with soil. Cover the boxes with black plastic and keep them in a cool, dark spot, where the temperature ranges from 45°-64°F (7°-18°C).

Pests and diseases

Crown rot (anthracnose) can affect rhubarb. Watch for spindly, pale leaves and stalks and cavities in the crowns. Remove infected plants immediately; do not re-plant rhubarb in the same spot.

Rhubarb curculios puncture the stalks and bore down into the crown and roots. Pick and destroy these pests whenever observed.

2 The plants do not normally need watering. The crop should be ready for harvesting after six weeks. Before forcing the crowns again, let them crop normally for at least two years.

Rhubarb 'Valentine'

STRAWBERRIES

Delicious and easy to grow, strawberries are one of the most popular fruits. Strawberry shortcake is synonymous with summer.

Strawberries are divided into four distinct categories: Day-neutral strawberries bear steadily from early summer through frost, but they won't set fruits when summers are hot; they are sensitive to weed competition and drought. Everbearing strawberries, which produce a succession of modest crops between early summer and fall, are best adapted to warm climates. June-bearing strawberries yield one large harvest in early summer to midsummer. Alpine strawberries offer small berries throughout the summer, and they are often prized for their rich, sweet flavor.

In a large garden strawberries can be picked from late spring to midfall if a number of different cultivars are planted. But even the smallest garden can accommodate strawberry plants, for if ground space is lacking, they can be grown in containers ranging from specially designed strawberry pots to hanging baskets and window boxes.

DAY-NEUTRAL, EVER-BEARING, AND JUNE-BEARING STRAWBERRIES

Strawberries will grow in most soils, although they prefer rich, well-drained, slightly acid soil.

Plant early-bearing cultivars in a sheltered spot and the main crop in an open, sunny bed that faces south.

▲ **Strawberry pots** Special terra-cotta strawberry pots with holes in the sides are ideal where space is limited. They give maximum returns as well as making an attractive garden feature.

▼ **Strawberry 'Earliglow'** This June-bearing type is resistant to disease and ripens as early as late spring.

◄ **Harvesting strawberries**
Pick the berries as they ripen, leaving immature fruits to swell. Growing different cultivars together will ensure steady, long-lasting production.

▲ **Planting strawberries** Dig holes 2 in (5 cm) deeper than the roots. Mound soil in the hole's bottom, then spread the roots over it so that the base of the plant is level with the surface. Fill in with soil, taking care to avoid burying the crown where the leaf stems meet.

Dig the bed thoroughly two or three weeks before planting. Work in a bucketful of well-rotted manure or compost per sq yd/m. Fork in a general fertilizer — about ¾ lb (340 g) of 5-10-10 per 10 sq yd (8.4 sq m) — and rake to a fine tilth, with the soil broken up into a fine, even crumb.

Change the site of the strawberry bed every three years to prevent the buildup of diseases and to give the soil a rest.

Planting

Day-neutral, everbearing, and June-bearing strawberries are generally purchased as bare-root plants. Both fall-dug and spring-dug plants are available; fall-dug plants are generally more vigorous. Make sure you buy plants that have been certified to be free of viral diseases.

Strawberries usually give a quicker return than other garden fruits do. In the South, plants set out in late summer will fruit early the following summer. In the North, plant strawberries in early spring. Day-neutral and everbearing cultivars will begin producing fruits by late summer and will yield a regular harvest the next year. June-bearing cultivars

will bear fruits the second summer after planting.

Space the plants approximately 1½ ft (45 cm) apart, with 2½ ft (75 cm) between the rows.

After planting, pinch off all flowers for the first three or four months. This will allow the plants to build up size and strength before they begin bearing fruits.

The strawberries in these three categories — day-neutral, June-bearing, and everbearing — will usually offer good crops for three seasons. After that, replace the plants with fresh stock from the nursery; otherwise you will have a shrinking harvest.

Care and maintenance

Water the plants thoroughly just after planting and whenever there is a dry spell. As the fruits begin to ripen, water sparingly and only in the morning, thus preventing mold from attacking the berries.

Six weeks after planting, feed the plants with 10-10-10 fertilizer at the rate of 2 lb (900 g) per 100 ft (30 m) of row. In subsequent years feed everbearing and June-bearing plants in late spring

and again a month later, using 5-10-5 at the rate of 2½ lb (1.1kg) per 100 ft (30 m) of row. The day-neutral types will require fertilization with ammonium nitrate, about 1-2 lb (450-900 g) per 100 ft (30 m) of row; feed them monthly from May through September.

After five to six weeks in the ground, the new plants will begin to sprout sprawling stems or "runners." These runners will produce small new plants, or "daughter plants," at their tips and then go on to form more new plants. Allow each runner to form only the first daughter, since this will bear better fruits than subsequent daughters. To root the daughters, peg the runner down with a U-shaped wire. Allow each parent plant to throw off no more than five daughters. Evenly space the plants 9 in (23 cm) apart.

▶ **Block planting** Instead of planting in long rows, set young runners in blocks 2½ ft (75 cm) apart in all directions. This saves space in irregular-size plots.

▲ **Fruit protection** To keep the berries clean and clear of the soil, use special strawberry mulch mats. Once all danger of frost is definitely past, tuck the mats underneath the berries. Alternatively, you can spread black plastic or straw over the ground between plants; such mulches also smother weeds.

Mulch around the strawberry plants with straw to suppress weeds, and scatter slug pellets around the plants when the developing strawberries are heavy enough to weigh down the trusses (the clusters of fruits).

Protect strawberry plants from birds and squirrels by covering them with nylon netting supported by stakes.

Harvesting
Pick strawberries in the morning when they are still cool. To avoid bruising them, make sure you pinch through the stem rather than the end of the berry.

Clearing the bed
When the crop is over in the fall, clear up the strawberry bed.

With June-bearing cultivars in the first and second years, cut off the old leaves and any unwanted runners. Rake off the old straw and leaves — if you compost this material, do so as far as possible from the berry patch so that the compost pile doesn't serve as a haven for pests and diseases. Cultivate the soil between the rows.

At the end of the harvest in the third season, dig up the strawberry plants and dispose of them.

Propagation
It is possible to propagate day-neutral, everbearing, and June-bearing strawberries by dividing existing plants or by transplanting daughter plants; however, as the stock degenerates with age, this is not a recommended practice. Instead, order vigorous and certified disease-free new plants from the nursery.

Forcing strawberries
Growing strawberries under cover can help extend the harvest in the North.

Polyethylene tunnels In late winter or very early spring, place hoops of heavy-gauge wire over the rows of plants and cover with clear plastic film (available from garden centers). This should ripen the crop up to three weeks earlier than strawberries grown in the open. To keep the harvest going longer, you can cover day-neutral or everbearing strawberries in early fall.

Cold frames In mid- to late summer you can plant newly rooted runners directly into the soil in the cold frame, spacing them 1 ft (30 cm) apart. Keep the clear plastic or glass cover on the cold frame from midwinter onward, opening it during the day in warm spells but closing it again before dark.

▲ **Forcing strawberries** For earlier and later strawberry harvests in gardens in the North, make peaked "hot caps" with panes of glass fastened together with special clips (available from catalogs and some garden centers); alternatively, create tunnels by stretching clear covers of plastic film over wire hoops.

◄ **Rooting daughters** Peg the runner down to the soil with a U-shaped wire and pinch off the outer end of the runner, which would otherwise go on to form more daughters. After four to six weeks, when the daughter has rooted, sever the connection to the parent plant and transfer the daughter.

▼ **Towerpot strawberries** Multilevel containers can hold up to 12 strawberry plants. These towers (available from catalogs and some garden centers) save space, and many have useful features such as self-watering devices.

▲ **Alpine strawberries,** with small flowers and fruits, are highly ornamental.

▲ **Strawberry** 'Ozark Beauty'
◄ **Strawberry** 'Rugen'

Pests and diseases

Aphids, spider mites, and plant bugs are common pests, causing stunted growth and yellowing of leaves; spray with an approved insecticide when these pests appear. Slugs, snails, and beetles — and birds — eat the fruits.

Strawberries are subject to such viral and fungal diseases as verticillium and red stele. You should remove and dispose of any infected plants.

Botrytis, a common disease, rots the fruits; the fungus appears at flowering time, when plants should be sprayed with sulfur or a fixed copper fungicide. Spacing the plants properly enhances air circulation and helps prevent the spread of this disease.

ALPINE STRAWBERRIES

The flowers and fruits of alpine strawberries are smaller than those of the other types of strawberries, but these plants have several advantages. They are very decorative and can be grown as an edging to a flower border. They also seed themselves freely and are rarely troubled by pests and diseases. Finally, they survive in partial shade and are more cold hardy than most other strawberries, flourishing in zones 3-9.

Alpine strawberries thrive in rich, well-drained, slightly acid soil. Raise them each year from seeds (most cultivars don't produce runners), or buy the young plants in spring.

Growing alpines

The soil and site preparation for alpine strawberries is much the same as for other types of strawberries. Sow seeds in early fall in pots of seed-starting mix. Alternatively, sow in early spring indoors at 68°F (20°C).

Germination is erratic, but the seedlings should be ready for transplanting by late fall. Transplant into flats of potting mix at 1 in (2.5 cm) intervals.

Overwinter the plants in a cold frame or cool sunporch before planting them out in mid- to late spring. Plant every 1 ft (30 cm) in rows the same distance apart.

Protect with hot caps if there is frost about when they start flowering in late spring. Keep the soil moist, and feed every two weeks.

Alpine strawberries fruit over a long period, producing small red berries continuously or in batches from summer to fall. The late berries are usually larger than early-summer fruits.

Strawberry 'Sequoia'

Summer feast Fresh, tasty vegetables, from juicy tomatoes to crisp zucchini, can be grown in your own garden.

Vegetables

Homegrown vegetables are far superior in flavor and freshness to those bought at a supermarket, and the choice of varieties is much greater. They have better texture and a higher vitamin content, and you can control which chemicals, if any, are applied as they grow.

In addition, homegrown vegetables can be real money savers, particularly in the South or Southwest, where the harvest may run year-round. If the harvest exceeds your immediate needs, then use these fresh-picked vegetables for freezing or canning.

Tending a vegetable plot may be a little more time-consuming than looking after a flower garden, but it doesn't require special skills. Besides, at harvesttime there is a satisfying sense of achievement. Essential factors, though, include properly prepared soil and a sunny and open site. It is almost impossible to fail if you have fertile soil, sow seeds at the proper time, and thin out seedlings before they crowd each other.

In a large garden it is sensible to grow vegetables in a crop-rotation cycle, with brassicas (cabbages and their relatives) following beans, peas, and salad vegetables, and root crops taking over from the cabbage family. Crop rotation is good for the soil and discourages the build-up of soil-borne diseases and insect pests. Root crops occupy the ground for longer than most other vegetables, but you can grow fast-maturing crops (lettuce, spinach, and radishes) between the rows while the roots are small.

In a small garden use a sunny patio for growing vegetables in containers or grow bags. Tomatoes, leaf lettuces, peppers, and eggplants are ideal for container growing. Cucumbers can be trained up a sunny wall, and radishes can occupy a kitchen window box.

Herbs are easy to grow and fascinating to experiment with in the kitchen. They are often grown in a section of the vegetable garden. A plot of 7 ft × 7 ft (2.1 m × 2.1 m) is ample for most gardeners, but place them where they won't interfere with crop rotation. You can also grow herbs in a flower pot or window box.

To help you determine if a particular plant will thrive in your area, we've given you zones that correspond to the plant hardiness map on page 176.

PLANNING A KITCHEN GARDEN

Fresh vegetables, fruits, and herbs have a flavor rarely matched by those from the store, and even a small garden can yield good crops year after year.

Gardeners grow vegetables and herbs for fresh, full-flavored food. Southern gardeners can harvest most vegetables year-round; in the North, the use of a cold frame or plastic row covers makes out-of-season crops possible.

Siting a kitchen garden

Choose a light, airy spot for a vegetable plot; it should get plenty of sun and not be shaded by trees or high fences. On exposed sites use hot caps or plastic row covers to protect seedlings in early spring and late fall.

You can grow some vegetables on a plot that is in the shade for up to half a day, but plant shade-tolerant crops such as raspberries and salad greens. But even these won't bear as well in the shade.

Avoid planting fruit trees too close to the garden. They can rob the soil of water and nourishment needed by the vegetables.

A central path (3 ft/90 cm wide) made of a solid material, such as flagstones or concrete pavers, is useful for walking on and wheeling a cart. Other paths can be narrower so as not to impinge on the planting area. To make temporary ones, simply tamp down the soil; you can dig it up later on.

A bed can be made any width but keep it narrow enough so you can weed and plant without stepping in the bed. Make a bed that is accessible from only one side 3 ft (90 cm) wide, one accessible from two sides 4 ft (1.2 m) wide.

▼ **Vegetable plot** Every inch of space is utilized in this small plot. A brick-edged bed, surrounded by fruit bushes, yields a good crop of vegetables.

FIRST YEAR OF A THREE-YEAR CROP ROTATION PLAN

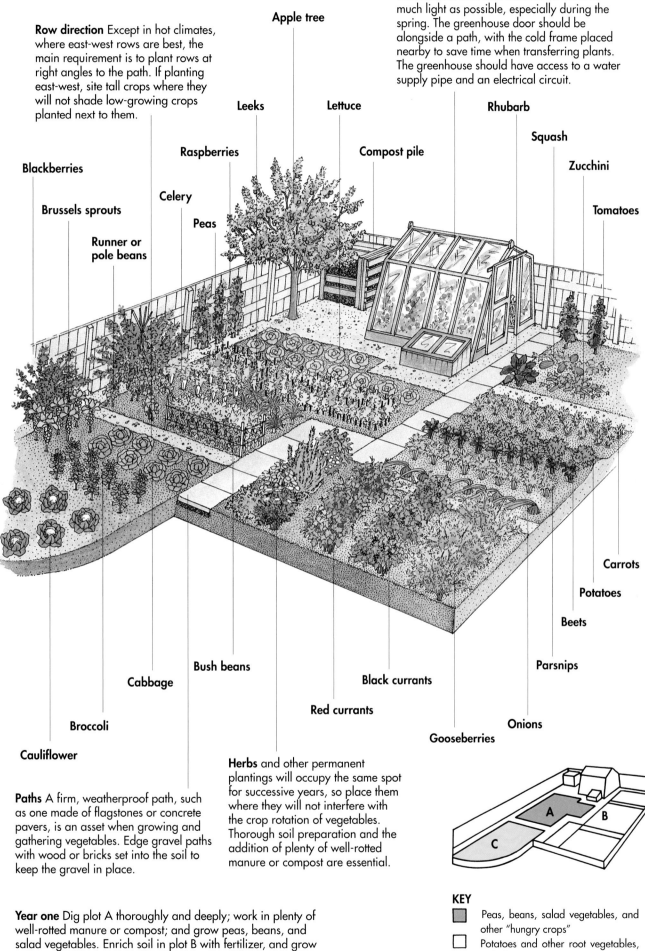

Row direction Except in hot climates, where east-west rows are best, the main requirement is to plant rows at right angles to the path. If planting east-west, site tall crops where they will not shade low-growing crops planted next to them.

Greenhouse and cold frame Both need as much light as possible, especially during the spring. The greenhouse door should be alongside a path, with the cold frame placed nearby to save time when transferring plants. The greenhouse should have access to a water supply pipe and an electrical circuit.

Apple tree

Leeks

Lettuce

Compost pile

Raspberries

Rhubarb

Squash

Zucchini

Tomatoes

Blackberries

Brussels sprouts

Celery

Peas

Runner or pole beans

Cauliflower

Broccoli

Cabbage

Bush beans

Black currants

Red currants

Gooseberries

Onions

Parsnips

Beets

Potatoes

Carrots

Paths A firm, weatherproof path, such as one made of flagstones or concrete pavers, is an asset when growing and gathering vegetables. Edge gravel paths with wood or bricks set into the soil to keep the gravel in place.

Herbs and other permanent plantings will occupy the same spot for successive years, so place them where they will not interfere with the crop rotation of vegetables. Thorough soil preparation and the addition of plenty of well-rotted manure or compost are essential.

Year one Dig plot A thoroughly and deeply; work in plenty of well-rotted manure or compost; and grow peas, beans, and salad vegetables. Enrich soil in plot B with fertilizer, and grow root crops. Enrich soil in plot C with lime and fertilizer, and grow brassicas (plants in the cabbage family).

KEY
- Peas, beans, salad vegetables, and other "hungry crops"
- Potatoes and other root vegetables, including onions
- Brassica crops

SECOND AND THIRD YEARS OF CROP ROTATION

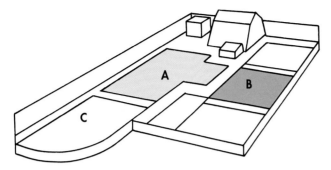 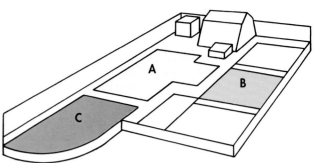

Year two Dig plot B thoroughly and deeply, and work in plenty of compost or manure for peas, beans, and salad crops, which follow the root vegetables. Feed plot C with fertilizer for root crops. Apply fertilizer and lime to plot A for brassica crops.

Year three Turn the soil deeply; dig in manure or compost in plot C for peas, beans, and salad crops. Feed plot A with fertilizer for the root crops. Prepare plot B with fertilizer and lime for the brassicas. Start the cycle again in year four.

Where a bed is much narrower at one end (the lie of the land may demand such a shape) use the shorter rows for crops such as lettuces and radishes; plant them in small sowings at regular intervals for successive harvests.

The direction of the row is usually not important. Crops that overwinter under plastic row covers get the most sun when grown in east-west rows; this direction is also slightly better for gardens exposed to westerly or easterly winds. Vegetables, especially tall ones, get more sunlight in summer when grown in north-south rows. This arrangement is good for northern gardens, where sunlight is precious, but not for southwestern gardens, where too much sun is fatal.

A water supply is vital for a kitchen garden, not only to increase the yield and prevent crop failure, but also to germinate seeds. If the plot is far from the house and its water supply, install a new water line to the garden.

Site a greenhouse or cold frame in the sunniest spot, with the axis running east-west or north-south and the door on the least exposed side. Seedbeds, your nursery for seedlings, should face east. Place the compost pile in a shady spot.

If the garden is on a windy site, you'll need some form of windbreak around it; a low hedge 2 ft (60 cm) high is usually adequate.

Crop rotation

Divide the garden into plots A, B, and C. Grow different groups of vegetables in each plot each year in a three-year crop-rotation cycle. This system helps the soil to remain fertile and prevents the buildup of soil-borne pests and diseases. Crop rotation does this by guaranteeing that no one type of plant is grown in the same spot two years in a row; since pests often prey on a particular crop, any that overwinter in the soil will be without food the following spring.

Plot A In the first year, grow "heavy feeder" crops in plot A; they need soil enriched with organic matter such as well-rotted manure or compost. These include beans, corn, lettuces, peas, radishes, and spinach. Most are sown in spring and early summer; some can be harvested in time for a second crop later in the year.

Plot B Use plot B for root vegetables, such as beets, onions, potatoes, and turnips. These prefer soil enriched with organic matter from a previous crop and treated with fertilizer in the current season. Sow them in spring and early summer and harvest them in time for the plot to be re-enriched with organic matter for peas and beans the next year.

Plot C Use plot C for brassicas: broccoli, cabbage, cauliflower, and kale. They prefer soil enriched for a previous crop and treated with lime and fertilizer in the current season. Brassicas are often sown in spring in a seedbed, planted out in summer, and harvested from fall to the following spring.

Each year move the cropping plan to the next plot — the rotation in each plot is thus peas and beans, root crops, and brassicas.

Onions and shallots grow in any good soil; plant them in the root crop plot. Grow large onions in the pea and bean plot.

Plan a permanent plot for long-term crops, such as asparagus, squashes, and tomatoes, which do not fit into the rotation system.

Allocate fruit bushes and herbs permanent sites. Grow herbs in a bed of their own or in clumps.

Catch and succession crops

Main crops in a rotation plan don't use the plot the whole year; there is often temporarily vacant space in which you can grow catch crops and succession crops.

Catch crops include vegetables that grow quickly in the early part of the season. You can sow a catch crop of scallions, for instance, in the brassica plot in early spring before you plant out the winter cabbage in midsummer.

You can also plant fast-growing catch crops between rows of slow-growing vegetables; pull them up as the slower ones need the space. Lettuces and radishes, for example, can be grown between rows of parsnips or Brussels sprouts. Don't grow a catch crop that covers the whole area with foliage, or the main crop will be smothered.

Succession crops are sown or planted after a main crop is cleared. For example, a main crop of green peas sown in early spring and picked by early summer can be followed by leeks.

Preparing a new plot

Clear and prepare the site for a new garden in fall or during a dry and frost-free period in winter. It will then be ready for sowing and planting the following spring. Work out a crop-rotation plan.

Clear away all debris. If subsoil has been brought to the surface by builders, redistribute it over the whole garden. Cut down all tall grass and weeds. Skim off the turf (if any) with a spade, cutting 1 in (2.5 cm) under the surface; you can stack and compost it.

Dig the soil thoroughly. For plot A, add well-rotted manure or garden compost to the top 8-10 in (20-25 cm) of soil at a rate of one bucketful per sq yd/m. Remove the roots of all perennial weeds; quack grass, dandelions, thistles, and the like will resprout from any bits of root left behind.

Soils for vegetables

The ideal soil for growing vegetables is loam — a well-balanced mixture of sand, silt, clay, and humus. It does not dry out quickly nor get waterlogged, and it has an open, spongy texture. Good loam is easily worked and needs only the regular replacement of essential nutrients in the form of manure or compost and fertilizers.

Most vegetables grow best in neutral soil (neither acid nor alkaline) or in slightly acid soil. Treat strongly acid soils with lime; use a soil-testing kit to check the amount required. The final pH reading should be between 6.5 and 7.0. Excessively alkaline soil is best improved with liberal amounts of sphagnum peat or applications of sulfur.

Sandy soil is loose and does not hold water well. It warms up quickly in spring in time for early crops but also dries out quickly. Essential nutrients are easily washed out and so need constant replacement. Sandy soil requires more frequent fertilization; blend it with compost (or some other organic matter) to help it retain water and nutrients.

Clay soil is dense, slow to warm up in spring, and moisture retentive. It may be rich in nutrients, but because it is poorly drained, roots are starved of oxygen. Dig in plenty of well-rotted manure, compost, sharp sand, or weathered ashes to lighten clay soil and to improve drainage. Add lime if the soil is excessively acidic.

Alkaline soil is common in the West. It is usually shallow and quick-draining, and so may be nutrient-poor. In the Southwest it is often underlaid with a layer of hardpan, such as caliche. Break up any hardpan and work in plenty of well-rotted manure or compost. If the soil is extremely

alkaline, add sulfur or dig in liberal amounts of sphagnum peat. **Peat or muck soil** is usually acid and may be poorly drained. Make drainage trenches around beds to carry off extra water. Treat with lime and apply a good general-purpose fertilizer, as peat and muck soils lack essential phosphorus and potassium.

HERBS

Many herbs are used for culinary purposes, adding flavor, color, and aroma to food. Others go into medicinal or cosmetic preparations or are dried for potpourris.

Cultivation

In general, herbs need ordinary well-drained soil and full sun. Pale-leaved and variegated forms prefer dappled shade, and mints do well in shade.

Marjoram and rosemary thrive on alkaline soil, and borage, chamomile, and thyme do well on sandy soil. Loamy soil is ideal for angelica, lemon balm, parsley, chervil, and sweet cicely.

In spring you can sow annual herbs from seeds. Follow instructions on the packet; sowing times and required temperatures for germination vary from herb to herb. Increase chives by division.

Perennial and shrubby herbs are usually purchased as plants raised from cuttings. For the best results, plant out in spring or fall.

A mulch of shredded bark or other organic matter will retain soil moisture and smother weeds.

For culinary, leafy herbs, pinch off flower buds as they appear to keep the leaves flavorful. Trim shrubby herbs after flowering. In spring cut back straggly plants.

▶ **Vegetable rows** Grow vegetables in orderly rows (or in a block for each kind) to make hoeing and harvesting easier. Regularly water in the early morning.

ASPARAGUS

An asparagus bed takes 3 years to develop, but it repays the wait by bearing spears for at least 20 years.

Few vegetables can compare in flavor with tender homegrown asparagus. Its shoots, known as spears because of their shape, can be enjoyed on their own, either raw or cooked, or as an ingredient in soups, salads, and other dishes.

Sadly, the asparagus harvest lasts only six weeks, making it a brief seasonal treat to enjoy and relish. However, the asparagus plant — one of the few perennial vegetables — should continue to a second phase. After harvesting the first shoots in early summer, leave the rest to grow on. They will grow into attractive fernlike foliage, which turns golden yellow in fall; but more importantly, they build up food reserves in the crowns for the crop in the following year.

Planning the crop
Asparagus will grow best in a fairly open site that is sheltered from wind. Because it needs rich, well-drained soil, the initial preparation of the asparagus bed is extremely vital for success with the plants in years to come.

The fall before planting, dig a bed 4 ft (1.2 m) wide; this will be wide enough to accommodate two rows of asparagus. Dig compost or well-rotted manure into the soil to one spade's depth (10 in/ 25 cm) at the rate of approximately a bucketful per sq yd/m.

If you have acid soil, add lime to make it neutral or slightly alkaline. In fall or winter, after digging, add the lime at the rate suggested by a soil-testing kit.

If your soil has a tendency to become sticky or waterlogged, make a raised bed enclosed by boards, stones, or concrete blocks.

The following spring, rake the bed level and work in superphosphate at a rate of 5 lb (2.3 kg) per 100 sq ft (9 sq m).

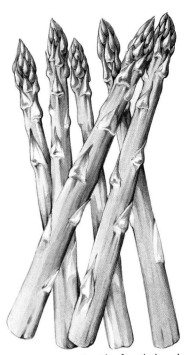

▲ **Asparagus tips** The fragile heads of asparagus spears need careful handling. They are the most treasured part of this succulent delicacy.

Growing asparagus
Most asparagus are bought for transplanting as one- or two-year-old plants or "crowns." Don't transplant crowns older than this, as they are difficult to establish and often die. One-year-old crowns are the easiest to transplant and they soon catch up with two-year-old crowns. Each mature plant, those more than three years old, will generally yield one average helping of spears a week.

Although asparagus can be grown from seeds, you must wait an extra year for the first harvestable spears. In addition, some seedlings will be female, and these do not produce as well as male plants; all-male plantings produce 25 to 30 percent more spears than mixed-sex plantings. For this reason it is best not to start these plants yourself, but instead start with plants of an all-male hybrid.

Asparagus crowns are shipped from nurseries around midspring and you should plant them as soon as they arrive.

In ground already prepared, dig trenches about 8 in (20 cm)

◄ **Asparagus fern** The top growth of culinary asparagus closely resembles the indoor asparagus fern. It turns a golden color in fall.

deep and 3 ft (90 cm) apart; make them wide enough for the roots to spread out flat. Replace some of the soil to form a domed base.

Remove the crowns from their packaging, and set them approximately 1½ ft (45 cm) apart in the trenches. Spread out the roots over the domed base, then immediately cover with soil — never let the crowns dry out.

Partially fill the trenches with 3 in (7.5 cm) of fine soil, and firm the surface. Leave the remaining soil at the sides of the trenches.

For the first year, lightly hoe to keep down weeds. Make sure you water thoroughly in dry spells. When asparagus spears appear, leave them to grow into ferns. In mid- to late fall, when their stems turn yellow, cut the ferns down to within 1 in (2.5 cm) of the soil, and mulch with well-rotted manure or compost. Ridge up the soil left at the sides of the trenches over the crowns.

The following spring, top-dress the asparagus rows with 10-10-10 fertilizer at a rate of 2½ lb (1.1 kg) per 100 sq ft (9 sq m). Again, leave the spears to grow into ferns before cutting them down when they turn yellow in fall. Then add a mulch of compost and ridge up the soil.

In the third spring after planting and before the shoots appear, pile 8-12 in (20-30 cm) of fine soil on top of the plants and smooth it into ridges. The soil must not be too heavy, or the asparagus spears will bend as they struggle upward. You can lighten heavy soil by mixing in organic matter or gritty sand.

The soil ridges will encourage the production of longer spears and blanch the asparagus, keeping the underground part of the spears white. The spears will turn purple or green, depending on the cultivar, where they appear above the soil. This third season of growth marks the beginning of the harvest.

Harvesting

The harvesting season may start in early spring and can extend to early summer, depending on the local climate. In the third year take only one or two spears from each plant; pick none later than the beginning of early summer.

Harvest the plants when approximately 5-8 in (13-20 cm) of the spears show above the surface. Again, asparagus spears will become stringy and not suitable for eating if they are allowed to grow too far above the soil. Cut or snap off the spears just below ground level; take only spears that are thicker than a pencil — thinner shoots should be allowed to grow into ferns.

When the emerging spears start getting thinner, it is time to stop harvesting. Always allow later spears to grow and develop their ferny foliage, and wait until the stems turn yellow in fall before cutting them to 1 in (2.5 cm) from the ground. Remember that the size of the following year's harvest depends on the amount of food that the present year's ferny top growth can manufacture and store in the roots. Fertilize established asparagus beds just after the end of the harvest season and again in early fall, applying 2½ lb (1.1 kg) of 10-10-10 per 100 sq ft (9 sq m) each time.

A special serrated asparagus knife is available that cuts deep down to the base of the asparagus shoot without disturbing too much soil. If you don't have this

---

▼ **Asparagus spears** Tall spears, like those below left, are too woody and stringy to be edible; leave them to develop foliage and to help build up the crown. The tender young spears below right are ready for cutting and eating.

Asparagus 'Jersey Giant'

GROWING ASPARAGUS FROM CROWNS
FIRST YEAR

1 Dig trenches 8 in (20 cm) deep, 3 ft (90 cm) apart, and wide enough for the crowns. Replace part of the soil to form a domed ridge.

2 Spread out the roots over the ridge, then quickly cover with 3 in (7.5 cm) of soil before they dry out. Leave the rest of the soil at the side of the trench.

3 Leave the first year's growth until the ferns start to turn yellow in fall. Then cut them down to about 1 in (2.5 cm) from the ground.

SECOND YEAR

5 The following spring, top-dress the rows with 10-10-10 fertilizer at a rate of 2½ lb (1.1 kg) per 100 sq ft (9 sq m).

6 When spears appear at the end of late spring, do not harvest. Once again allow them to grow out as ferns to build up reserves in the crowns.

7 Cut ferns when they turn yellow in fall, as before. Clear the bed entirely of any weeds with a hoe, and ridge up soil over the crowns.

THIRD YEAR

9 Spears growing within the ridge are blanched but they color when they surface. Cut only one or two spears from each plant during the first harvest.

10 Always cut or snap spears off; never pull them out. Use an asparagus knife or small trowel at a 45° angle to cut below the surface of the soil to the spear's base.

11 Stop harvesting at the beginning of early summer, as the emerging shoots become thinner. Fertilize to encourage healthy development of ferns.

4 After cutting down, mulch with well-rotted manure or compost. Ridge up the remaining trench soil 2-3 in (5-7.5 cm) deep over the crowns.

8 Add an extra topdressing of compost in fall. In spring, before shoots appear, mound 8-12 in (20-30 cm) of fine soil over the crowns and smooth.

12 Let the ferns grow up, and treat as before. Future crops depend on this slow buildup of the crowns. The fourth year is the first real harvest.

Blanched asparagus

type of knife, use a small trowel. Cut the spears at an angle. Alternatively, snap the spears at the base with your fingers.

Cut spears should be 5-8 in (13-20 cm) long. Cut the spears as they are ready. Be patient if you don't have enough for a meal right away. Keep the spears you have harvested standing in water in the refrigerator until you accumulate a sufficient number.

In their prime the small fat heads on the tips of the spears should be tightly compressed, above moist and glistening green, purple, or white stems. Any trace of brown on the cut edge of the stem indicates that the asparagus is past its best.

Wash the asparagus very carefully to avoid damaging the fragile tips. Trim the woody parts from the bases of the stems. Green stems only need washing; remove the hard exterior from white and purple stems by thinly peeling from the top downward.

Pests and diseases

The most troublesome pest is the asparagus beetle. If it occurs during the harvesting season, which is usually in early summer, hand-pick or spray with rotenone or pyrethrum.

Asparagus rust will produce reddish-brown spots on stems and leaves; fusarium wilt can stunt spears, causing lesions; and crown rot can turn spears brown at the soil line. Keep your plantings free of these problems by buying disease-free stock of resistant cultivars, maintaining good soil drainage, and keeping the soil pH at 6.0 or above.

CULTIVARS TO CHOOSE

'Jersey Giant': all-male hybrid; large green spears; resistant to rust, fusarium wilt, and crown rot.

'Jersey Knight': all-male hybrid; large green spears with purple tips; resistant to rust; tolerant of fusarium wilt, crown rot, and root-rot fungi.

'Martha Washington': traditional favorite; both male and female plants; long, thick spears tinged purple; large crops; very reliable.

'UC 157': all-male hybrid developed for growing in the South and Southwest; deep green spears have uniform tips; exceptionally productive.

BEANS, BROAD AND BUTTER

Broad beans thrive where springs are long and cool. Butter beans are a better crop for the South.

Broad beans, or favas, are an easy and rewarding crop in the Northwest or Northeast, where springs are long and cool. Sown early, they furnish a double harvest: pick and cook the half-grown pods whole; later shell out the mature seeds and eat like lima beans.

Butter beans are a better crop for a spring in the South; they are sensitive to frost and need warm weather to mature properly.

Planning the crop

Both types of beans need full sun and fertile, well-drained soil enriched with organic matter.

In the North sow broad beans four to six weeks before the last frost, when the soil reaches at least 40°F (4.5°C). In the South grow as a fall or winter crop. The seeds rot in waterlogged ground, so avoid cold, wet soils. Raised beds, which warm more quickly in the spring, are ideal for beans. A double row 10 ft (3 m) long provides 20 lb (9 kg) of broad beans.

Sow butter beans only after all danger of frost is past; that date may come early in the year in the Deep South.

Preparing and planting

Dig the soil thoroughly the fall or winter before sowing; incorporate one bucket of garden compost or well-rotted manure in every sq yd/m. Two weeks before sowing, rake in a low-nitrogen fertilizer (the ratio of numbers on the label should be 1:2:2, as in 5-10-10). Feed only at the rate recommended on the label; too much fertilizer will encourage big plants that yield fewer beans.

Dust the seeds with a legume inoculant. Plant broad beans 1 in (2.5 cm) deep and 10 in (25 cm) apart, in rows 2-2½ ft (60-75 cm) apart. Depending on the cultivar, butter beans will grow into bush (dwarf) or climbing ("pole") plants. Space bush butter beans about 1 in (2.5 cm) deep and 3 in (7.5 cm) apart, in rows 2-2½ ft (60-75 cm) apart; set rows of pole types at intervals of 3-4 ft (90-120 cm).

Many gardeners plant beans in double rows; this leads to bigger harvests, especially in arid climates, where the broader mass of foliage protects plants and soil from dehydration. To grow broad beans in double rows, plant seeds at the same depth and intervals, but space the second row 9 in (23 cm) away for dwarf cultivars and 1½ ft (45 cm) away for taller-growing types. Each pair of rows should be 2½ ft (75 cm) away from the next pair. Plant rows of bush butter beans 1 ft (30 cm) apart, in pairs 2½ ft (75 cm) apart. Climbing butter beans do not flourish in double rows.

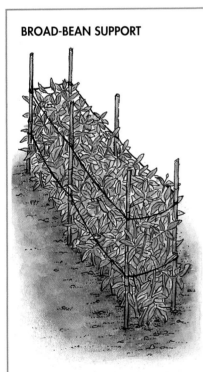

BROAD-BEAN SUPPORT

Tall-growing broad-bean cultivars need support. While the plants are small, insert two stakes at the end of each row and at 1 ft (30 cm) intervals along the rows. As the plants grow, run string around the stakes to support the developing plants. Support dwarf broad beans only on windy, exposed sites.

▲ **Succulent broad beans** Pick when young and tender — about the thickness of a little finger. If the scar on the pod is dark brown, the beans will be tough. You can cook young plant tops like spinach.

Support Broad beans need support so they are not blown about and damaged by winds. Flank the rows with stakes, and wrap a string around the stakes 8-10 in (20-25 cm) above the ground to gently confine the vines. Add more string at 6 in (15 cm) intervals as the plants grow taller.

You can grow bush butter beans unsupported, but provide trellises for pole types. At planting time, drive 4 ft (1.2 m) tall stakes into the ground every 4 ft (1.2 m) along the row of seeds;

Broad bean 'Aquadulce Claudia'

PEST CONTROL

▲ **Discouraging black bean aphids**
Pinch off the growing tips when the lowest bean pods are 1 in (2.5 cm) long and there are four sets of flower trusses at the top of the stems.

---

run a string between stakes 8 in (20 cm) above the ground. When the bean tendrils fasten themselves to the string, add another string to the stakes 8 in (20 cm) higher. Add strings as needed.

Successive plantings To extend the harvest, divide the space for the beans into several parcels; plant them one after another at two-week intervals. The number of sowings depends on the length of the bean season. Avoid planting broad beans in late spring in New England; summer heat will abort the harvest. Determine when the heat will end your harvest, then count back the number of days needed for the seeds to reach harvest (look for this number on the seed packet). This date should mark your last sowing.

Fall-sown broad beans In the South and in California, grow broad beans as a fall or winter crop. Sow seeds in mid- to late fall in the South and after the beginning of the fall rains in California.

Care and management
Mulch between rows after the seedlings emerge. Water the plants thoroughly during periods of drought; hoe regularly around the plants to keep down weeds.

When the lowest broad-bean pods are 1 in (2.5 cm) long and there are still flowers at the top of the stems, pinch off the growing tip of each plant to encourage pod development. (These young tips are good cooked lightly.) Pinching also removes the part of the plant likely to harbor a pest, the black bean aphid. You may still need to spray with insecticidal soap.

Harvesting
Pick the first broad-bean pods when 3 in (7.5 cm) long and cook them whole. Feel the pods gently with your fingers to gauge the size of the beans inside. Keep picking as and when required.

Harvest butter beans when the pods are large and plump but bright green and fresh looking.

Pests and diseases
Black bean aphids gather in thick masses to feed on new growth at the top of each plant. Mexican bean beetles and Japanese beetles can defoliate plants; use floating row covers to keep them out. Spider mites cause yellow stippling of foliage; spray the leaf undersides with insecticidal soap.

Anthracnose, bacterial blight, and mosaic virus may cause bean crops to fail. Plant resistant cultivars and rotate crops to prevent infection. Remove and destroy infected plants immediately; wash hands and tools before touching other bean plants.

CULTIVARS TO CHOOSE

Broad beans
'Aquadulce Claudia': 90 days from sowing to harvest; white beans in 5 in (13 cm) long dark green pods; sow in early spring or fall.

'Masterpiece': 90 days; large green seeds in 8-10 in (20-25 cm) long pods on 3 ft (90 cm) tall plants.

'The Sutton': 84 days; white beans with good flavor; 1 ft (30 cm) tall; good in small garden and good yield; grow in single rows.

'Toto': 63 days; 8 in (20 cm) long pods on dwarf, upright plants.

'Windsor': 65-75 days; large beige beans on plants 2-3 ft (60-90 cm) tall; plant in spring or fall.

Butter beans
'Baby Fordhook': 70 days from sowing to harvest; small lima-type beans in 2¾ in (7 cm) long pods on 14 in (36 cm) tall bushes.

'Dixie Butterpea': 75 days; richly flavored white beans in medium pods on vigorous bush-type plants.

'Sieva': 72 days; small green beans, borne three or four to a pod on vigorous climbing plants.

BEANS, GREEN AND SHELL

Green beans and shell beans are easy to grow and yield heavy crops from midsummer onward.

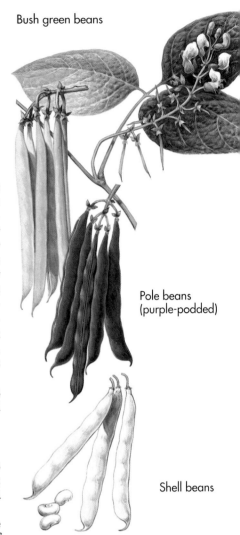

Bush green beans

Pole beans
(purple-podded)

Shell beans

These two types of bean — the green (or "snap") beans, which are grown for their edible pods, and the shell beans, which are grown for their edible seeds — are popular with American diners and gardeners. Rightly so, too, for they suit almost any palate and succeed in most regions.

Green beans are often called snap beans, because their pods are snapped into pieces and then cooked and eaten. These beans mature within 45 to 60 days of sowing. They are ideal for northern areas, where the growing season is short, and for a quick crop for the South or even a catch crop to grow after an earlier crop has been harvested. Included in this group are the old-fashioned string beans and the yellow wax beans.

Shell beans are grown for their seeds, which may be eaten fresh at harvesttime or frozen or dried

for winter use. Shell beans take longer to mature than green beans do: 68 days for 'French Flageolet' beans to over 100 days for some kidney beans. Despite their long season of growth, shell beans are a traditional staple of many northern gardens. Some cultivars thrive even in northern New England and the upper Midwest; other types of shell beans perform well in the South, while some, such as pinto beans, are standbys of southwestern gardeners.

Green beans and shell beans require similar cultivation and will be treated together here.

Site and soil preparation
Most soils are suitable, as long as they are not too heavy or too acid; a fertile and well-drained soil in a sunny and sheltered spot is best.

The fall before sowing, dig the plot deeply, adding a bucketful of well-rotted manure or compost per sq yd/m. Work in lime at the rate of 3 oz (85 g) per sq yd/m. A couple of weeks before sowing, apply 5-10-10 fertilizer at the rate of 1½ lb (680 g) per 100 sq ft (9 sq m), then rake the soil to a fine texture.

Sowing and planting
Cold, wet soils often prevent the seeds from germinating. If the soil is cold or if the season is late, cover the bed with black plastic for a few weeks to warm it up.

Because green and shell beans are cold sensitive, don't sow them outdoors until a week or so after all risk of frost has passed, usually in late spring. Treat seeds with a legume inoculant before sowing.

Sow seeds 1-1½ in (2.5-3.75 cm) deep. Plant bush-type (dwarf) green beans and shell beans at

◄ **Dwarf green beans** Ready for harvesting within 10 weeks of sowing, pick green (and shell) beans when pods are young, tender, and 4 in (10 cm) long.

intervals of 3-6 in (7.5-15 cm) in rows 1½-2½ ft (45-75 cm) apart; the interval between the rows will depend on the vigor of the cultivar. Sow pole-type or climbing green beans and shell beans at intervals of 6-10 in (15-25 cm); space the rows 4-8 ft (1.2-2.4 m) apart. Again, the vigor and height of the cultivar will determine the interval between the rows.

Erect supports for pole types at the time of planting. Use a trellis system (see p.82) or use tepees of four 6 ft (1.8 m) poles. Tie the poles together at the top; stand them with the free ends 3-4 ft (90-120 cm) apart and drive them a few inches into the soil. When using tepees, sow the seeds in hills or mounds, one by each pole. Sow six to eight seeds in each hill; thin the seedlings after germination so that each hill has three.

Sow another batch of seeds three weeks later, with successive sowings every three weeks until two to three months before the first killing frost of fall is expected. These successive sowings ensure a more manageable harvest.

Mulch around the stems in early summer. Water often in the flowering period to help the pods develop fully over a long period.

Harvesting
Green beans and shell beans produce crops within 8 to 10 weeks of sowing, and many yield pods up to 8 weeks between early summer and midfall. The more they are picked, the more they produce.

Look over the plants every couple of days for young, tender beans. Pick them when the pods are 4 in (10 cm) long. If left too long, the pods become stringy, the

beans turn starchy, and the plants stop producing.

When picking, hold the stem with one hand and pull the pods downward with the other. Alternatively, use scissors.

To dry shell beans, leave the pods on the plants until they turn brown and you hear the seeds rattle when you shake them. Shell the beans and spread them out on sheets of paper to dry thoroughly. Store them in an airtight container; seal in with them a packet of dried milk, which absorbs any slight residual moisture. Kept in a cool, dry place, the beans will last for 10 to 12 months.

Pests and diseases
Aphids, beetles, and spider mites are the main insect pests; see p.83 for a description of these and the principal diseases of beans.

CULTIVARS TO CHOOSE

Green beans, bush types
'Contender': 43 days from planting to harvest; thick pods; bears early.

'Goldkist': 56 days; yellow wax beans; disease-resistant plant.

'Provider': 50 days; tender pods; disease-resistant plant.

'Royal Burgundy': 51 days; purple pods turn green when cooked.

Green beans, pole types
'Blue Lake': 55 days; 6 in (15 cm) long, flat pods on 8 ft (2.4 m) tall plants; large crops; matures early.

'Kentucky Wonder': 60 days; 6 in (15 cm) long pods, 5 ft (1.5 m) plants.

'Romano': 70 days; wide, flat pods; vigorous plant; climbs 7 ft (2.1 m).

Shell beans, bush types
'French Flageolet': 68 days; small green beans, 8 to 10 to a pod.

'French Horticultural': 75 days; red-splotched white beans; dwarf plant.

'Jacob's Cattle': 88 days; maroon-speckled white beans.

Shell beans, pole types
'Jeminez': 67 days; red-tinted dark green pods; harvest as green beans or shell for eating fresh or dry.

'King of the Garden': 85 days; lima-type beans; climbs 10 ft (3 m).

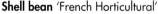
Shell bean 'French Horticultural'

Bush green bean 'Contender'

Climbing green bean 'Blue Lake'

BEANS, RUNNER
Runner beans are an old-fashioned favorite, valued for their tasty crops and for the flowering screen they provide.

Runner beans are also known as scarlet runners because many cultivars have scarlet flowers; however, some cultivars do bear white blossoms. All are decorative, and in fact runner beans are often grown as ornamental annual vines in the United States.

Runner beans are attractive trained up strings or netting around a porch. They will quickly climb up a fence, hiding it with fresh green foliage and flowers. In the vegetable garden a tepee of runner beans in full flower makes a spectacular focal point. But it is a mistake to ignore the delicious beans that follow the blossoms.

Tall-growing runner beans normally reach a height of 8-10 ft (2.4-3 m), although they can be grown on the ground without support if the growing points are pinched off when the plants are about 1 ft (30 cm) high.

Runner beans come into season when most green beans come to an end. They have larger, coarser pods than the green beans, but they are equally flavorful.

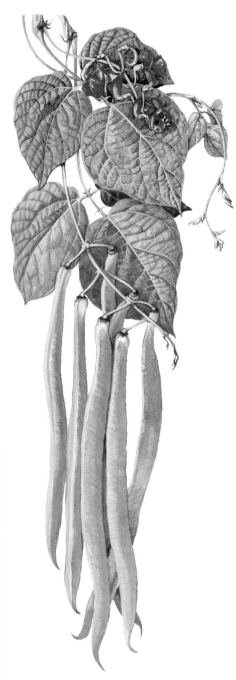

▲ **Runner beans** Common cultivars produce 10-16 in (25-40 cm) long pods, which are sometimes stringless. The blossoms may be scarlet or white.

◀ **Bean support** Tepees are an ideal and attractive way of supporting runner beans and are particularly suitable for small plots. Use 8 ft (2.4 m) high wooden poles or bamboo stakes, pushing them into the ground at 2 ft (60 cm) intervals in the shape of a circle. Pull the tops together and tie them with string.

Site and soil preparation

Runner beans grow best in a sunny spot, but they are cold sensitive and in the North need shelter from the wind. Wind protection also assists pollinating insects, ensuring a better crop of beans.

Most garden soils, if properly prepared, are suitable for growing runner beans, though a deep, rich soil is best. For heavy clay, dig the ground deeply the winter before sowing and work in plenty of compost or well-rotted manure; leave the soil rough so frost can break down the clods.

A month or two before sowing, dig a straight or circular trench, 1½-2 ft (45-60 cm) wide, on the chosen site. Remove the topsoil to one spade's depth (10 in/25 cm), then work a bucketful per sq yd/m of garden compost or well-rotted manure into the trench bottom, digging the soil to another spade's depth. Replace the topsoil, but leave the site of the trench with a slight depression, which will help to retain water and prevent the roots from drying out in summer.

A couple of weeks before sowing rake in 5-10-10 fertilizer at a rate of 2 oz (57 g) per sq yd/m.

Staking and supporting

Unless you intend to keep the vines pinched back, runner beans need plenty of room to climb; supports should be at least 6 ft (1.8 m) high, but 8-10 ft (2.4-3 m) is a better height. Such a structure must be firmly anchored, too, if it is to withstand the wind.

A-frame trellis Runner beans are often supported by stakes set on both sides of a double row. Insert the stakes before the seeds are sown. Bamboo stakes about 8 ft (2.4 m) high are excellent for this where available, but ordinary hardwood poles work well too.

At 1 ft (30 cm) intervals, push stakes or poles into the ground (the beans will be planted at their feet); establish two rows of stakes or poles, 1½ ft (45 cm) apart. Cross opposing stakes or poles just above their halfway mark and lash them together with wire or strong string. This will ensure that pods on the upper parts of the plants, where there is most growth, will hang down and out, making them clearly visible for harvesting. To strengthen the structure, set a pole horizontally along the tops of the crossed

pairs; tie this stabilizer in place. Allow 5-6 ft (1.5-1.8 m) between each set of trellising (and each double row of beans).

Tepees Push an 8 ft (2.4 m) high stake into the center of a circle about 5 ft (1.5 m) in diameter. Attach strings from the top of the stake to pegs placed in the ground at 2 ft (60 cm) intervals around the edge of the circle.

Alternatively, use poles instead of strings, dispensing with the central stake and tying the poles firmly together at the top.

Netting Set up a row of sturdy 8 ft (2.4 m) high poles along the bean trench at intervals of 5-6 ft (1.5-1.8 m); leave 2½ ft (75 cm) between rows. Staple plastic, string, or wire netting to the poles. This will form a rigid, wind-resistant structure.

Alternatively, support beans against netting fixed to a permanent wall or fence.

Sowing and planting

Runner beans are cold-sensitive plants and should not be put outside until all danger of frost is past, so find out when the last

▲ **Net support** Push a row of strong 8 ft (2.4 m) tall poles well into the ground, 5-6 ft (1.5-1.8 m) apart. Attach plastic, string, or wire netting firmly to them.

PINCHING

When the runner beans reach the top of their supports, start pinching back the growing tips. This stops the climbing stems from growing any more, encourages side shoots and bushiness, and increases flowering (and therefore the number of pods).

If you grow runner bean cultivars on the ground without supports, pinch out the growing tips as soon as the plants reach a height of about 1 ft (30 cm).

spring frost is predicted in your region. In the North, where the growing season is short, it may be advantageous to get runner beans off to an early start by sowing them indoors.

Sowing indoors To produce an earlier crop in the North, sow an early cultivar, such as 'Enorma,' in early spring to midspring. Sow the seeds about 1 in (2.5 cm) deep in 5 in (13 cm) pots of sterilized potting soil.

Place the pots in a warm spot or heated propagating unit to germinate the seeds. Then transfer the small plants in their pots to a cold frame or cool but sunny windowsill. Harden off cold-frame plants by gradually opening the top of the frame and increasing the ventilation on warm days. Harden off windowsill pots by setting them outside in a sheltered spot for gradually increasing intervals of time on warm days.

When the danger of frost is past, transplant the seedlings to their positions in the garden. Use a trowel to dig holes for each seedling, and water them in well.

If you need to protect young plants in the early stages from the wind, attach a sheet of clear plastic, 2-3 ft (60-90 cm) high, to the outside of the supports.

Sowing outdoors The first outdoor sowing can be made as soon as the soil has warmed and the danger of frost is past. Put the supports in place, and make drills 2 in (5 cm) deep. Sow two seeds at intervals of about 6 in (15 cm), with a few extra at each end to fill in any gaps.

After germination, pull up the weaker of each pair of seedlings. Use these extra plants, if necessary, to fill in gaps where neither seed has germinated.

After sowing and transplanting, water the soil thoroughly and then scatter slug pellets.

Looking after the crop

As the plants grow, spread a 1 in (2.5 cm) deep mulch of straw, leaf mold, compost, or shredded bark around the plants. This helps prevent the soil from becoming too dry, and also smothers weeds.

Twine the runners (climbing shoots) counterclockwise around the supports — this is the natural way for the plants to climb. If necessary, carefully tie them in place loosely with string. When the plants reach the top of their supports, begin to pinch back the growing tips.

You may choose to grow some of the normally tall-growing cultivars as short and bushy plants. This means pinching back the growing tips when the plants are 1 ft (30 cm) high and then growing the beans as bushes without supports. Space the plants about 2 ft (60 cm) apart. In general, it is better to grow climbing cultivars on supports, since more beans are produced and the pods will grow longer and straighter. If bush-type plants are desired, grow one of the dwarf cultivars, such as 'Gulliver,' which grows no more than 1 ft (30 cm) tall naturally.

Runner beans need frequent watering, so don't let the soil around them dry out.

Harvesting

Runner beans are ready to harvest from midsummer onward. Pick the beans every couple of days so that they don't have a chance to mature fully — if even a small number are allowed to mature, this will stop the flower-producing process.

An ideal size for harvesting the pods is 6-8 in (15-20 cm) long: if you pick the pods at this stage, a season of eight weeks should be guaranteed. The more you pick the beans, the more the plants will produce.

After you harvest the last of the beans, cut the foliage off at ground level. Because the roots are a valuable source of nitrogen, leave them in the ground.

Pests and diseases

The major problem with runner beans is the failure of flowers to set seeds. Dryness at the roots, a lack of pollinating insects, or birds pecking off buds are the usual causes.

See p.83 for details on other bean pests and diseases.

CULTIVARS TO CHOOSE

Tall-growing cultivars

'Case Knife': 65 days from sowing until harvest; white flowers; flat, stringless, 8 in (20 cm) pods.

'Desiree': 65 days; broad, fleshy, entirely stringless pods, about 10-12 in (25-30 cm) long; excellent flavor; large harvest; white flowers.

'Enorma': 65 days; slender pods of fine flavor and shape; heavy crop of pods up to 20 in (50 cm) long, but harvest under 12 in (30 cm) long; good for freezing or eating fresh; scarlet flowers.

'Ivanhoe': 65 days; straight, thick pods to 1½ ft (45 cm) long; scarlet flowers and lilac-pink seeds.

'Lady Di': 65 days; long, slender, fleshy, stringless pods; slow seed development; large harvest.

'Scarlet Emperor': 75 days; smaller pods than average but sweeter flavor; outstanding scarlet flowers; large harvest.

Dwarf cultivar

'Gulliver': 60 days; large harvest; smooth, crisp, stringless pods on plants 15 in (38 cm) high.

Runner bean 'Scarlet Emperor'

Runner bean 'Desiree'

BEETS

These sweet-flavored roots furnish both spring and fall harvests, and you can cook their leafy tops for a delicious bonus.

There are two types of beets: cultivars with globe-shaped roots, which are usually grown for eating freshly boiled in summer and fall, and cultivars with long roots, which are harvested in fall and stored for winter use. Both types grow best in cool, moist weather and should be treated as an early-spring or even winter crop where summers are very hot. A row 20 ft (6 m) long can yield 25 lb (11 kg) of globe-shaped beets or 45 lb (20 kg) of the long-rooted beets.

Beets will grow in partial shade but thrive in an open, sunny site. While they produce higher yields on a light, sandy loam, you can grow them on heavier soils if the ground is prepared well beforehand. Dig the plot in fall or early winter before sowing. Cover the plot with well-rotted manure to a depth of 2-4 in (5-10 cm), then turn it in with a spading fork. Never use fresh manure in preparing soil for beets; it may cause them to grow small, forked roots.

If aged manure is not available, use compost, but supplement it with 5-10-10 fertilizer applied at a rate of 3-4 cups (720-960 ml) per 20 ft (6 m) of row. If a soil test indicates acidic soil, add enough lime to raise the pH to 7.0.

Growing beets
In the South sow beets in very early spring or late winter, while the soil is cool, about 50°F (10°C).

◀ **Types of beets** Beets come as both round globe cultivars and long-rooted cylindrical types. In addition to red beets there are yellow ones. All beets are easy to grow and thrive in light, well-drained, loamy soil and an open, sunny site. Avoid freshly manured sites, where the roots will fork.

Globe-shaped beet

Long-rooted beet

In the North sow beets a month before the last spring frost; make successive sowings every two weeks until the weather turns hot. Warm temperatures may inhibit the germination of seeds sown for fall crops. To counteract this, soak the seeds overnight before planting. Then saturate the soil at planting time; keep it covered until the seedlings emerge.

A beet "seed" is actually a cluster of one to four seeds. Because they germinate as a group, sow seeds sparingly, ½ in (1.25 cm) deep and 2 in (5 cm) apart. Allow 1 ft (30 cm) between rows.

The seedlings will sprout in clusters, so pinch or snip off all but one from each group. About a month later — when the roots are the size of golf balls — give the beets a second thinning. Pull up entire plants to leave the remaining ones 4 in (10 cm) apart.

The rows should be kept free of weeds. Always use a hoe, and avoid damaging the tender roots. Excessive dryness can produce woodiness and smaller yields, so make sure that the plot is watered frequently, at least weekly in hot weather. Mulching will improve moisture retention. Too much water can be bad, too; a very rainy spring may cause the roots to split.

HARVESTING BEETS

1 Pull globe-shaped beets by hand as needed. Ease out long-rooted beets with a garden fork, but take care not to damage the roots.

2 Twist off the foliage, leaving 2 in (5 cm) attached to the roots to prevent "bleeding." Store the roots in a box of sand in a frost-free spot.

Harvest greens from the beets as they grow; you can snip off up to a third of a beet's leaves without damaging the plant. Harvest the roots when they reach 1½-3 in (3.75-7.5 cm) diameter. If the roots stay in the ground longer, they will lose their sweet flavor.

Harvesting and storing

Harvest globe-shaped cultivars by hand as required. Once out of the ground, shake off any soil and discard damaged roots. To remove the leaves, hold the base of the leaves in one hand and twist off the remainder with the other; leave a 2 in (5 cm) crown of leaves attached. If you cut or twist off the leaves too close to the root, they will "bleed" — the roots will lose their juiciness and flavor.

Lift long-rooted cultivars by placing a garden fork alongside the row and gently breaking up the soil so that the roots can be removed without damage. After twisting off the tops, store the roots in boxes of sand in a frost-free place. If you are short of storage space, beets can be left in the ground and lifted as needed.

Pests and diseases

The black bean aphid is the main pest. Leaf miners sometimes tunnel into the leaves; if they do, remove infested foliage. A boron deficiency in the soil can be the source of stunting or black spots and brown hearts in the roots; treat deficient soil with household borax; mix 1 tablespoon with 3 gal (11.4 L) of water and apply it to 100 ft (30 m) of row.

CULTIVARS TO CHOOSE

Globe-shaped cultivars

'Boltardy': 59 days from sowing to harvest; fine-textured, deep red roots; heat resistant; can be sown early; stores well.

'Burpee's Golden': 56 days; golden orange with yellow flesh that does not bleed; excellent greens.

'Detroit Dark Red': 63 days; standard main-crop globe cultivar; sweet, crisp flesh; can be stored over winter.

'Little Ball': 50 days; early maturing; small; sweet and tender, perfectly round roots are ideal for canning or pickling.

'Monogram': 60 days; rich red color; smooth skin; each seed cluster produces one seedling only, no thinning necessary.

'Red Ace': 55 days; a vigorous hybrid with large, sweet red roots and flavorful greens; disease-resistant plant.

Long-rooted cultivars

'Cylindra': 60 days; 8 in (20 cm), oval-shaped roots; deep red flesh with excellent storing qualities; good for slicing and canning.

'Forono': 70 days; good flavor and texture; cylindrical roots; slow to become woody and stores well.

Globe beet 'Burpee's Golden'

Globe beet 'Boltardy'

Long beet 'Forono'

BROCCOLI

Hardy and adaptable to poor soil, broccoli produces big harvests of vitamin-rich florets through spring and fall.

The growing interest in a healthy diet is giving broccoli an ever-greater popularity in the United States. Broccoli is rich in vitamins A, B, and C, as well as calcium and iron. The home gardener, however, may prefer to plant broccoli simply because it is easy to grow and productive.

Broccoli comes from a wild cabbage species, *Brassica oleracea*, and its cultivation is similar to that of its relatives, the cabbages, cauliflowers, and kales. Like all members of the brassica family, broccoli needs a long, cool growing season, though it is not as cold hardy as cabbage or kale. In the northern and central parts of the United States, broccoli does well as a spring and fall crop. In the warmer parts of the country, it is better to grow broccoli as a winter crop.

Plant breeders have created a host of different broccoli types; in general they are divided into one of two groups. The common broccolis have grayish-green leaves and fleshy, edible stems that support large central heads of tightly clustered flower buds, which may be green, bluish green, or purple. Sprouting broccolis produce wilder-looking plants with leafy stems and many clusters of edible flower buds, but no central head. Common broccolis produce big harvests in a convenient form; sprouting broccolis yield their smaller, leafier heads ("florets") over a longer season. If you harvest the mature florets every few days, the plants can continue to produce over a period of at least two months.

A related vegetable that closely resembles broccoli and may be grown in the same way is the purple cauliflower, sometimes called broccoliflower. Since this takes up to 110 days to mature, it is best grown as a fall crop in most areas. At maturity it produces a big central head of purple florets that tastes like broccoli. After this is

cut, the plant yields a second crop of top-quality side shoots.

Site and soil preparation
While you can grow broccoli on poor soil and in cold areas, it will grow best in fertile, loamy soil and in a sunny spot. Choose a site sheltered from the wind; otherwise staking may be necessary to support the plants.

▲ **Sprouting broccoli** Purple or white sprouting broccoli produces numerous small heads or spears 1-2 in (2.5-5 cm) wide. Cut these with a length of stem, and cook them in a bunch. Harvest regularly to prevent flowering and to stimulate further young growth.

Broccoli prefers an organically enriched, well-fertilized, alkaline soil. Unless the soil was enriched for a previous crop, in the fall or winter before planting dig in well-rotted manure or compost, about half a bucketful per sq yd/m.

If a test shows the soil to be acid or neutral, treat it with ground limestone at a rate of 5 lb (2.3 kg) per 100 sq ft (9 sq m) for each point you wish to raise the pH (e.g., from 6.0 to 7.0). One or two days before planting broccoli, fork in a dressing of 5-10-10 fertilizer at a rate of 3-4 lb (1.4-1.8 kg) per 100 sq ft (9 sq m).

Starting seeds indoors

You can buy seedlings to transplant into the garden, but you will have a greater choice of cultivars (and save some money) if you start from seeds. Depending on your climate and the season, start the seeds indoors or sow them directly into the garden.

In areas where winters are frigid, springs are short, and summers are hot, start the seeds indoors. Sow seven to nine weeks before the expected date of the last spring frost. Plant the seeds ¼ in (6 mm) deep in peat pots full of sterilized seed-starting mix. Moisten the pots and soil, then set them in a sunny area with a temperature of 60°-65°F (15.5°-18.5°C). Seedlings should emerge in about five days.

A month before the date of the last spring frost, harden off the seedlings by setting them outside for increasing lengths of time. Three weeks before the last frost date, plant them in the garden at intervals of 1-2 ft (30-60 cm) and in rows 2-3 ft (60-90 cm) apart; plant closer on fertile soil and farther apart on poorer, sandier soil. If frost threatens, cover the seedlings overnight with paper bags, cones made of newspaper, or hot caps made by cutting the bottoms off 1 gal (4 L) plastic milk jugs.

Direct seeding

In areas with long, cool springs or when broccoli is grown as a fall or winter crop, the best harvests are secured by sowing the seeds directly into the garden rows. Sow spring crops about two months before the expected date of the last spring frost; sow fall crops about 85 days before the expected date of the first fall frost. Sow winter crops as the weather cools in midfall.

Plant the seeds ¼ in (6 mm) deep; use two to five seeds per 1 ft (30 cm) and space the rows 2-3 ft (60-90 cm) apart. Water the soil thoroughly. Once the seedlings

Common broccoli forms large heads of densely packed buds. Once these are cut, small but edible side shoots sprout from the leaf bases.

develop their second set of leaves, thin them out until they are 1-2 ft (30-60 cm) apart.

Care

Broccoli seedlings are very sensitive to drought, so be sure to irrigate whenever the soil dries out.

Fertilize three weeks after setting out seedlings or about five weeks after direct seeding. Apply 1 tablespoon of balanced fertilizer per plant, mixing it into the surrounding soil 4-5 in (10-13 cm) out from the stems.

Continue watering regularly in dry spells; keep weeds down by hoeing. To save weeding time, put a mulch down between the rows.

Harvesting

Broccoli heads are actually clusters of immature flower buds. With cultivars of common broccoli, cut the large central head while it is deep green (or bluish green or purple) and the buds are tightly closed. If the buds start to yellow, you waited too long.

Cut the head back to a point just below where the flower stems start to separate. Small but tasty side shoots will then sprout from upper leaf axils.

When the florets on sprouting types are in a tight-bud stage, cut them just above the point where the stem becomes tough.

Purple broccolis turn bright green during cooking but retain their distinctive nutty flavor.

Pests and diseases

Broccoli is mostly a problem-free crop. Aphids, cabbage root maggots, imported cabbageworms, cabbage loopers, and flea beetles may attack it. Insecticidal soaps are an effective treatment for aphids; Bt (*Bacillus thuringiensis*) is effective for cabbageworms and cabbage loopers. Floating row covers help exclude flea beetles and cabbage root maggots.

Clubroot can be a problem, especially in poorly drained or acidic soil. To prevent it, rotate crops and lime the soil before planting.

CULTIVARS TO CHOOSE

Green sprouting

'De Cicco': 75 days from seed to harvest; 3-4 in (7.5-10 cm) central head and numerous side shoots; different shoots ripen over several weeks for extended harvest.

'Spring Raab' ('Rapine'): 70 days; many dime-size green florets; does not develop central head; flavorful but the plant can be quick to bolt in warm weather.

Purple sprouting

'Purple Sprouting': 220 days; 2-3 ft (60-90 cm) plant bears small purple florets; hardy to 10°F (-12°C); good fall or winter crop.

'Purple Sprouting Red Arrow': 95 days; heavy-bearing plant.

'Rosalind': 60-65 days; early maturing for spring or fall crop; relatively fine texture and color.

White sprouting

'Late White Sprouting': 105 days; golden-white florets; compact plant produces large crop.

Common

'Corvet': 90 days; large, round light green head, uniform and of fine quality.

'Emperor': 80 days; early-maturing, strong-growing plant; suitable for poor soil; thick, dark green domed head.

'Everest': 83 days; 6 in (15 cm), domed green head; disease resistant; good for fall harvest in the Northeast.

'Green Comet': 55 days; deep green head, large and tight; early, from late summer.

'Green Valiant': 92 days; large, domed green head; side shoots to 3 in (7.5 cm) wide.

'Packman': 75 days; especially large head and good side-shoot production; early crop.

'Romanesco': 85 days; lime-green head; harvest as whole head or individual florets; suitable for northern regions.

'Shogun': 102 days; dark green dome-shaped head; tolerant of cold weather; crops into late fall.

Common broccoli 'Corvet'

Sprouting broccoli 'Late White Sprouting'

Sprouting broccoli 'Purple Sprouting'

Common broccoli 'Romanesco'

BRUSSELS SPROUTS

Members of the brassica family, Brussels sprouts are a hardy, cool-weather crop. Plant both early- and late-maturing cultivars for a long harvest.

Although rarely seen in gardens in the United States, Brussels sprouts, which are rich in vitamin C, are one of the best fall crops for northern gardens. A frost actually sweetens the sprouts, and the harvest can extend well into the winter months. Gardeners in the Southeast can overwinter plants and harvest a spring crop as well.

You can have Brussels sprouts ready for a continuous harvest of weeks or months by sowing early- and late-maturing cultivars.

Each 10 ft (3 m) row of plants can yield 16 lb (7.3 kg) of sprouts.

Planning the crop

Brussels sprouts prefer an open, sunny site and fertile soil with a neutral to just slightly acid pH; a pH of 6.5 is ideal.

To give the soil time to settle, dig the bed for Brussels sprouts several weeks before planting. If it wasn't enriched with manure for a previous crop, dig in well-rotted manure or compost.

On acid soils, add ground limestone a couple of weeks before planting; apply the lime at the rate called for by a soil test. As a rule, ground limestone applied at a rate of 5 lb (2.3 kg) per 100 sq ft (9 sq m) will raise the pH one point (e.g., from 6.0 to 7.0). Blend the lime into the soil thoroughly.

◄ **Brussels sprouts** Said to have first originated in Belgium, Brussels sprouts yield fresh green vegetables loaded with vitamin C throughout winter. The modern F1 hybrids are reliable and compact, producing large numbers of uniform, firm, and tasty button sprouts. Sow early- and main-crop cultivars for sprouts from fall through to spring.

HARVESTING BRUSSELS SPROUTS

1 As plants mature, remove yellowing leaves and "blown" sprouts from the lower part of the stem to improve air circulation. Loose-leaved sprouts are tasteless and best discarded.

2 Harvest the lower sprouts first, while they are small (not much larger than walnuts) and while their leaves are still tight. Harvest after a slight frost for the best flavor.

Sowing and planting

The easiest way to grow Brussels sprouts is to buy young plants from a garden center. Unfortunately, these seedlings usually appear for sale in the spring, even though Brussels sprouts succeed far better as a fall or winter crop in most regions. Raising your own transplants can solve that problem and allows a greater choice of cultivars. Direct seeding in the garden is possible, but it is better to start the seeds indoors to help the plants escape an infestation of flea beetles.

For a fall crop (ideal in the North), count back 90-100 days from the expected date of the first fall frost to determine when to set the transplants into the ground;

▲ **Straw mulch** Brussels sprouts need fertile soil manured for a previous crop. Straw mulch protects roots from frost, sprouts from mud. To improve soil, dig in straw at end of the season.

▲ **Spring greens** Pick the top growth of the Brussels sprout plant at the end of the season, after all the sprouts are harvested. Cook and serve like cabbage and other greens.

sow the seeds four weeks earlier. Plant them ½ in (1.25 cm) deep in flats filled with sterilized seed-starting mix. Water well and set the flats under fluorescent lights.

In two weeks, when the seeds germinate and produce their first pairs of leaves, separate the seedlings; transplant them to 2½ in (6.25 cm) peat pots full of sterilized potting soil. Grow the seedlings indoors, under lights or on a sunny windowsill, for two weeks; transplant to the outdoor bed.

At the end of this period harden the seedlings off for a few days before planting them in the beds. Set them at 2 ft (60 cm) intervals in rows 3 ft (90 cm) apart. Firm the soil down around the plants; water it well, making sure that it settles in around the roots.

In southern areas, where Brussels sprouts are grown as a winter or spring crop, seed them directly into the garden bed. Figure out the sowing date by counting backward from the time of harvest. For a crop in late winter, count backward the number of days listed on the seed packet as the time required for the plants to reach maturity. Add two weeks to the total; Brussels sprouts take longer to mature in winter.

When sowing directly, plant the seeds ½ in (1.25 cm) deep, four or five seeds to 1 ft (30 cm), in rows 3 ft (90 cm) apart. When the seedlings reach a height of 4-5 in (10-13 cm), thin them so that the remaining seedlings are spaced 2 ft (60 cm) apart in each row.

Water young plants regularly in dry weather. Side-dress monthly with 5-10-10 fertilizer at a rate of 1-2 tablespoons per plant.

The plants grow upward in spikes. Sprouts form around the spikes, maturing from the bottom up. When sprouts are approximately half the harvestable size, snip off the leaf under each one to give the sprout growing room. If your growing season is short or if the sprouts are slow to mature, snip off the topmost, terminal bud of the spikes. This forces the plants to put their energy into bud production.

Harvesting
Slice sprouts off the spikes as they ripen, working from the bottom up. Ready-to-harvest buds will be no bigger than walnuts. Be sure to cut the sprouts while they are still tightly packed, before they start to open. Sprouts taste better if they have been touched by frost.

Pests and diseases
Brussels sprouts are attacked by aphids, cabbage root maggots, cabbage whiteflies, caterpillars, and flea beetles. Clubroot can be a problem, especially in acidic soil.

Brussels sprout 'Jade Cross'

CULTIVARS TO CHOOSE

'Fortress': 130 days from seed to harvest; large yield of dark green sprouts; cold-hardy type.

'Jade Cross': 97 days; best for short-season garden; large yield of medium-size sprouts on short plant.

'Lunet': 115 days; medium-large firm sprouts; one of the most productive cultivars.

'Prince Marvel': 100 days; early-maturing type; small, hard sprouts; good for winter crop.

CABBAGE

With red, green, and Chinese types to choose from, as well as crinkled-leaf savoys, cabbage is one of the most varied crops.

Another cool-weather crop, cabbage flourishes if planted in early spring or fall. A traditional mainstay of northern gardeners, cabbage can be grown in the South as a winter crop, or if more heat-tolerant cultivars are planted, as a very early spring crop. Some types of cabbage, in particular tight-headed cultivars, such as 'Danish Ballhead,' keep for as long as five to six months if stored in a cool place, such as a root cellar, where the temperature is 32°-40°F (0°-4.5°C).

Types of cabbage

Cabbage heads may be round, conical, or flattened on top. They range in color from dark to light green and white, as well as pink to purple. The leaves may be smooth or, in savoy cabbages, crinkled. At maturity the heads may weigh anywhere from 1 lb (450 g) up to as much as 60 lb (27 kg). The larger heads are exceptional; a 16 lb (7.3 kg) cabbage is remarkably large for a home garden. Generally, cultivars with round or flat heads tend to grow larger, while conical-headed cabbages tend to be smaller.

Cabbages are categorized by the rate at which they mature. So-called early cultivars are

Savoy cabbage

Summer cabbage

Winter cabbage

Spring cabbage

Red cabbage

BRASSICA COLLARS

Carefully fit brassica collars made of tar paper around the stems of young cabbages to protect them from cabbage root maggots. A floating row cover will also keep away flea beetles.

ready to harvest roughly 60 to 80 days after seedlings are set out in the garden, midseason cultivars in 80 to 90 days, and late cultivars in 90 to 110 days.

The cold hardiness of cabbages varies considerably from cultivar to cultivar. Some cultivars can withstand temperatures as low as 10°F (-12°C), and late types, such as 'Danish Ballhead,' can be stored by simply leaving them in the garden as long as the temperature does not drop below 20°F

(-6.5°C). Typically, the savoy cultivars are the most cold resistant.

Site and soil preparation

All cabbages need a sunny, open site in well-drained, alkaline soil. While early types thrive on light, sandy soil, later-maturing types require a heavier, more moisture-retentive soil.

Start cabbages in flats and packs or in peat pots indoors — ideally, place them under fluorescent lights — then transplant

TRANSPLANTING CABBAGE

1 When the young plants are ready for transplanting, prepare holes for them at 12-15 in (30-38 cm) intervals in rows 1-2 ft (30-60 cm) apart; the spacing varies with the size of the cultivar.

2 Set the plants carefully in the holes, and firm them in place before watering in thoroughly. Hoe regularly to remove weeds, and water conscientiously to ensure that the soil remains evenly moist.

them to the position in the garden where they will mature.

If your vegetable garden is new, with cabbage as the first crop to be grown in that part of the plot, enrich the soil by working in well-rotted manure or compost, half a bucketful per sq yd/sq m, several weeks before planting. If the garden is an established one and the cabbage is replacing a leguminous crop, such as peas or beans, or it is taking over from salad greens in a rotation plan, the plot won't need enrichment of this sort.

Test the soil before planting, and if it is acidic, raise the pH with ground limestone. The rule of thumb is to apply ground limestone at a rate of 5 lb (2.3 kg) per 100 sq ft (9 sq m) to raise the pH one point (e.g., from 6.0 to 7.0). Use a spading fork to blend the lime into the soil thoroughly.

A week before setting out the seedlings, fertilize the cabbage bed with 5-10-10, applying it at a rate of about 3-4 lb (1.4-1.8 kg) per 100 sq ft (9 sq m).

Sowing and planting

If you are planning to raise a spring crop of cabbage, you must make sure it is ready to harvest before hot weather sets in. For the best results with a spring crop, it is usually advisable to plant an early cultivar.

Check the expected date of the last spring frost for your region and sow your cabbage seeds 50 to 60 days before that date. Plant the seeds ¼ in (6 mm) deep in a shallow pot, or flat, filled with sterilized seed-starting mix. Sow the seeds 2 in (5 cm) apart. Water the flat, then set it on a sunny windowsill where the temperature remains constant around 60°-70°F (15.5°-21°C). Or better yet, set the flat in a heated propagation unit or set it underneath fluorescent lights and on top of a soil-heating cable that is set to 75°F (24°C). The seeds should germinate in four to five days in such conditions.

As soon as the seedlings emerge from the seed-starting mix, move the flat to a cooler spot where the temperature stays between 55°-65°F (13°-18.5°C). Or turn off the heating cable and make sure the fluorescent lights are at least 1 in (2.5 cm) above the seedlings. Too much heat encourages the seedlings to become overly tall (leggy).

As soon as the seedlings develop their first pair of leaves, transplant them into plastic cell packs or peat pots filled with sterilized potting mix, planting them a little deeper than they were in the seed flat to further ensure that they won't become leggy.

Keep the seedlings indoors until two to three weeks before the last spring frost date, then harden them off by setting them outside for gradually increasing periods of time for a few days. Next, plant the seedlings in the prepared bed, setting them at intervals of 12-15 in (30-38 cm) in rows 1-2 ft (30-60 cm) apart. If frost threatens, cover the newly transplanted seedlings overnight with hot caps (plastic 1 gal/4 L milk or water containers with their bottoms cut off) or with cones made of newspaper.

Start a fall or winter crop in flats, or direct-seed — that is, sow the seeds directly into the outdoor bed where the cabbage will grow. Where winters are moderate, midseason or late-maturing cultivars are the best choice. Sow the seeds in early summer in the North and in mid- to late summer in central and southern regions.

If the plants are started indoors, the procedure for sowing a fall crop is identical to that for a spring crop. For direct-seeding, sow two or three seeds every 1 ft (30 cm) of row, ¼-½ in (6-12 mm) deep. Tamp the soil down over the seeds and moisten it. After the seedlings emerge and grow four to five leaves, thin them to 1½-2 ft (45-60 cm) between plants.

Care

After planting out young cabbage plants, fit them with collars (see illustration, facing page) or drape a floating row cover of spunbonded polypropylene over each row of plants, supporting the cover with stakes or wire hoops. The collar protects against cabbage root maggots; the row cover protects against the maggots and flea beetles as well.

A month after planting, side-dress the plants with a balanced fertilizer, such as 10-10-10, applying it at a rate of 1 lb (450 g) per 25 ft (7.5 m) of row.

To help keep the soil moist and cool, apply a 2-3 in (5-7.5 cm) thick layer of organic mulch, such as straw, around the plants. This is especially important with cabbage. It is the soil temperature more than the air temperature that causes the plants to bolt — that is, to send up a flower stalk instead of forming a head.

Irrigate the plants during dry weather, but try to keep the moisture level in the soil even; uneven watering may result in sudden growth, and this can lead to the cabbage heads splitting. Do not irrigate during periods of cool weather or during high humidity. In these situations the water won't evaporate promptly, and prolonged wetting of the foliage can promote disease.

Harvesting

You can begin harvesting as soon as the cabbage heads reach soft-ball size and feel firm to the touch. In the home garden, many cultivars can grow up to 6-8 lb (2.7-3.6 kg), several times the size of store-bought heads. Savoy cabbages are at their best after a slight frost.

Pests and diseases

The main diseases of cabbages are clubroot and leaf spot. Cabbage root maggot, cabbageworms, cabbage loopers, and flea beetles are the most troublesome pests.

CHINESE CABBAGE

Though grown in Asia for centuries, Chinese cabbage is fairly new to American gardeners — in spite of being a versatile vegetable and easy to grow.

Chinese cabbage is divided into two main groups: heading types (Pe-tsai) and nonheading types (Pak Choi). Heading types may be short and round (similar to Western cabbages) or tall and torpedo-shaped. The nonheading types will form tall, loose bundles of leaves.

BLANCHING CHINESE CABBAGE

In midsummer, after the hearts begin to swell, tie the outer leaves of each Chinese cabbage together around the base and top with soft rope or string. Be sure to water the cabbages regularly if the weather is hot.

The short, round heading types are used for cooking, while the tall, slender ones may be cooked or used as salad greens.

Pak Choi, a nonheading Chinese cabbage, is open-leaved, and the white leafstalks are invariably bare and fleshy. These tender stalks can be eaten along with the leaves. The outer leaves of Pak Choi are steamed, boiled, or stir-fried. The inner leaves can be used raw in salads.

Chinese greens, also known as mustard spinach, usually have fairly open heads. You can boil and serve the mature leaves like spinach or spring greens, or you can stir-fry them; or pluck the young, tender, mild-flavored leaves and eat them raw.

Site and soil preparation

The basic cultivation requirements for all types of Chinese cabbage are the same as for ordinary cabbage or any other brassicas. The bed should be in an open, sunny spot with well-drained, slightly alkaline soil.

On a new plot, dig in a light dressing of well-rotted manure or compost. In a crop-rotation system, where Chinese cabbage follows a legume or salad crop, no extra manure or compost is required. But test the soil pH, and apply lime if needed. Fertilize the bed before sowing with 5-10-10; apply it at a rate of about 3-4 lb (1.4-1.8 kg) per 100 sq ft (9 sq m).

Sowing and growing

Chinese cabbage usually resents transplanting, so it is best to sow this cabbage where you plan to grow it. It may succumb to fall

▲ **Chinese cabbage** The leaves on the nonheading Chinese cabbage above form tall, loose bundles. Sown in summer, all types of Chinese cabbage are ready for eating in the fall.

frosts unless protected with hot caps on cold nights, but the cabbage will bolt easily if you sow it too early in the summer.

Sow most cultivars in late summer or fall, planting seeds ½ in (1.25 cm) deep in rows spaced 2 ft (60 cm) apart. As soon as the seedlings are large enough to handle, thin them to intervals of 12-15 in (30-38 cm). Sow early-maturing cultivars, especially nonheading types, in early spring. Avoid planting them in very early spring; the plants may bolt, producing flower stalks instead of forming a head. Except in areas with long, cool springs, such as the Pacific Northwest, spring plantings face the threat that an early spell of warm weather may cause heads to deteriorate before they reach full size.

Water Chinese cabbage well during dry spells, and hoe the bed regularly to eliminate weeds. Protect the plants from slug and snail damage by sprinkling a commercial slug bait regularly when the weather is warm. If the cabbage heads or clusters of leaves become loose, raise the outer leaves around them and tie them gently in place with soft twine or string. This will prevent the center of the heads from becoming dark green and tough.

Harvest the crop when the heads are firm and before they show signs of bolting.

Cabbage 'Golden Acre'

Cabbage 'Early Jersey Wakefield'

CULTIVARS TO CHOOSE

Early
'Early Jersey Wakefield': 63 days from transplanting to harvest; conical, weighing 2-3 lb (0.9-1.4 kg).

'Golden Acre': 64 days; medium-size, firm round head; big harvest.

'Julius': 75 days; savoy-type blue-green head; 4-5 lb (1.8-2.3 kg).

'Puma': 64 days; tender, mild flavor; round, split-resistant head; weighs 2-4 lb (0.9-1.8 kg).

Midseason
'Charmant': 85 days; dark bluish, split-resistant head; full, rich flavor; weighs 3-6 lb (1.4-2.7 kg).

'Roundup': 86 days; round head, 3-9½ lb (1.4-4.3 kg).

'Ruby Ball': 80 days; firm, sweet flavor; purplish-red, round head; weighs 5-6 lb (2.3-2.7 kg).

Late
'Danish Ballhead': 100 days; dark green head, 8 in (20 cm) in diameter; its head holds well in the field in winter.

'First Early Market': 218 days; hardy to 10°F (-12°C), best for winter crop; conical head, 1-1½ lb (450-680 g); bolt-resistant plant.

'Savoy King': 90 days; flat-topped head, delicious flavor; cold-hardy.

'Late Flat Dutch': 100 days; solid, flattened blue-green head, white interior; 10-14 in (25-35 cm) in diameter; stores well.

'Meteor': 110 days; solid, with sweet flavor; deep purple head, 7-8 in (18-20 cm) in diameter; excellent cold tolerance.

Chinese cabbage
'Jade Pagoda': 72 days; 16 in (41 cm) tall head, 6 in (15 cm) in diameter; bolt-resistant plant.

'Lettucy': 45 days; open head of Pak Choi type with ruffled green leaves and creamy yellow interior; good spring crop; weighs 3 lb (1.4 kg) per head.

'Wong Bok': 80 days; crisp and tender; light green foliage; short, round head, 6-7 in (15-18 cm) wide and 10 in (25 cm) tall; resistant to drought and heat; best for fall harvest.

Cabbage 'Savoy King'

Cabbage 'Ruby Ball'

CARROTS

Easy to grow and highly nutritious, carrots can be enjoyed virtually year-round if different cultivars are sown at regular intervals.

Carrots come in many lengths and shapes. There is the short 'Thumbelina,' whose roots form 1-1½ in (2.5-3.75 cm) balls; 'Royal Chantenay,' with tapered roots and wide shoulders; 'Scarlet Nantes,' with cylindrical roots; and the conical-rooted 'Danvers.'

These differences in shape and root length are more than cosmetic; they affect the way carrots perform and determine which will do best in particular soils.

Short, round carrots are sweet and succulent. They are a good choice for shallow or heavy clay soils. They take as little as seven weeks to mature. A crop sown in early spring may be ready for picking in early summer.

Intermediate-length, thick-shouldered types do well in shallow or heavy soils but take longer to mature. The cylindrical types store well, keeping their flavor for a long time in the cellar or if left in the ground after maturing as a late-fall crop. The longest cylindrical or tapered cultivars bear top yields of high-quality roots; they mature in 10 weeks or more and need deep, rich, pebble-free, sandy loam or peat soils.

Soil and site preparation

Carrots flourish in crumbly, light, well-drained soil that was turned and dug the fall before sowing. Lighten heavy clay soil by mixing in a generous dose of compost or well-rotted manure.

A week before sowing, break up heavy clods of soil and rake the topsoil to a fine tilth. Apply a general-compound fertilizer, such as 5-10-10, at a rate of 1 lb (450 g) per 50 sq ft (4.5 sq m).

Plant in a sunny spot. If you are rotating crops, choose a site enriched for a previous crop, such as brassicas, but don't apply any more manure at planting time; it gives carrots a hard skin and can cause the roots to fork.

Sowing seeds

Carrot seeds are tiny and hard to handle. You can use easy-to-sow pellet seeds, or mix regular seeds with a handful of clean sand.

Avoid standing on prepared soil as you sow; this will compact it.

The seeds will germinate in soil temperatures between 40° and 95°F (4.5°-35°C) but do best in moist soil at 80°F (26.5°C). Three to four weeks before the expected

Intermediate-rooted

Short-rooted

Long-rooted

▲ **Carrot types** These root vegetables come as short, intermediate, or long-rooted varieties. Within these groups the carrots can be cylindrical in shape with a blunt end, tapered to a point, or almost globular. Cylindrical-rooted types and the small round-rooted ones are best for heavy soils; long, tapering roots need deep, light soils.

THINNING AND HARVESTING CARROTS

1 When the plants are large enough to handle, thin them out in two stages: first to 1 in (2.5 cm) and later to 2 in (5 cm) apart for short-rooted types, to a final spacing of 4 in (10 cm) for other types. Work in the evening or on a cloudy day to avoid attracting carrot rust flies.

2 When pulling carrots, hold the foliage with one hand; using a garden fork with the other hand, ease the carrots out of the ground. Leave mature roots in the ground for several weeks in summer; store crops that mature in late fall in this fashion right into and through the winter.

date of the last spring frost in your area, start sowing; but save the bulk of your seeds for later, when germination will be better. To guarantee a continuous harvest, sow every two weeks. Keep in mind that carrots maturing in midsummer heat lose flavor and vitamins. Plan for the heaviest crops to mature in the cooler fall weather. Determining when to sow a cultivar is simple: count backward from the desired harvest date for the number of days listed under "days to maturity" in the seed catalog or on the packet.

For tender carrots in late fall and early winter, sow cylindrical-rooted cultivars in late summer; cover with tunnels of clear plastic on heavy wire hoops after thinning out seedlings in early fall.

The seeds need 10 days or more to germinate, and you must keep the soil continuously moist during that period. For early-spring sowings, cover the moistened soil with a sheet of clear plastic, removing it as soon as the seedlings emerge. Summer sowings may benefit from being covered with sheets of dampened burlap.

Looking after the crop
When they are large enough to handle, thin out the weaker seedlings. Thin short-rooted cultivars 2 in (5 cm) apart, intermediate- and long-rooted types 4 in (10 cm) apart. Keep the soil cultivated and weeded. Apply an organic mulch after the plants are well up; when they are 6 in (15 cm) tall, feed them with a general-purpose, water-soluble fertilizer.

Harvesting and storing
Begin harvesting as soon as the roots reach ½ in (1.25 cm) in diameter. Leave roots in the ground until you need them. Carrots keep their flavor in the ground for several weeks after maturing.

Leave carrots maturing in late fall in the ground into winter. In cold northern regions, bury the rows under 1 ft (30 cm) of dry hay after frost cuts down the carrot greens. This keeps the soil from freezing, allowing you to dig it up.

Pests and diseases
Carrot pests are cutworms, carrot rust flies, carrot weevils, leafhoppers, and parsley worms.

Splitting and forked roots are usually caused by heavy, poorly drained, or stony soils.

CULTIVARS TO CHOOSE

Short-rooted
'Amsterdam Forcing': 60 days from seed to harvest; juicy root with little core.

'Kinko 4': 55 days; 4 in (10 cm) long, conical root; sweet flavor and excellent texture.

'Thumbelina': 50 days; small, round root; grow in heavy soil.

Intermediate-rooted
'Royal Chantenay': 70 days; 5-6 in (13-15 cm) long root, 2 in (5 cm) wide at the top and tapering; dark orange color; sweet flavor, good for juice.

'Scarlet Nantes': 70 days; 6 in (15 cm), cylindrical to slightly tapered root; bright orange; sweet flavor and crisp texture.

Long-rooted
'Danvers': 70 days; conical root, 1½ in (3.75 cm) wide at top and 6-7 in (15-18 cm) long; rich orange; grows well in heavier soil; keeps well in soil at maturity.

'Processor II': 67 days; similar to 'Danvers' but 2 in (5 cm) longer.

Intermediate-rooted 'Scarlet Nantes'

Intermediate-rooted 'Royal Chantenay'

Long-rooted 'Danvers'

CAULIFLOWER

**Delicate in flavor and versatile,
cauliflower is a popular vegetable, but it is a
demanding crop for the home gardener.**

Cauliflower is the most difficult member of the cabbage family to bring to harvest. Any setback, such as a period of drought, can cause it to "button," forming small heads on stunted plants. It is also important to plant the right cultivar for your climate. Northern gardeners do best with fast-maturing types; Southerners need slow-maturing cultivars for their winter crops, heat-resistant ones for fall or spring crops.

If you choose wisely, however, and are conscientious in tending the plants, your reward will be cauliflowers sweeter and milder in flavor than any from the store.

Cauliflowers are divided into three groups: early-maturing, late-maturing, and overwintering cultivars. Early cultivars are suitable for spring crops and do best in temperate maritime climates. Late cultivars are better adapted for planting as a fall crop, the most successful way to raise cauliflowers in cold climates. Overwintering cultivars are suited to planting in fall in areas with mild winters; harvest them in late winter or early spring.

Planning the crop

Cauliflower needs rich, loamy, deep soil. Grow the plants on soil enriched with well-rotted manure

▼ **Cauliflower florets** The crisp, creamy white head of a cauliflower is protected by a nest of green-blue leaves.

or compost the previous year for a leguminous crop, such as peas or beans. If you are planting in a new area, work in plenty of well-rotted manure or compost. In either case, dig the beds well ahead of time. For a spring planting, you should spade up the soil the previous fall, so that winter frost can break down the clods.

Choose a sunny site, open but not exposed; avoid frost pockets (low-lying areas that trap cold air on chilly nights). This is important for overwintering crops. The soil pH should be neutral, between 6.5 and 7.5. If a soil test indicates acidity, treat the soil with ground limestone at a rate of 5 lb (2.3 kg) per 100 sq ft (9 sq m) for

CULTIVATION

1 Select young plants with four or five leaves and a good ball of soil on the roots. To check that the plants are set firmly, tug a leaf — it should tear.

2 Water the plants well, and keep watering through the growing season. If the plants dry out, they will produce undersized heads lacking in flavor.

3 When the florets begin to form, fold in two or three of the large outside leaves to cover the florets. This will prevent sunlight from turning the florets yellow.

GROWING MINI CAULIFLOWER

Mini cauliflowers, such as 'Cargill Early Maturing,' are easy to grow and good for a small plot. One mini cauliflower makes a single helping and is ideal for freezing. Sow the seeds in well-prepared ground, 6 in × 6 in (15 cm × 15 cm) apart, and harvest when 1½-3½ in (3.75-8.75 cm) wide.

To harvest mini cauliflowers over an extended period, sow them several times at two-week intervals from two to three months before the expected date of the first fall frost. Alternatively, sow an early-maturing cultivar, such as 'Garant,' and plant it with a late-maturing cultivar, such as 'Dominant.'

each point you wish to raise your soil's pH (e.g., from 6.0 to 7.0). A day or two before planting, fork in a dressing of 5-10-10 fertilizer at a rate of 3-4 lb (1.4-1.8 kg) per 100 sq ft (9 sq m).

Grow about 14 cauliflowers in a 20 ft (6 m) row. Plant a mixture of cultivars, maturing at different times, for a longer harvest.

Sowing indoors
Start spring crops indoors four to six weeks before the expected date of the last spring frost. Sow the seeds in peat pots full of sterilized seed-starting mix. Plant the seeds ¼-½ in (6-12 mm) deep, and set the pots in a sunny window or underneath fluorescent lights. If necessary, use bottom heat (such as an electric soil-heating cable) to keep the soil at 70°F (21°C). Lowering fluorescent bulbs until they stand just a few inches over the pots may accomplish the same thing.

Keep the pots evenly moist at all times. Raise the lights, turn off the heating cable, or move the pots to a cooler windowsill once the seedlings germinate and produce their first pair of leaves.

About two weeks before the last spring frost, harden off the seedlings by setting them outdoors each day in a sheltered location for gradually increasing intervals of time.

Cold-frame sowing If you have a cold frame, you will find it ideal for starting cauliflower seedlings.

Prepare the soil as for sowing outdoors. Scatter the seeds lightly and cover with a ¼ in (6 mm) layer of sifted soil or seed-starting mix. Keep the transparent cover on the frame closed until germination takes place, then allow a little ventilation in mild weather.

When they are large enough to handle, thin the seedlings to 2 in (5 cm) apart. Cover the frame with an old blanket during nights with hard frosts. Keep the plants in the frame and ventilate in mild weather until they are planted out around midspring.

Planting out Use a trowel to make holes 1½ ft (45 cm) apart in a prepared bed, spacing the rows 1½ ft (45 cm) apart.

Before you transplant a seedling, it should have four or five leaves. If transplanting it from the cold frame, make sure it has a good ball of soil around the roots. Check the plant for a growing point — a small half-folded leaf at the tip of the stem. Plant carefully without disturbing the root ball, so that the stem is covered up to the lowest leaf. Firm the soil down well by pressing with your heel close to the stem.

Water well, and keep watering as necessary. Dried-out plants will produce undersized heads.

Sowing outdoors
For a fall or overwintering crop, sow seeds directly into the garden. In the North sow the seeds two to three months before the first fall frost date. In the South delay sowing until the weather cools with the onset of fall.

To protect the seeds from rotting in damp soil, plant in small mounds, or hills, of soil set about 2 ft (60 cm) apart, with five seeds in each hill. Keep the hills moist. Once the seedlings emerge and are growing strongly, remove all but the most vigorous one.

Keep the plants well watered. Fertilize four weeks after thinning them, applying 1 tablespoon of balanced fertilizer per plant; mix it into the soil, about 4-5 in (10-13 cm) out from the stems.

When the florets begin to form, fold two or three of the large outside leaves over them to prevent sunlight from turning the florets yellow or frost from turning them brown. Leave the covering in place until the florets are nearly mature. Some cultivars are self-blanching; they produce incurved leaves naturally and need no assistance from the gardener.

Harvesting and storing
Cut the heads while firm — left too long, the florets will begin to separate. The morning is the best time for cutting, when the heads still have dew on them. In frosty weather, wait until midday.

Pests and diseases
Cauliflower is attacked by aphids, cabbage root maggots, cabbageworms, cabbage loopers, and flea beetles. Brassica collars (see p.96) can reduce their incidence.

Cauliflower is also vulnerable to clubroot, damping-off, downy mildew, hollow stem disorder, leaf spot, and root-rot fungi. You can use chemical treatment for most of these, but healthy, strongly growing plants are less likely to succumb to disease.

CELERY

A summer crop in the North and a winter crop in the South, celery is particular about temperatures but otherwise easy to grow.

Climate plays more of a role in determining your success with celery than with almost any other crop. Celery needs a long growing season, from 120 to 150 days, and it won't tolerate high heat or too many cool nights. Indeed, a series of nights with temperatures below 55°F (13°C) may cause celery plants to go to seed prematurely, ruining their flavor and texture.

For this reason, celery is best grown in areas where temperatures are moderated by closeness to a large body of water, either a lake, a river, or the ocean. Michigan and Florida are leading producers of celery. In Michigan it is a summer crop, in Florida a winter crop. Raising celery in the central parts of the country, in much of the Midwest or in the upper South, can be challenging.

Traditionally, it was necessary to blanch celery; the stalks, but not the leaves, were kept in the dark as they grew to give them a tender texture and mild flavor.

▲ **Celery stalks** Crisp and juicy celery can be eaten raw in salads or cooked as a vegetable. Harvest summer crops of self-blanching cultivars before the first frosts. Trench-grown celery is insulated by its soil covering and the flavor is actually improved by frost.

This was often done by planting celery in a trench, then hilling the earth up around the stalks as they extended upward.

Nowadays, a number of self-blanching cultivars are available to home gardeners. These need no special treatment to produce mild-flavored, tender stalks. Self-blanching celery is grown in an ordinary bed, but plants are set in blocks instead of rows so that they shield each other from the light. Only those on the outside are shaded with straw.

Blanching does provide an important advantage to gardeners growing celery where temperatures dip overnight as the crop matures. The hilled-up earth will

◀ **Blanching celery** Tie cardboard or black plastic collars around the stems to blanch them. Self-blanching celery is grown in ordinary garden beds; old-fashioned blanching types are grown in trenches to improve the flavor.

insulate the stalks, protecting them from a brief cold snap.

Soil and site preparation

Celery grows best in a sunny spot with rich soil.

For self-blanching cultivars, work in a bucketful of well-rotted manure or compost per sq yd/m a few weeks before planting.

For blanching cultivars, dig a trench in midspring in preparation for a spring crop, in early summer for a fall crop, or in midfall for a southern winter crop. The trench should be 1 ft (30 cm) wide for a single row of celery and 2 ft (60 cm) wide for a double row.

Dig the trench 1 ft (30 cm) deep, and place the excavated soil on each side of it. Fork up the bottom of the trench, and work in well-rotted manure or compost at the rate of a bucketful per sq yd/m. Replace some of the soil so

GROWING SELF-BLANCHING CELERY

1 Buy transplants at the garden center or start them yourself indoors. Set them in a block so that they are 9 in (23 cm) apart in all directions. Be sure to water them in well.

2 Self-blanching celery plants do not need their stalks buried or covered. The inner plants in a block are shielded from the light by the outer ones. Pack those on the outside with straw in midsummer.

▲ **Harvesting self-blanching celery** Push the protective straw to one side and lift the required number of plants with a garden fork. Afterward pile the straw around the newly exposed plants to continue the blanching.

that the base of the trench is 6 in (15 cm) below true ground level. Save the rest of the soil for burying the stalks later.

Sowing and planting

Transplants can sometimes be bought at garden centers, but you will have a greater choice of cultivars if you start plants yourself. Sow them 8 to 10 weeks before the last spring frost for a spring crop, in May or June for a fall crop, in midfall for a winter crop.

Soak the seeds in warm water overnight, then sprinkle them thinly over a shallow pot or flat of sterilized seed-starting mix. Cover them with an extra ⅛ in (3 mm) of mix. Moisten the mix and set the pot or flat on a sunny windowsill or under fluorescent lights, keeping it at a temperature of about 65°F (18.5°C).

When the seedlings reach a height of 2 in (5 cm), transplant them to individual peat pots full of sterilized potting mix. Keep the pots moist, and two weeks before the last spring frost, begin setting them outside for gradually increasing intervals of time to harden off the seedlings.

Set the pots into the garden a week before the last spring frost, but cover the seedlings with hot caps on chilly nights. If the seedlings are of a self-blanching cultivar, set them 9 in (23 cm) apart in each direction so that a block is formed. If the seedlings are of a blanching cultivar, space the plants 9 in (23 cm) apart along the center of the prepared trench.

If planting double rows, allow about 1½ ft (45 cm) between them. Water the plants in well.

For a fall crop, follow the same procedure, but plant the seedlings out in June or July and provide them with some protection from the sun on hot, humid days.

Self-blanching celery

To encourage the main shoots to grow vigorously, remove any side shoots from the base of the plants as they appear.

To blanch the outer rows, pack straw around the outside plants in midsummer. (Shade from the exterior plants helps blanch plants in the center of a block.) A mulch of straw among the plants will help to keep the soil moist and cool. Take care that the soil doesn't dry out. Celery is a heavy feeder, so fertilize the plants every two to three weeks; sprinkle 1 teaspoon of 5-10-10 around each plant.

Trench-grown celery

When the plant reaches 12-15 in (30-38 cm) high, cut off any suckers growing from the base of the plants, then loosely tie black plastic, corrugated cardboard (with the smooth side facing inward) or newspaper around each clump of stems. Water thoroughly, then with a spade draw soil from the ridges at the sides of the trench to form a slight slope reaching about halfway up the stems of each plant. Avoid getting soil into the heart of the plants.

Three weeks later, pile more soil around the plants, up to the base of the leaves. Be careful not to pile earth higher than the base of the green leaves.

DOING WITHOUT TRENCHES

For just a few plants, grow celery on a level bed instead of digging trenches. When the plants are 12-15 in (30-38 cm) high, trim off any suckers, then tie corrugated cardboard (with the smooth side innermost), newspaper, or black plastic around the stems. Pack earth down inside this collar to exclude light still further.

Add additional earth in three more weeks, and slope the soil to form a ridge. If frost threatens, lay straw along the ridge tops of late celery to give it some additional protection.

To maintain steady growth, water the plants freely, especially during dry spells in fall.

Harvesting

Start digging out self-blanching celery at the end of summer. Pile up the straw against newly exposed plants. Dig out all self-blanching cultivars before the onset of severe fall frosts.

It takes six to eight weeks from the first hilling up with soil to blanch trench-grown celery. After this, dig up plants as needed, but replace the soil against remaining plants to protect from frost.

Pests and diseases

Parsleyworms, carrot rust flies, and soil-borne nematodes are the worst insect pests. Two fungal diseases, early and late blight, begin as small yellow dots on the leaves; severely infected plants may die. Weekly applications of fungicides limit the effect of the diseases, but the best prevention against diseases and pests is regular crop rotation.

GROWING CELERY IN A TRENCH

1 Dig a trench, piling dug-out soil along side. Fork up the bottom; work in compost or manure. Add soil until the bottom is 6 in (15 cm) below ground level.

2 Plant out young seedlings in late spring or midsummer. Space the plants 9 in (23 cm) apart along the center of the trench. Water in well.

3 When the celery plants are 12-15 in (30-38 cm) high, trim off any suckers from the base and loosely tie newspaper, corrugated cardboard, or black plastic around the stems.

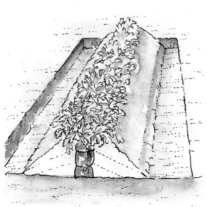

4 With a spade, draw soil about halfway up the stems of the plants and form a slight slope. Three weeks later, hill up a little deeper; do so again after another three weeks.

Celery 'Lathom Self-Blanching'

Trench-grown 'Hopkins Fenlander'

CULTIVARS TO CHOOSE

Self-blanching

'Golden Self-Blanching': 115 days from transplanting to harvest; creamy stalks; nutty flavor; stringless; early-maturing type.

'Greensleeves': 125 days; smooth, long green stalks; large crops.

'Hercules': 85 days; tall, vigorous plants; crisp, sweet stalks.

'Improved Utah 52-70': 98 days; dark green stalks; thick and juicy.

'Lathom Self-Blanching': 120 days; yellow stalks; vigorous; early-maturing type; resistant to bolting.

'Ventura': 80 days; bright green stalks; high-yielding plant.

Trench-grown

'Giant Pascal': 110 days; large pure white stalks; very hardy.

'Hopkins Fenlander': 105 days; stringless pale green stalks; trench-grown or self-blanching.

CELERIAC

◄ **Celeriac** A turnip-rooted relation of celery that has the same distinctive flavor, celeriac is easy to grow. Its knobbly roots are ready for harvesting and storing in late fall. Cook and serve celeriac like other root vegetables, or use them in soups, stews, and salads.

Celeriac is a turnip-rooted form of celery. Its swollen roots, with creamy white flesh, have a flavor similar to celery's and are particularly good in soups, stews, and salads. Although it is not often seen in supermarkets, celeriac is an easy crop for home gardeners to grow.

Soil and site preparation

Celeriac needs a long growing season and prefers well-drained soil in a sunny spot. The winter before planting, enrich the site with well-rotted manure or compost at the rate of one bucketful per sq yd/m.

Sowing and planting

Sow seeds in a shallow pot or flat in early spring. Before sowing, press down the sterilized seed-starting mix to make it level and firm, then sprinkle the seeds thinly over the top and cover with a shallow layer of mix. Water, then set the pot or flat on a cool windowsill at a temperature of 50°-55°F (10°-13°C).

When the seedlings are ½ in (1.25 cm) high, prick them out into flats of sterilized potting mix, spaced 1½ in (3.75 cm) apart in all directions. Keep the flats indoors or in a greenhouse for three or four weeks, then harden them off.

Set the plants out at 12-15 in (30-38 cm) intervals in rows the same distance apart. Plant the seedlings with the roots completely buried; the leaves should just rest on the surface of the soil.

Looking after the crop

Water the plants well in the early stages. Make sure to hoe often to kill weed seedlings, which can seriously check growth.

Feed every second week with a water-soluble fertilizer, following the instructions on the product label and applying it either just before or just after watering.

To ensure that roots develop properly, remove any side shoots above ground from late summer to midfall.

Harvesting

Dig the roots as they are needed during the fall months, leaving them in the ground as long as possible so that they reach an optimum size of about 1 lb (450 g), when the sweet celery flavor is most pronounced. There is no advantage in using celeriac roots when they are still young, and older roots tend to become woody and hollow.

In late fall dig up all the remaining roots, cut off the foliage, and store in damp sand in a cool shed or cellar.

Cultivars to choose

There isn't much difference between cultivars, but some to look out for are 'Brilliant,' 'Diamant,' and 'Monarch.'

Pests and diseases

The principal pests that attack celeriac are carrot rust flies, slugs, and snails. Leaf spot is the most common disease.

CHICORY

Members of the same family, ordinary chicory, Belgian endive, and radicchio offer an assortment of summer and winter salad greens.

Chicory, a hardy perennial, flourishes as a roadside weed throughout North America, though it is native to Europe. It appears in the vegetable garden in three forms: as a lacy-leaved, slightly bitter green, as Belgian endive (a small blanched head of greens), and as the red-leaved radicchio.

The ordinary lacy-leaved chicory, grown outdoors for harvest in fall and winter, produces heads that resemble those of cos lettuce.

Belgian endives are also grown outdoors but are then usually blanched indoors in complete darkness, though they may also be forced outdoors.

A third type of chicory, which has been gaining in popularity, is radicchio. This nonforcing form produces a small, round, cabbagelike head with red leaves.

Planning the crop
Chicory does best in a sunny, open site. The plants have deep roots and prefer a medium to light, moderately rich soil. If possible, choose a patch of soil that was already enriched with organic matter for a previous crop. Alternatively, dig in well-rotted manure or compost before sowing, although such rich soil may encourage Belgian endive to form forked roots, which are less suitable for forcing.

Rake in a general fertilizer, such as 5-10-10, a few days before sowing; apply it at a rate of 2 lbs (900 g) per 100 sq ft (9 sq m).

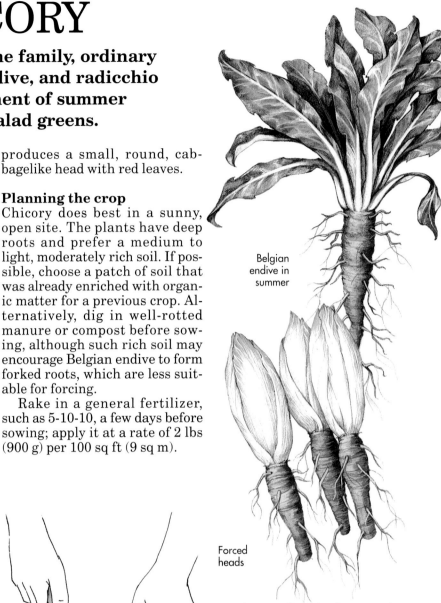

Belgian endive in summer

Forced heads

▲ **Belgian endive** After forcing and blanching, this type of chicory will produce pale, crisp heads with a delicious mild flavor.

FORCING BELGIAN ENDIVE

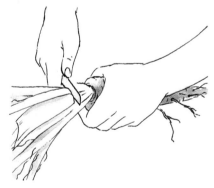

1 Lift plants in mid- or late fall, when leaves die down. Cut off foliage 1 in (2.5 cm) above the crown of the roots.

2 Shorten the roots to 6-9 in (15-23 cm), trimming off the lower end. Rub off side shoots at the top; leave the main crown.

3 Force the roots a few at a time. Put four or so in a 9 in (23 cm) pot of soil or potting mix; leave the crowns exposed.

4 Cover with an inverted pot. Harvest four weeks later, when 6 in (15 cm) high. Cut or snap them off at the base.

Cultivation
Sow seeds of all types in midspring in the North and in late summer in the Deep South. Sow thinly ½ in (1.25 cm) deep, allowing 1½ ft (45 cm) between rows.

Hoe on a regular basis to keep down weeds, and water the soil thoroughly in dry weather. When the seedlings are large enough to handle, thin them until they are 6 in (15 cm) apart for Belgian endive, or 1 ft (30 cm) apart for nonforcing cultivars. Continue to hoe regularly, and water thoroughly during prolonged dry spells.

Forcing indoors Lift Belgian endives from the soil with a fork in mid- to late fall, when the leaves die down. The roots should be 1 ft (30 cm) long, 2 in (5 cm)

Chicory 'Crystal Hat'

Radicchio 'Rossa di Treviso'

across the top, and shaped like parsnips. Discard any that are forked or less than 2 in (5 cm) wide at the top.

Reduce the roots to a length of 6-9 in (15-23 cm). Remove side shoots; cut off any leaves to 1 in (2.5 cm) above the crown. Store the roots until needed for forcing in a cool, frost-proof shed, packed horizontally in a box of sand, or put them in a shallow outdoor trench beneath a layer of soil.

If the weather is mild, stack the roots outdoors to wait for a hard frost, which will break their dormancy and make them easier to force later.

Force the roots, a few at a time, from late fall to early spring. Put four or five roots in a 9 in (23 cm) plastic pot, packing moist soil or potting soil around them but leaving the crowns exposed.

Water the roots lightly. Cover the pots with black plastic film, boxes, or inverted pots. Make sure that light is completely shut out, or the endives will turn green and develop a bitter taste.

Place the pots in a greenhouse, shed, or garage, at a temperature of 45°-61°F (7°-16°C). Pale heads will sprout from the crowns.

Harvesting and storing
The heads of Belgian endives will be ready within four weeks from

the start of forcing, when they are about 6 in (15 cm) high. Cut or snap off at crown level. They are best eaten raw or cooked immediately after harvesting. Smaller secondary heads may follow, if the potting soil is watered after the first harvest and the cover replaced. Discard the roots after the second crop has been harvested.

Cut nonforcing leaf chicory in late fall and early winter in the North and in mid- to late winter in the Deep South. Chicory is ideal for winter salads and can be stored for several weeks in a cool, frost-free shed.

Radicchio
Radicchio needs a long, cool growing season and should be sown in midspring in the North (where it will mature in late fall) and in late summer in the Deep South (where it will mature from winter to early spring). To ensure that the plants will head up properly, cut them back to the ground in early fall in the North.

Red cultivars are hardy and can often be left outdoors all winter in areas where temperatures stay above 10°F (-12°C).

Pests and diseases
Chicory is seldom troubled by diseases. Aphids, cutworms, slugs, or snails may attack them.

CULTIVARS TO CHOOSE

Chicory
'Catalogna': 49 days from seed to harvest; nonforcing cultivar good for fall or spring crop.

'Crystal Hat': 70 days; oval cos-lettuce-like head; heat and frost tolerant; sweet, tangy flavor.

'Sugarloaf': 80 days; cos-lettuce-like head; firm heart; crisp leaves.

'Zuckerhut': 75 days; cos-lettuce-like head; store in refrigerator or frost-free shed to three months.

Belgian endive
'Flash': 110 days; crisp creamy white head.

'Witloof': 110 days; good for forcing outdoors; cone-shaped golden head; pick green leaves for salads.

Radicchio
'Alouette': 100 days; round, tight head; deep red-and-white leaves.

'Giulio': 80 days; needs no cutting back; burgundy head, white veins.

'Rossa di Treviso': 100 days; green in summer, red in cold weather.

'Rossa di Verona': 100 days; deep red in winter; can force indoors.

CORN, SWEET

Fresh homegrown sweet corn is delicious, and the attractive tassellike flowers look decorative in the garden.

Sweet corn, which we commonly call corn, is an essential part of summer picnics and a symbol of Thanksgiving harvests. It is Central American in origin, but it was brought as far north as New England by Native Americans long before Europeans arrived.

The sugar in the kernels of older cultivars starts to turn to starch as soon as an ear is picked. But new "supersweet" cultivars not only start sweeter, they also keep their sugars far longer. Still, many gardeners prefer the flavor of such traditional favorites as 'Silver Queen'; these old-timers tend to be more vigorous plants.

Planning the crop

Corn needs a sunny site and well-drained, fertile soil. A slightly acid soil is an advantage; usually this crop does not benefit from an application of lime.

In the winter before planting, enrich the bed with well-rotted compost or manure at the rate of one bucketful per sq yd/m. A few weeks before planting or sowing, rake in a general-purpose fertilizer, such as 10-10-10, at a rate of 10 lb (4.5 kg) for every 500 sq ft (45 sq m).

Grow corn in a block, not in long rows. The blocks make it easier for the light, airborne male pollen to reach female flowers.

Each plant bears male and female flowers. Male flowers grow at the tops of the plants, while the silky female flower tassels hang from the tops of immature ears.

Growing corn

Sow corn directly into the prepared bed as soon as the soil warms to 60°-65°F (15.5°-18.5°C). This may be as early as late January in the Deep South or not until late spring in the North. The old rule of thumb — plant the corn when oak leaves are the size of a squirrel's ear ($^{1}/_{2}$ in/1.25 cm long) — works reasonably well.

For a lasting harvest, sow a new block of corn every two weeks until midsummer. Plant blocks of different cultivars at least 25 ft (7.5 m) apart, or sow them so that they mature at least 10 days apart.

Sowing

Sow the seeds 1 in (2.5 cm) deep in spring and 4 in (10 cm) deep in midsummer. Plant three kernels together every 7-15 in (18-38 cm), in a block measuring 8 ft × 10 ft (2.4 m × 3 m). When the seedlings emerge, thin them to one plant every 12 in (30 cm) for dwarf cultivars, one to every 15 in (38 cm) for standard cultivars. Remove unwanted seedlings by snipping them off at ground level.

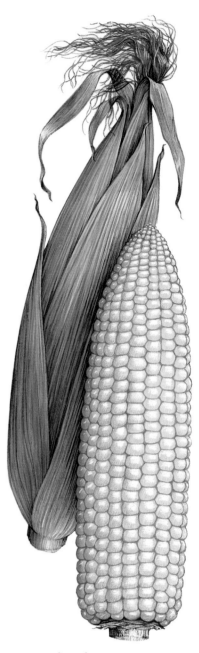

▲ **Corn on the cob** Homegrown sweet corn is far superior to supermarket produce. Its tender, succulent kernels taste sweet rather than starchy.

SOWING AND HARVESTING

1 For an early start in the North, sow seeds, two per pot, in midspring. Pinch off the top growth of the weaker of the two seedlings when they emerge.

2 After planting out, remove any side shoots from the base to direct all energy into ear production. Pinch the shoots off when they are about 6 in (15 cm) long.

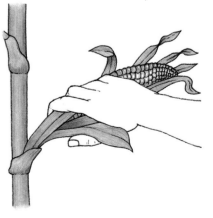

3 The ears are ready for picking when kernels pricked with a fingernail exude a creamy liquid. Twist the ears away from the plants or snap them sharply down.

Sowing indoors

Northern gardeners can start their crop a few weeks early by sowing seeds indoors in peat pots filled with seed-starting mix. Plant two seeds per pot, moisten, then enclose the pots in a plastic bag and set them in a warm, dark spot, such as by the furnace. As soon as the seedlings emerge, remove the pots from the bag, set them on a sunny windowsill, and pinch off the top growth of the weaker of the seedlings in each pot (avoid disturbing the roots).

When the plants are about 6 in (15 cm) tall, harden them off. Plant them when they reach a height of 2-4 in (5-10 cm) and all danger of frost has passed. Set dwarf cultivars 12 in (30 cm) apart each way and standard plants about 15 in (38 cm) apart each way, in blocks measuring at least 8 ft × 10 ft (2.4 m × 3 m).

Care

Water during dry spells, giving the plants 1 in (2.5 cm) of water per week. Control weeds by frequent shallow hoeing until the plants are knee-high, then apply an organic mulch. On windy sites, mound soil around the base of the plants to provide extra support.

Fertilize the plants when they reach 8-10 in (20-25 cm) tall, applying 2 lb (900 g) of ammonium nitrate per 100 ft (30 m) of row. Repeat this treatment when the tassels appear.

Remove any side shoots that grow from the base of the plants, pinching them off when they are about 6 in (15 cm) long.

Harvesting

The ears will be ready for harvesting in late summer or early fall, when the tassels wither and turn dark brown.

Pierce a kernel with your fingernail to test for maturity. When ripe, the kernel should exude a creamy (not watery) liquid.

Twist the cobs off the plant to remove them, and eat or freeze immediately. They become dry and lose their flavor if stored.

Pests and diseases

Seed corn maggot may attack seedlings, which wilt and collapse at ground level. Corn earworms, European corn borers, and flea beetles are other common pests.

Common diseases are bacterial wilt (this is spread by flea beetles), smut, leaf blight, and maize dwarf mosaic virus. The best countermeasure for these diseases is to plant only resistant corn cultivars.

Ornamental corn

Some cultivars of corn have variegated foliage or colored ears. These ornamental varieties are usually not edible but make an attractive addition to bedding displays and herbaceous borders. The ripe ears can be dried and used as winter decoration.

▲ **Pollination** The silky female flower tassels are pollinated by male flowers at the top of the plants.

▲ **Harvesting** You can tell that corn ears are ready for picking when flower tassels shrivel and turn dark brown.

Corn 'Seneca Chief'

CUCUMBERS

Crisp and juicy cucumbers are an essential ingredient of summer salads, and gherkin types are ideal for pickling.

Cucumbers are a hot-weather crop that flourishes in subtropical conditions: long, sunny summer days and warm nights. They are ideal for the South but can be raised successfully in the North if you plant early-maturing types. They are also an excellent winter crop, bearing well when planted in a greenhouse or cold frame.

This is a most productive crop. A single slicing cucumber plant may yield 30-40 lb (13.5-18 kg) of cucumbers. It also offers considerable variety: there are spherical lemon cucumbers, tiny warty gherkins, and giant slicing types that produce straight, smooth-skinned fruits 1 ft (30 cm) long. Look for the parthenocarpic cultivars, which set fruits without pollination. These are especially good for greenhouse cultivation, since there are no pollinating insects in that environment.

Selecting cultivars
The standard cucumber cultivars produce both male and female flowers, and though only the females set fruits, they need the pollination of male flowers to do so. Some new cultivars bear only female flowers and are especially productive; however, each packet includes a few marked seeds of a standard cultivar, and at least one of these must be planted among the all-female plants to provide them with pollen. Of course, if you plant parthenocarpic cucumbers, you need not worry about ensuring pollination.

Another new development is the "bush" cucumber. It produces compact plants that are ideal for small gardens.

OUTDOOR CUCUMBERS
Choose a warm, sunny site with well-drained soil. A few weeks before sowing seeds, make "planting pockets." Dig holes, 1 ft × 1 ft (30 cm × 30 cm) square, 2-3 ft (60-90 cm) apart. Fill the holes with a mixture of well-rotted manure or compost and fine loamy soil. Rake into the soil a general fertilizer, such as 5-10-10, at the rate recommended on its label.

Cultivation
When the soil has warmed and all danger of frost has passed, sow three or four seeds 1 in (2.5 cm) deep and 3 in (7.5 cm) apart in the middle of each of the pockets.

Greenhouse cucumber

▶ **Cucumber types** Cylindrical-shaped greenhouse cucumbers have smooth skin; outdoor types are shorter, and many old-fashioned warty cucumbers have been superseded by smooth-skinned types. The crisp, juicy lemon cucumbers somewhat resemble the fruit they are named after.

Lemon cucumber

Outdoor cucumber

Remove all but the strongest seedling from each group.

Looking after the crop

Irrigate regularly to keep the soil evenly moist, or the fruits may develop a bitter taste. Four weeks after planting, sidedress by sprinkling a few handfuls of compost or 1 tablespoon of 5-10-10 around each plant. Apply a thick layer of organic mulch, such as straw.

Harvesting

For the best flavor, harvest cucumbers before they reach their maximum size. Depending on the cultivar, pick from midsummer until early fall.

Pests and diseases

Cucumber beetles are a common insect pest. Cover young plants with floating row covers, but remove these as the vines begin flowering to give pollinating insects access to the blossoms. Inspect the plants daily, picking and destroying any beetles you find.

Bacterial wilt is spread by the beetles. Other diseases include fusarium wilt, mosaic virus, powdery and downy mildew, and anthracnose. Crop rotation is the best prevention.

CUCUMBERS IN THE GREENHOUSE

Use parthenocarpic cultivars (sometimes listed in catalogs as seedless cucumbers), since they do not require pollination. You can grow all-female cultivars too, but they require hand-pollination (see p.62) and you must grow them with a standard cultivar.

Cucumbers require a constant temperature of 70°F (21°C); start them from midfall through early spring. Sow seeds in 3 in (7.5 cm) pots of seed-starting mix, setting a single seed on edge about ½ in (1.25 cm) deep in each pot.

Fill 10 in (25 cm) pots with a sterilized potting mix, or set grow bags filled with potting mix on the greenhouse floor. To train the cucumbers, stretch horizontal wires between greenhouse supports above the pots or bags, and shade from late spring onward.

When the seedlings develop two true leaves, transplant them to their growing positions and fix a stake beside each plant.

Shade the plants from strong sunlight, water them well, keep the air moist by spraying the greenhouse floor twice a day, and maintain good ventilation. Once the fruits begin to swell, feed the plants with a water-soluble fertilizer every second week.

COLD-FRAME CUCUMBERS

Prepare the soil inside the frame by late spring, and set the plants out a few weeks later, using cultivars recommended for cultivation in a cold frame or cold greenhouse. Sow seeds by late spring in the same way as for greenhouse cultivation, and leave them to germinate in the cold frame.

Transplant the seedlings, setting them at 3 ft (90 cm) intervals along the higher side of the frame. Replace the frame lid and cover the glass with shading. Open the lid 2 in (5 cm) on the sheltered side during warm days; close it to just a crack at night.

Water the plants frequently, and spray the inside of the frame twice a day during hot weather.

Harvesting

Harvest greenhouse cucumbers before they reach their maximum size; use them right after cutting.

Pests and diseases

Cucumbers are susceptible to spider mites and whiteflies.

CULTIVARS TO CHOOSE

Slicing
'Bush Champion': 55 days from sowing to harvest; compact, good for grow bags and tubs or small gardens; ribbed dark green fruits 10 in (25 cm) long.

'Jazzer': 48 days; sweet fruits, 7½-8 in (19-20 cm) long; productive, disease-resistant plant.

'Marketmore 86': 56 days; 8 in (20 cm) long, dark green fruits on compact vines.

'Sweet Alphee': 55 days; 4-5 in (10-13 cm) long, tender fruits; eat unpeeled; mostly female flowers, needs no pollinator; long harvest.

'Tasty Green': 62 days; tender-skinned fruits, 10-12 in (25-30 cm) long; mildew-resistant plant.

Pickling
'Conquest': 50 days; gherkin- to dill-pickle-size fruits; disease-resistant vines; requires pollinator.

'Vert de Massy': 53 days; little-finger-size fruits; pickle whole.

'West India Gherkin': 60 days; 2 in (5 cm) long, 1 in (2.5 cm) thick fruits; mild flavor; vigorous vines.

Lemon
'Lemon': 70 days; globular fruits with yellow skins; mild, sweet flesh.

Greenhouse
'Euro-American': 55 days; seedless fruits, 10-12 in (25-30 cm) long; disease-resistant plant.

'Little Leaf': 55 days; seedless, pickling-size fruits; good where clouds interfere with pollination; disease-resistant plant.

'Orient Express': 59 days; slim 10-12 in (25-30 cm) long fruits; resists diseases; good on trellises.

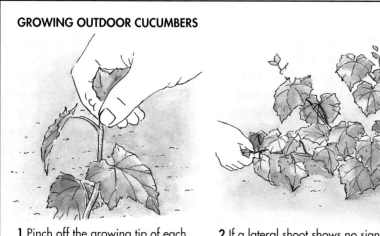

GROWING OUTDOOR CUCUMBERS

1 Pinch off the growing tip of each plant after six or seven leaves appear; this will encourage fruit-bearing lateral shoots to develop.

2 If a lateral shoot shows no sign of fruiting by the time the sixth or seventh leaf appears, pinch off the tip. Do not remove male flowers.

EGGPLANT

A warm-weather crop that flourishes in the South, eggplant also bears well in the North if started early indoors.

The eggplant was named for the fruits of old cultivars, which are egg-shaped, and yellow, white, green, brown, or purple. Modern cultivars have larger fruits; most are pear-shaped or long and thin.

All types of eggplant need a sunny spot and three months of warm weather to produce a good crop. These conditions are easy to provide in the South or Southwest, though eggplant needs ample irrigation in dry climates.

In the North sow eggplant seeds indoors six to nine weeks before the date of the last frost; transplant outside after soil and daytime air temperatures warm to 70°F (21°C). Raised beds and a black plastic mulch warm soil more quickly. Beware of setting seedlings out early, when nighttime temperatures still drop below 50°F (10°C). Exposure to cold weather will stunt young plants and prevent them from bearing later on.

Sowing seeds indoors

Eggplant is usually started in a pot, since seeds sown directly into the garden don't prosper.

Soak the seeds overnight, then sow them ¼ in (6 mm) deep in peat pots (two or three seeds per pot) full of a seed-starting mixture. Moisten the pots by standing them in warm water, then set them on a heating cable or over a radiator to keep the soil at a temperature of 75°-80°F (24°-26.5°C).

When seeds sprout in 8 to 10 days, move them to a warm and sunny windowsill. If more than one seed sprouts in a pot, snip off all but one seedling as soon as a second set of leaves appears. Begin setting seedlings outside in a sheltered spot for a few hours each day when air temperatures reach 70°F (21°C).

Site and soil preparation

Eggplant grows best in fertile, well-drained soil and in a spot with full sun. Dig compost into the soil, a bucketful per sq yd/m. A week before planting, feed the soil 2-3 lb (0.9-1.4 kg) of 5-10-5 fertilizer per 100 sq ft (9 sq m).

If you live in a climate where the soil stays cool late into the spring, cover the bed with a sheet of black plastic; bury the edges to hold it in place. This absorbs solar radiation and warms the soil.

Set seedlings 2½-3 ft (75-90 cm) apart in all directions. If the bed is covered with black plastic, cut an X-shaped slit into the plastic and plant right through it. Water in seedlings with a half-strength solution of soluble fertilizer.

Care

Young plants need 1 in (2.5 cm) of water a week. In rainless weather apply this as a long, slow soak with a drip irrigation system or a sprinkler. Water in early morning, before the sun is hot.

Unless the bed is mulched with black plastic, cover it with 1 in (2.5 cm) of organic mulch, such as shredded leaves, after the soil warms fully (about four weeks after planting the seedlings).

Northern gardeners should snip off the bottom three or four suckers at the joints where lower leaves meet the main stem. This

▲ **Purple eggplant** The most familiar type of eggplant is long and purple, but some have egg-shaped white fruits.

will confine the plant's strength to its primary growth.

Harvesting

Begin harvesting eggplant when it is half-grown: 4-5 in (10-13 cm) long with standard types, smaller with miniature types. Younger fruits have a better texture than older ones. If the fruits grow to full size, pick them before the skins turn dull. This is a sign that seeds are forming inside; the flesh will be tough and flavorless.

Cut off the fruits carefully with a sharp knife. Eggplant can be kept for about two weeks.

Pests and diseases

Flea beetles attack foliage on young plants; floating row covers help keep these pests out, and a spray of pyrethrin corrects severe infestations. Spider mites attack in dry weather; wash off plants by spraying them daily with water.

Fusarium wilt can kill plants. The best prevention is a three-year crop-rotation plan.

CULTIVARS TO CHOOSE

'Black Beauty': 85 days from setting out seedlings to harvest; large purple-black fruits with fine, pale yellow flesh.

'Early Bird': 50 days; large, oval purple fruits; bears early, continues to frost; will grow in containers.

'Easter Egg': 65 days; egg-shaped white fruits eventually turn yellow.

'Ichiban': 61 days; 1 ft (30 cm) long, slim purple fruits; exceptional quality and flavor.

'Little Fingers': 84 days; light purple fruits, 1 in (2.5 cm) thick, to 7 in (18 cm) long; borne in clusters of three to four.

'Rosa Bianca': 88 days; pear-shaped, medium to large white fruits with lavender; best flavor.

ENDIVE AND ESCAROLE

Crisp and tender endive and escarole make a pleasant change from lettuce in spring and fall salads.

Endive 'Green Curled'

Endive and escarole are related to chicory, and they serve a similar role at the dining table, providing a green with a bit of bite that livens up a salad. You can grow them as a spring crop but they are ideal for a fall harvest, since frost helps temper the leaves' flavor, making them sweeter. The leaves are easy to blanch.

Planning the crop
Although endive and escarole are closely related, they are different in appearance. Curly endives, such as 'Green Curled' and 'Salad King,' have cut and curly leaves; escaroles, such as 'Full Heart Batavian' or 'Nuvol,' have broader, less frilled foliage.

Endive and escarole thrive in sandy, well-drained soil that has been enriched with organic matter for a previous crop.

Sow both in spring where summers are cool. Start the seeds indoors in flats of seed-starting mix two months before the last spring frost. Thin the seedlings to 6 in (15 cm) apart. Four weeks before the last spring frost, plant them outdoors, 1 ft (30 cm) apart and slightly deeper in the soil than they were growing in the flats.

For a fall crop, sow the seeds directly into the garden 90 days before the first fall frost; sow in midsummer in the North, in early fall in the Deep South and the warmer regions of the West. Sow the seeds thinly, ½ in (1.25 cm) deep, three per inch (2.5 cm) in rows 15 in (38 cm) apart. Water seedlings thoroughly, and thin in stages to 12-15 in (30-38 cm) apart. Continue to irrigate regularly. A lack of water makes the leaves tough and bitter.

Blanching the crop
Endive must be blanched to make it palatable. The first plants are ready 12 weeks after sowing, or when they are 1 ft (30 cm) in diameter. When the leaves are dry, gather them together with the leaves upward; tie them loosely with string halfway up the leaves. This method excludes light from the heart and inner leaves but does not blanch the whole head.

To exclude light altogether, cover each endive with an overturned bushel basket or pot.

When the leaves turn creamy white, the endive is blanched and ready for cutting and eating. Blanch escarole in the same way.

Harvesting
Use leaves right after cutting, since they toughen quickly and regain their bitter taste when exposed to light. Keep any surplus in a black plastic bag in the refrigerator for up to three days.

Pests and diseases
If slugs and snails attack the plants during blanching, encircle the plants with coarse sand.

BLANCHING ENDIVE OR ESCAROLE

Choose a sunny or windy day when the leaves of mature plants are dry. Gently pull the leaves upward and bunch them, then tie loosely with string.

Alternatively, blanch the plants under overturned flower pots. Leave a small gap at the bottom to let the plants breathe, but cover the drainage holes.

FLORENCE FENNEL

**Florence fennel is grown for its firm
and crisp bulbous stem base, which has a
delicious aniseed flavor and smell.**

Florence fennel, also called finocchio or sweet fennel, is an annual plant with ferny leaves, which make a decorative backdrop in any herb or vegetable garden.

The "bulb," actually a swollen stem base, is used raw in salads or cooked as a vegetable in soups. The leaves and seeds can be used for flavoring in the same way as those of common fennel. Because they are slightly more pungent, use them with discretion.

Site and soil preparation
Florence fennel prefers rich, well-drained but moisture-retentive soil in a sunny spot. Heavy clay soil is not suitable.

Dig well-rotted manure or compost into the ground the winter before planting. Right before sowing seeds or setting out seedlings, rake in a dressing of a general fertilizer, such as 5-10-10, at the rate given on the product label.

Because the bulb develops best in cool weather, grow Florence fennel as a spring crop in the North and as a fall crop in mild climates. A 10 ft (3 m) row, yielding 10 to 12 plants, is about the right amount for most families.

Cultivation
In the North start seeds indoors in peat pots six weeks before the last spring frost; grow seedlings

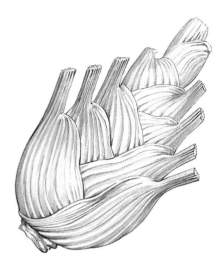

▲ **Florence fennel** The plump bulbs of Florence fennel are prized for their sweet aniseed flavor. Cultivars include 'Fino,' 'Herald,' 'Romy,' and 'Zefa Fino.'

on a sunny but cool windowsill. Harden off the seedlings and set out in garden beds two to three weeks before the last frost. Plant seedlings 1 ft (30 cm) apart.

In mild climates sow seeds directly into the garden in late summer for a fall harvest. Sow the seeds thinly in ½ in (1.25 cm) deep drills in rows 20 in (50 cm) apart. Thin the seedlings twice: to 9 in (23 cm) apart when they form their first true leaves, and a few weeks later to 1 ft (30 cm) apart.

Keep the plants well watered, or the stem bases will not swell. As they begin to develop, apply a 5-10-10 fertilizer at 2 oz (57 g) per sq yd/m and water in well. For milder flavor, blanch stem bases by hilling up earth around them, covering the stems to approximately three-fourths their height.

Harvesting
Use a sharp knife to cut the swollen stem bases when they are the size of tennis balls or larger. Continue to harvest as required. Cut off the leaves to use for flavoring or as garnish.

Pests and diseases
Florence fennel is generally trouble free, but look out for aphids and cutworms.

Florence fennel

GLOBE ARTICHOKES

**Though grown primarily for their edible buds,
artichokes have silvery leaves and fuchsia flowers, which make
them a good choice for flower borders.**

The edible parts of artichokes are actually the flower buds of a large, productive perennial.

Growing artichokes

Artichokes require rich, well-drained soil; cool, moist weather; and plenty of sun. Grow them as a summer and fall crop in mild coastal climates, as a winter crop in much of the South, and forced as annuals in the Northeast.

Prepare the beds for planting by digging in plenty of well-rotted manure or compost.

Plant roots purchased from mail-order nurseries in early spring in mild-weather regions. Set them 4-6 ft (1.2-1.8 m) apart in rows 6-8 ft (1.8-2.4 m) apart. Plant the roots with the upper buds just above the soil surface.

Where plants are planned as annuals, start plants from seeds. Soak seeds in room-temperature water for two days. Then chill them for one month — keep them in a plastic bag of moist sphagnum moss in the refrigerator.

Remove the seeds six to eight weeks before the last frost; sow them ½ in (1.25 cm) deep in 4 in (10 cm) pots of sterilized potting mix. Place the pots in a warm, south-facing window; keep moist.

◀ **Globe artichokes** The edible part of this handsome plant is the immature flower head. The plant grows more than 5 ft (1.5 m) in height and is valuable in the border, where its silver-gray foliage contrasts well with more colorful flowers. It grows best in a sheltered, sunny part of the garden. 'Green Globe' is a good cultivar to grow in warm climates; 'Grand Beurre' is a better selection for cold climates.

Harden off seedlings and plant them outside a few weeks before the last frost. Space the seedlings as with roots. Cover them with hot caps or newspaper cones on cold nights.

In late spring apply a mulch of manure or compost. Water well in dry weather. Every three to four weeks apply about 3 tablespoons of 5-10-10 fertilizer per plant.

Where plants are grown as perennials and bear in summer and fall, cut harvested stems back to ground level in fall and mulch with straw. Renew beds every third year with rooted suckers.

Harvesting

Harvest still tightly closed flower buds when they are about the size of oranges. Cut the buds with 1 in (2.5 cm) of stem.

The first cutting will prompt a second crop. The buds will be smaller but of excellent quality.

Pests and diseases

Aphids, caterpillars, slugs, and snails may attack artichokes.

RAISING NEW PLANTS FROM OLD STOCK

1 In spring remove strong, 9 in (23 cm) tall suckers from older plants. Cut through the crown; include some roots.

2 Transplant the suckers to their permanent growing sites. Pot up cuttings taken in fall and overwinter in a cold frame.

JERUSALEM ARTICHOKES

**Often marketed as "sunchokes,"
Jerusalem artichokes produce sweet-flavored
tubers that are cooked like potatoes.**

Jerusalem artichokes are nothing like true artichokes yet share the name because the tubers have a similar flavor. They are not from Jerusalem either; that part of the name derives from the Italian for sunflower, *girasole*. In fact, these plants are a kind of sunflower.

Cultivation

Plants are grown from seed tubers. Each plant yields about 3 lb (1.4 kg) of artichokes. Plant tubers 1 ft (30 cm) apart to produce 11 lb (5 kg) per yd/m. A warm spot in well-drained soil is best.

Prepare the soil by digging in plenty of well-rotted manure and raking it smooth.

Plant dormant tubers in late fall or early spring (two weeks before the last frost date). Set them 1 ft (30 cm) apart in furrows 4 in (10 cm) deep and 3 ft (90 cm) apart. Pull soil in to cover the tubers; pile it in a ridge 2 in (5 cm) high over the top. Add a general fertilizer, such as 5-10-5, to the ridge at the rate of 2 oz (57 g) per sq yd/m; hoe it into the surface.

When the plants grow to 6 in (15 cm) tall, draw up another 1 in (2.5 cm) of soil. Repeat this every two weeks until the ridge is 6 in (15 cm) high — tubers will form close to the surface.

Support the plants with stakes and wires; water them well. Pinch off flower buds before they open.

Harvesting

The tubers are ready for lifting when the plants' leaves yellow and fall. Cut the stems back 1 ft (30 cm) from the ground.

Leave the tubers in the ground until winter. When harvesting, dig up all the tubers. Any left behind will resprout, aggressively invading nearby garden spaces.

Pests and diseases

The tubers may be attacked by cutworms; root-rot fungi can occur in wet soil.

▶ **Jerusalem artichokes** Easy to grow and prolific, these vigorous plants bear starch-free potato-like tubers.

GROWING JERUSALEM ARTICHOKES

1 Plant tubers at 1 ft (30 cm) intervals in 4 in (10 cm) deep furrows in rows 3 ft (90 cm) apart. The tubers grow best in a warm site and well-cultivated soil but will tolerate other soil conditions.

2 Use a hoe to start forming a shallow ridge along the row of plants when they are 6 in (15 cm) high. Continue drawing soil around the plants every two weeks or so until the ridge is 6 in (15 cm) high.

3 In early summer support the plants by inserting stakes at each end of the row. Secure wires between them, spaced 1 ft (30 cm) apart, and tie the plants to these with soft garden string or twine.

KALE

**Kale is one of the hardiest of greens,
surviving frost and poor soil. For the best flavor,
pick the leaves when they are young.**

Kale — a member of the brassica, or cabbage, family — is rich in vitamins and nutrients, especially iron and vitamins A, C, and E. It thrives in semishade and in cloudy climates. In addition, kale tolerates poor soil and is rarely troubled by the pests and diseases that often afflict cabbage.

An ideal fall and winter crop, kale tolerates even hard frosts, staying green long after other vegetables have died back to the ground. Actually, kale tastes best after exposure to frost.

In areas with not-too-severe winters, kale may carry on right through to spring, providing greens when other leafy vegetables are hard to come by. Even as far north as zone 6, a cold frame is all the winter protection a planting of kale needs. While the leaves of kale may differ — they are either plain or curly — the plants grow in the same way and have the same flavor.

A 15 ft (4.5 m) row of either curly or plain cultivars should yield about 9 lb (4.1 kg) of leaves. Harvest them while young and tender, after the first frost.

Cultivation
Kale grows best on well-drained, loamy soil with a pH of 5.5-6.8. Soil that is more acidic will promote clubroot disease in kale; amend it with lime. Ideally, the soil should have been enriched with manure or compost for a previous crop. After digging the plot thoroughly, apply a 5-10-10 fertilizer at the rate of about $1\frac{1}{2}$ cups (360 ml) per 25 ft (7.5 m) of row.

In the North sow the seeds six weeks before the first fall frost for a fall and winter harvest. In the South sow the seeds in early fall for a winter to spring harvest. Where summers are cool, sow in early spring. Sow the seeds $\frac{1}{2}$ in (1.25 cm) deep in rows spaced about $2\frac{1}{2}$ ft (75 cm) apart.

When seedlings are large enough to handle, thin them to stand 2 ft (60 cm) apart with standard cultivars, $1\frac{1}{2}$ ft (45 cm) apart with dwarf cultivars. Keep

Plain-leaved kale

Curly-leaved kale

◄▼ Winter kale
Rich in both iron and vitamin C, the leaves of kale can be used for soups, in purées, in stir-fried dishes, boiled in a little water, or steamed and served as a green. Raw young kale sprigs are tasty in winter salads — simply toss freshly chopped leaves in a lemon dressing.

the soil well watered, and hoe the soil to control weeds. After the first fall frost, mulch around the plants with a thick layer of straw.

Harvesting
Kale is ready for cutting as soon as the leaves are the size of your hand and while they are still young and tender. Discard yellowing and very large leaves. Avoid picking the terminal bud at the top and center of the plant.

Kale tastes better after a frost. You can use young leaves in salads. Cook older leaves as a green or add them to soups.

When the plants start to flower, pull them up, chop the tough stems into small pieces to speed decay, and put them on the compost pile.

Pests and diseases
Although generally trouble free, kale may be infested by imported cabbageworms, flea beetles, Mexican bean beetles, and aphids. Clubroot is a common disease.

CULTIVARS TO CHOOSE

Curly
'Dwarf Blue Curled Scotch': 55 days from seed to harvest; tightly curled, dark green leaves.

'Siberian': 50 days; frilly leaves; cold-hardy plant; slow to bolt.

'Winterbor': 60 days; curly green leaves; very cold-hardy cultivar.

Plain
'Red Russian': 50 days; purplish stems with gray-green leaves.

KOHLRABI

This versatile vegetable has a pleasant nutty flavor. Resembling a turnip in appearance, it is quick and easy to grow and is well worth a place in the vegetable garden.

Kohlrabi resembles a root vegetable or bulb, but the edible part is actually a swollen stem base. Like other members of the brassica family, kohlrabi succeeds in shallow soils where such root crops as turnips or carrots fail.

Although the flesh is white in all kohlrabies, some cultivars have pale green or purple skins. All have a delicate flavor, best described as a cross between a turnip and a cabbage. Kohlrabi is ideal for people who prefer mild-tasting vegetables.

The young stem bases can be boiled or steamed and served as an accompanying vegetable, or they can be used raw — coarsely grated or cut into strips — in salads. The young leaves can be boiled like spinach.

It is not a particularly large plant, reaching only 1 ft (30 cm) in height when fully grown.

Kohlrabi matures in only 8 to 12 weeks from sowing and withstands fall frosts. In areas with temperate climates, some cultivars can be left in the ground throughout winter. It is an unusual, delicious, and easy-to-grow vegetable, provided it is planted in rich soil and never runs out of water. It can even be sown as a second crop after a bed has been cleared of other, earlier crops.

Planning the crop

Kohlrabi grows best in fertile, well-drained soil. If the soil is either sandy or heavy (a clay), fork in a generous quantity of compost, then hoe in a 5-10-10 fertilizer at a rate of 1½ cups (360 ml) per 25 ft (7.5 m) of row.

Acid soil should be treated with lime or ground limestone to bring it up to a slightly alkaline level — about pH 7.5. Allow several weeks to elapse between the applications of fertilizer and lime.

Growing kohlrabi

Spring crops may be directly sown into the garden beds four to six weeks before the average date of the last spring frost. Sow the seeds ½ in (1.25 cm) deep, about 10 seeds per 1 ft (30 cm) in rows spaced 1 ft (30 cm) apart. Thin the seedlings to 9 in (23 cm) apart when they are large enough to handle. It is important to keep the plants well watered, especially during very dry spells. Kohlrabi needs generous amounts of water throughout the growing season for the stems to swell.

In areas where springs are short and summers are hot, sow the seeds indoors six to eight weeks before the average date of the last spring frost. Sow the seeds in peat pots full of sterilized seed-starting mix; keep them moist, and set the pots on a sunny but cool windowsill. When the seedlings develop their first pair of leaves, thin to one seedling per pot. Harden off the seedlings, then set them out in the garden a week or two before the last frost date, protecting them with hot caps or cones of newspaper on cold nights.

For a fall crop, sow seeds in the garden 10 weeks before the average date of the first fall frost.

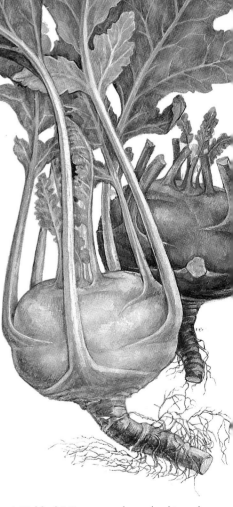

▲ **Kohlrabi** Green- and purple-skinned cultivars all have white flesh. Kohlrabi is easy to cook and has a mild, nutty flavor.

Purple-skinned kohlrabi 'Purple Vienna'

CULTIVARS TO CHOOSE

White or green skin
'Early White Vienna': 50 days from seed to harvest; pale green skin; especially delicate flavor and crisp texture; early-maturing; particularly resistant to bolting.

'Express Forcer': 42 days; early-maturing; tolerates warm weather.

'Grand Duke': 45-50 days; white flesh with mild, sweet flavor; early.

'Kolpak': 50 days; flesh has a sweet flavor, slow to become fibrous or pithy.

'Winner': 53 days; large bulbs with light green skins and white flesh; exceptionally productive.

Purple skin
'Purple Vienna': 50 days; foliage is marbled with purple; crisp white flesh; with its purple skin it adds a decorative touch when grated raw in salads — if picked when leaves are very young and tender.

'Rapid': 60 days; bright purple skin; bulbs exceptionally slow to turn woody; sweet flavor.

Harvesting
Pull the plants out of the soil when the bulbous stems reach a diameter of approximately $1\frac{1}{2}$ in (3.75 cm). These young stems are tender and have the best flavor. If allowed to grow larger, they often become tough and woody.

Young leaves can be cooked like spinach, but remove the leaves and stalks of older plants and dispose of them on the compost pile.

Kohlrabi will keep for two weeks if it is put in a plastic bag and refrigerated.

Pests and diseases
Kohlrabi is subject to all the pests that afflict the cabbage family: imported cabbageworms, cabbage root maggots, cabbage loopers, flea beetles, and cutworms. Because it is quick to mature, however, kohlrabi more often escapes the pests' notice. Aphids may be troublesome but can be dislodged with a strong jet of water or a spray of insecticidal soap.

Diseases to watch for, though they are rarely severe, are club-root, damping-off, black rot, leaf spot, whiptail, and wire stem. Maintaining a neutral to slightly alkaline soil and following good cultural practices are the best preventive measures.

HARVESTING AND STORING

If sown in early spring or late summer, thinned to allow room for each bulb, and kept well watered, kohlrabi will be ready for harvesting 8 to 12 weeks after sowing. When bulbs reach $1\frac{1}{2}$ in (3.75 cm) in diameter, pull whole plants from the soil or dig them up carefully with a spading fork. Once the leaves are trimmed from the bulbs, store them in a dry, cool place for about two weeks. You can pick young leaves for steaming or stir-frying.

LEEKS

Easy to grow, and hardy even through northern winters, leeks (a member of the onion family) are a worthwhile vegetable for a small garden.

Leeks have a sweet, mild flavor. Though they take 90 to 130 days to grow, they can be cultivated in regions with short summers, for an early frost improves their flavor. Northern growers sometimes overwinter leeks in the garden, supplying only a blanket of straw as protection.

Leeks are generally free of pests and diseases and will tolerate a variety of growing conditions. They are productive, too: a 10 ft (3 m) row will yield an average of 10 lb (4.5 kg) of leeks.

Site and soil preparation

Leeks grow in most soils, if they are neither compacted nor badly drained. Choose a sunny spot. Dig the bed well, mixing in compost or well-rotted manure at the rate of a bucketful per sq yd/m.

Leeks are commonly grown from seeds, which are sown in the early spring in the North and in the fall in the South.

In the North sow the seeds indoors two to three months before the last frost. Plant the seeds ½ in (1.25 cm) deep in flats or shallow pots filled with sterilized seed-starting mix. Moisten thoroughly, and keep the flats at 65°-70°F (18.5°-21°C) during the day and at 55°-60°F (13°-15.5°C) at night.

When the seedlings are 3 in (7.5 cm) tall, thin to 1 in (2.5 cm) apart; at 5 in (13 cm) tall, thin to 2 in (5 cm) apart. When the seedlings are 8 in (20 cm) tall, transplant them into the garden. Set them into the bottom of holes 6 in (15 cm) deep and 6 in (15 cm) apart in rows 1½ ft (45 cm) apart. Use a dibble to make the holes, drop in the plants, and then gently fill the holes with water. Do not refill the holes with soil. This forces grit in among the leeks' leaves, which are difficult to clean. The amount of soil carried

► Tasty leek The most delicately flavored of the onions, the leek is hardy and easily grown. It thrives in any well-drained soil and benefits from a sunny site. In the North it yields a fall and winter harvest; in the South it matures in mid- to late winter.

► Harvesting leeks To prevent the stems from breaking, lift leeks out of the ground with a spade or fork — never wrench plants out by hand. Remove root ends and trim the leaves before cleaning.

into the holes by the water will hold the leeks in place. Subsequent watering and hoeing will complete the job.

In the South sow leeks directly into prepared garden beds. Plant seeds ½ in (1.25 cm) deep in rows 1½ ft (45 cm) apart, and thin seedlings to 6 in (15 cm) apart. Begin to hill earth up around the stems when the seedlings are 8 in (20 cm) tall.

Caring for the crop

Hoe the bed regularly to control weeds, and water well during dry spells. Continue blanching the stems by hilling more earth up around them. This should be done in fall in the North and in early winter in the South.

Fifty days or so after planting, feed the leeks by sprinkling 1 lb (450 g) of 10-10-10 fertilizer along each 25 ft (7.5 m) of row.

Harvesting and storing

Begin harvesting the leeks when they are ¾ in (2 cm) thick. Ease them out of the soil with a fork. Cut off the roots and trim back the leaves. Wash thoroughly.

Continue harvesting as needed. Leeks can remain in the ground throughout winter and continue to grow in the coldest months.

Pests and diseases

Onion fly is a common pest; smut, pink root, and downy mildew are the most common diseases.

CULTIVATING LEEKS

1 Make holes for seedlings 6 in (15 cm) deep and 6 in (15 cm) apart, using a dibble. Water plants in gently to avoid washing soil into leaves and stems.

2 To blanch and lengthen the stems, hill up earth around the plants regularly throughout the season. Harvest leeks when the stems are ¾ in (2 cm) thick.

CULTIVARS TO CHOOSE

Early
'Titan': 70 days from transplanting to harvest; vigorous plant; dark green leaves; white stems 6 in (15 cm) long.

'Varna': 50 days from sowing to harvest; developed for direct-seeding; stems up to 2 ft (60 cm) long; excellent yields.

Midseason
'Giant Musselburgh': 100 days from sowing; large, fat tender stems; exceptionally cold-hardy plant; good in North and South.

'King Richard': 75 days from transplanting; long, uniform white stems; can be pulled early.

Late
'Alaska': 105 days from transplanting; thick, long stems; nonbulbous; resists disease; goes until late spring.

'Durabel': 125 days; slow-growing and strong; exceptionally cold-hardy plant; mild flavor and tender texture.

'Laura': 115 days; medium-length white stems; very cold-hardy plant.

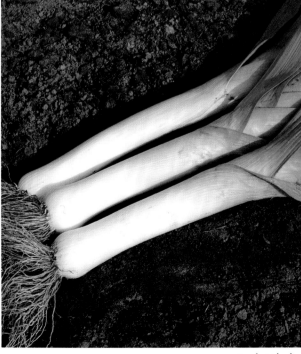

Leek 'Alaska'

Leek 'Giant Musselburgh'

LETTUCE
Crisp lettuce is the essence of a salad. By growing different cultivars, you can make the harvest last for months.

There is room for lettuce in just about every garden. It is one of the easiest vegetables to grow and does well in almost any soil. With just a little know-how you can ensure a regular supply and a wide choice of tastes and textures.

Types of lettuce
There are several different types of lettuce, each with slightly different growing requirements.

Butterhead is round, like a cabbage, with smooth, spreading leaves. It is exceptionally easy to grow and quick to mature.

Crisphead, or iceberg, lettuce resembles the butterhead type, but it has a large heart of crisp, curled leaves.

Cos, or romaine, lettuce is usually crisp in texture. It grows upright, with oblong leaves. Cos lettuce takes a little longer to mature than the other types do and needs more watering.

Loose-leaf lettuce has a profusion of leaves but no heart. Pick the leaves, which are curly and indented, a few at a time.

Greenhouse lettuce has been specially bred for growing in unheated greenhouses to mature from fall to spring.

Site and soil preparation
Fertile, well-drained soil and a sunny, sheltered site are best for lettuce. During the winter dig the site thoroughly, incorporating well-rotted manure or compost. Before sowing or planting in spring, rake the soil to a fine tilth and apply a general fertilizer at the rate of 2 oz (57 g) per sq yd/m.

Sowing and planting
Lettuce thrives at a temperature of 60°F (15.5°C) and will bolt (set seed) when the days get hot. For this reason, it's a spring and fall crop in most of the North, and a winter crop in the South and Southwest, although in some parts of the Pacific Northwest lettuce may be grown year-round.

For the earliest spring crop, start cos lettuce indoors, four to six weeks before the average date of the last frost. Sow two seeds

Crisphead

Cos

Miniature butterhead

Loose-leaf

Bronze-tinted butterhead

Butterhead

¼ in (6 mm) deep in small peat pots filled with sterilized seed-starting mix. Remove the weakest seedling from each pot, and gradually harden off seedlings before planting them out as soon as the soil is workable. Set transplants 6-8 in (15-20 cm) apart.

Follow this by direct-sowing seeds of cos, loose-leaf, and butterhead cultivars at two- to three-week intervals, then gradually switch to heat-resistant types, such as 'Buttercrunch,' as the weather warms. Crisphead lettuce needs cool weather to form heads and should be grown as a fall crop in the North or a winter crop in the South.

Sow seeds thinly ¼ in (6 mm) deep and 1 in (2.5 cm) apart. Thin the seedlings to 3-4 in (7.5-10 cm) apart for loose-leaf lettuce, 6-8 in (15-20 cm) apart for cos and butterhead cultivars, and 12-16 in (30-40 cm) apart for crispheads.

Interplanting In a small garden lettuce plants need not occupy a special bed. Plant them between slower-maturing vegetables, such as leeks or celery. The lettuce will be out of the ground before the other crop needs the space.

Fall crops In mid- to late summer sow cos or crisphead cultivars, such as 'Frosty,' in seed flats set out in a shaded screen porch, or sow directly into the garden. Check the days to maturity of your chosen cultivar, add 10 days because growth is slower in fall, and count backward that number of days from the first fall frost date to arrive at the correct date for sowing seeds.

Greenhouse crops Butterhead and crisphead cultivars can be sown in a cold frame or greenhouse from early fall onward, and grown there for harvesting in winter and spring.

CULTIVARS TO CHOOSE

Spring crop
'Bibb': 60 days from seed to harvest; soft green leaves in tender head with delicate flavor; inspired the name *butterhead*.

'Black Seeded Simpson': 45 days; loose-leaf, light green, frilled foliage; harvest small leaves early.

'Green Ice': 44 days; deep green, crinkled loose-leaf type.

'Paris White Cos': 74 days; 10 in (25 cm) tall, spoon-shaped leaves; dark green leaves; pale heart.

Summer crop
'Buttercrunch': 49 days; deep green, heat-tolerant butterhead, with crunchier texture than 'Bibb.'

'Cimmaron': 65 days; bronze-red cos; resists bolting; good summer crop in North.

'Iceberg': 82 days; large compact, curly-leaved head; tolerates heat.

'Red Sails': 45 days; bronze-and-red loose-leaf foliage; tolerates heat; also good in greenhouse.

'Red Salad Bowl': 47 days; loose-leaf with fringed, deep red foliage; slow to bolt; good in moderately hot weather.

'Salad Bowl': 47 days; similar to above but with green leaves.

Fall and winter crop
'Crispino': 57 days; green crisphead; tolerant of bad weather.

'North Pole': green butterhead; overwinters with protection for late-winter, early-spring harvest.

'Rouge d'Hiver': 58 days; large red-leaved cos type; matures quickly; heat-tolerant cultivar.

'Winter Density': 54 days; large head, intermediate between cos and butterhead; cold-hardy plant.

Greenhouse
'Sitonia': 60 days; green butterhead for fall and winter harvest.

'Titania': 60 days; green head; spring or summer harvest; disease-resistant cultivar.

Winter crops In mild regions direct-sow seeds in mid- to late fall for winter harvests.

Cultivation
Fertilize lettuce seedlings with a liquid fertilizer at transplanting time. Three to four weeks later (or three to four weeks after thinning direct-sown plants) sprinkle 1 teaspoon of 10-10-10 fertilizer around each plant.

Water regularly; do not let the soil dry out. Mulch deeply around the plants as temperatures rise in late spring to keep them cool.

Harvesting
Harvest loose-leaf lettuce as soon as the leaves are large enough to eat. Begin cutting heading types as soon as they form a firm heart.

Pests and diseases
Aphids, cutworms, and slugs are common pests. Poorly drained soil or overcrowding may bring on bottom rot, turning plants black and making them smell bad. Damp, overcast weather promotes botrytis, which appears as grayish-green or brown spots on the lower leaves.

Butterhead 'Bibb'

Crisphead 'Iceberg'

Loose-leaf 'Salad Bowl,' 'Red Salad Bowl'

MUSHROOMS

**Freshly picked homegrown mushrooms
have superb flavor. They are easy to grow from
prepared kits and take up little space.**

Button
mushroom

Cup mushroom

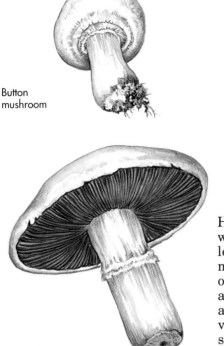

Flat mushroom

Harvesting mushrooms in the wild is a dangerous business, unless you take the time to master mushroom identification. On the other hand, growing mushrooms at home is virtually risk free — and it is easy. You provide an environment suitable only for a safe species and then inoculate it with the pure, laboratory-grown strain of mushroom you desire.

The classic culinary mushroom is the white button mushroom, which grows best in a medium of composted horse manure. This material is available inexpensively or for free if you live near a riding stable, and preparing it for inoculation is a simple process. The only equipment you will need is a few wooden boxes set in a shady corner of the backyard or in the back of a cool shed or cellar.

The best crops are harvested from growing media purchased from mushroom-grower supply houses (your county Cooperative Extension Service can supply you with names and addresses). Such suppliers can even provide kits of preinoculated media; they are relatively expensive but easy to use. Typically, all you need to do is to moisten a container already filled with the medium and inoculant, then set it in a suitable spot.

Homemade compost
It is fun, however, to start from scratch. For this, you must find fresh, strawy manure (many stables bed their horses on wood shavings, which make an unsuitable growing medium). Make sure that the manure has not been treated with pesticides. You will need 1 cu yd (0.75 cu m) of manure, or four garbage cans full.

Mix the manure thoroughly, moisten it with water, and pile it up outside. Within a day, it should start to heat up.

After about a week, turn the pile over and dampen it again. Repeat this process every two or three days until the manure becomes crumbly and no longer smells of ammonia. Check the temperature: 75°F (24°C) means it is ready. Pack it firmly into open boxes or tubs to a depth of 10-12 in (25-30 cm).

The compost is now ready for inoculation with the mushroom

◀ **Homegrown mushrooms** Delicious homegrown mushrooms are superior to store-bought ones. Expect two or three crops from one set of spawn.

GROWING MUSHROOMS

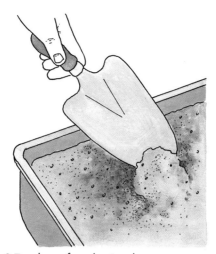

1 Insert pieces of spawn, the size of a walnut, 1 in (2.5 cm) deep and 10 in (25 cm) apart in boxes of compost at a temperature of 75°F (24°C). Water lightly; put the box in a dimly lit spot.

2 Ten days after planting the spawn, cover the compost with a 1 in (2.5 cm) layer of pH-adjusted, sterilized potting mix. Sprinkle regularly with water to keep the compost moist.

3 Harvest the mushrooms by gently twisting them free of the bed; cut any debris free with a sharp knife. Refill the holes with loose bedding material. Repeat until crops stop appearing.

spawn. This can be purchased from the same suppliers who sell the growing media and kits. You need at least 2 oz (57 g) of spawn for every 22 lb (10 kg) of compost.

Planting

Set the compost-filled boxes in a dimly lit, humid location with a steady temperature of 50°-55°F (10°-13°C). An unheated basement is ideal, but a shaded garage or shed may be suitable in the spring or fall.

Break the spawn into walnut-size pieces, and gently insert them in the compost, 1 in (2.5 cm) deep and 10 in (25 cm) apart. Water the compost lightly.

In a few days the spawn will start to spread fine threads — the mycelium, or mushroom tissue — throughout the box.

Ten days after planting, cover the compost with a 1 in (2.5 cm) layer of sterilized potting mix to help maintain the temperature and level of moisture in the bed. Check the pH of the potting mix before applying it, and if necessary add lime to raise it to 7.2-7.8.

Water regularly using a watering can with a fine-spray nozzle, maintaining dampness rather than soaking the compost.

For outdoor cultivation, on a warm, damp day between late spring and fall, lift small squares of lawn 2 in (5 cm) thick and 1 ft (30 cm) apart; insert a walnut-size piece of spawn into each hole and replace the turf. If the weather becomes dry, water the spawn area. Do not mow the lawn.

Harvesting

Mushrooms first appear as tiny pinheads three or four weeks after planting indoors.

Once they emerge, mushrooms will take 7 to 10 days to reach a good size for harvesting. A second and third flush, perhaps more, will follow over six to eight weeks.

When the mushrooms stop sprouting, use the compost as a garden mulch; it cannot be used again for growing mushrooms.

Pests and diseases

The larvae of mushroom flies may tunnel into the stalks and caps, making the plants inedible.

▼ **Mushroom culture** A regular, light supply of water is essential for a successful crop. A capillary watering system (available from greenhouse supply companies) allows mushrooms to take up water from a reservoir as needed.

CULTIVARS TO CHOOSE

Suppliers offer a fascinating range of spawn, from shiitake to oyster mushrooms, together with appropriate growing media. For growing on composted manure, order spawn of white button mushrooms (*Agaricus brunnescens*) or the related 'Porto Bello.'

ONIONS

The most versatile of all vegetables, onions come in so many cultivars that a fresh harvest is available year-round.

Few vegetables are cheaper at the store, yet onions are well worth growing at home. Homegrown onions taste better and offer a far greater range of flavors. And all this can be had for little work.

The secret to success in growing onions is choosing cultivars adapted to your climate. Then decide whether to grow them from seeds, which takes from six or seven months to a year, or to grow them from sets (immature bulbs), which takes about five months.

Onions need cool weather during the early part of their growth. The tops grow in cool weather, and bulbs form in warm weather.

Long vs. short day

The many types of onions include bunching onions, pickling onions, scallions (green onions), storage, and sweet onions. The most important distinction for gardeners is between long-day and short-day onions. Long-day cultivars require 13 to 16 hours of sunlight daily to thrive and produce the best bulbs; these are best adapted to cultivation as summer crops in the North. Short-day onions will flourish in areas where they get just 12 hours of sunlight each day and are best adapted for southern gardens, especially in the milder regions where onions are grown as a fall and winter crop.

Planning the crop

Onions need a site in full sun with well-drained soil. The larger storage and sweet onions need a deep loam that has been enriched with well-rotted manure or compost. For a spring planting, dig the plot deeply early in fall. Work in two buckets of well-rotted manure or compost per sq yd/m. Smaller onions — bunching onions, pickling onions, and scallions — grow in any fertile, well-drained soil. All onions grown from sets require less finely textured soil than seed-grown ones.

Onions grow best in a firm soil. Prepare the bed well in advance to give the soil a chance to settle. A week or two before planting,

fertilize the bed with 4 oz (115 g) of bonemeal and 2 oz (57 g) of sulfate of potash per sq yd/m. Or apply 10-10-10 fertilizer at a rate of 1 lb (450 g) per 20 sq ft (1.8 sq m).

Whether growing from seeds or sets, a 15 ft × 3 ft (4.5 m × 1 m) bed should produce 13 lb (6 kg) of onions, and good fertilization can increase the yield. A 10 ft (3 m) row of pickling onions will yield up to 150 onions.

Onions from sets

Plant onions from sets in midspring, after the danger of heavy frost has past, and harvest them

in late summer. Onion sets are immature bulbs that have been stored at high temperatures to induce dormancy and prevent the formation of a flower embryo. They have distinct advantages over seeds: they are easier to handle, are less likely to be attacked by mildew or aphids, and reach a harvestable size more quickly.

Buy onion sets that are not too big, about ½ in (1.25 cm) wide, as larger sets are more likely to bolt.

Never plant onion sets in cold or wet soil. If you have to delay planting, take the bulbs out of their packaging and spread them

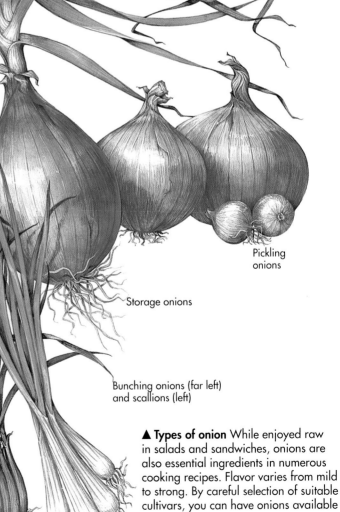

Pickling onions

Storage onions

Bunching onions (far left) and scallions (left)

▲ **Types of onion** While enjoyed raw in salads and sandwiches, onions are also essential ingredients in numerous cooking recipes. Flavor varies from mild to strong. By careful selection of suitable cultivars, you can have onions available at all times of the year.

GROWING ONION SETS

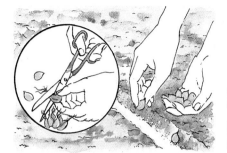

1 In midspring plant the sets in prepared beds. Snip the small roots off before planting. Firm the soil in well, then cover the bed with netting.

2 Bend the leaves down when they turn yellow. This will encourage early ripening. Take care, however, not to snap the leaves off.

3 Loosen the onions two weeks later by pushing a fork underneath the bulbs. Ease them out slightly, but leave them in the ground.

4 After another two weeks, lift out the bulbs and spread them out in a sunny spot to dry fully; remember to handle them carefully.

out in a cool, light place to avoid premature sprouting.

Plant the sets 1-2 in (2.5-5 cm) deep, 4 in (10 cm) apart, in rows 9-10 in (23-25 cm) apart. Set them pointed end up, and cover them with soil so that only the tips show. Firm down the soil, and cover the bed with netting or floating row covers to keep birds from pulling up the bulbs. Check the bed daily. Replace sets that have been lifted out of the soil as the roots grow. Hoe between the rows regularly, but hand-weed between young onions to avoid damage. Make sure they have enough water; in dry conditions, sets may bolt, flowering prematurely. Remove any flower heads.

Onions from seeds
Starting from seeds offers the gardener a larger selection of cultivars to choose from — this alone may justify the extra work.

The seeds of sweet onions can be sown directly into the garden. In the South plant in August for a late-winter harvest. In the North plant seeds four to six weeks before the average date of the last frost, setting them ½ in (1.25 cm) deep, one to three seeds per 1 in (2.5 cm), in rows 9-10 in (23-25 cm) apart. Thin emerging

seedlings to 4 in (10 cm) apart within the rows.

Because onion seeds are slow to germinate, many gardeners mix them with fast-sprouting radish seeds, which mark the row within a few days. The radishes also trap root maggots, which attack their roots but are removed when the radishes are pulled out, once the onions emerge.

Direct-seeded onions often produce smaller bulbs. If you want larger bulbs, sow the seeds indoors in 4-6 in (10-15 cm) deep flats of sterilized seed-starting mix, two to three months before the last spring frost date.

Plant seeds ¼ in (6 mm) deep in rows 1 in (2.5 cm) apart. Thin seedlings to ½ in (1.25 cm) apart in the row. Place the flats under strong fluorescent lights or in a cool, sunny window, and keep the seedlings well watered.

Feed regularly with a liquid fertilizer at the rate recommended on the product label, and keep the emerging leaves trimmed back to a height of 3 in (7.5 cm). Harden off the seedlings, and set them outside in the garden as soon as the danger of heavy frost has passed. You should plant them out 4 in (10 cm) apart in rows 9-10 in (23-25 cm) apart.

Growing onions
Conscientious weeding is important to the success of your onion crop. Use a sharp hoe to slice off the top growth of any weeds that appear — pulling up or digging out the weeds may damage the onions' roots.

As soon as the soil has warmed, put an organic mulch around the plants to control the weeds and to keep the soil moist.

Regular irrigation during periods of dry weather helps determine the size and quality of the harvest. Underwatered plants produce small, pungent bulbs, and really dry conditions may cause the bulbs to split. In general, apply a full inch (2.5 cm) of water weekly in rainless weather. Keep in mind that transplants are more vulnerable to drought than onions started from sets.

When the leaves reach 4-6 in (10-15 cm) tall and the bulbs just begin to swell, fertilize the onions again. Scratch out a shallow trench 3 in (7.5 cm) to one side of the row. Sprinkle into the trench 1 lb (450 g) of 10-10-10 fertilizer per 20-25 ft (6-7.5 m) of row.

You can treat scallions and bunching onions like leeks if you desire long white stems. Keep hilling up soil around the plants as they develop, adding more soil as the leaves grow taller.

Pickling onions yield best on sandy soil that has not been overly enriched with manure or fertilizer. A rich soil encourages large bulbs, but this is not desirable in the case of pickling onions, which are better when small.

Direct-seed pickling cultivars in midspring in a bed that has been raked to a fine tilth. Broadcast or sow the seeds two to three to 1 in (2.5 cm), ½ in (1.25 cm) deep, in rows 6 in (15 cm) apart.

Little thinning is necessary if the plants have sufficient space to form small bulbs. Harvest from midsummer onward.

Harvesting and storing
When the outer leaves of the onions begin to turn yellow, use the back of a rake to bend the tops over. This stops the sap from flowing up out of the bulb and concentrates the plant's energy into maturing the bulb.

Two weeks later push a fork gently under the bulbs to help loosen the roots. After another couple of weeks, lift the bulbs out altogether. Spread the bulbs out in a sunny place to dry thoroughly. In wet weather bring the bulbs indoors to dry in a warm, well-ventilated place, then move them to a cool, dry place to complete the process.

When the outer skins are completely dry, wipe off any remaining soil. Always handle the bulbs carefully to avoid bruising them. Do not trim off the tops completely, as they will be needed for stringing. Tie them to a length of rope or store the onions in netting hung in a cool, dry place.

Pests and diseases
Pests include onion thrip and onion maggots. Plants grown from seeds are more likely to be attacked by onion maggots than onions grown from sets. Common diseases are smut, basal rot, and pink root; the best insurance against them is crop rotation.

SHALLOTS
Shallots are smaller than onions. They are used for flavoring or pickling rather than as a vegetable. Shallots grow in bunches or clusters of 10 small bulbs.

Because they can be expensive to buy and difficult to find in supermarkets, shallots are an obvious choice for growing in a home garden. Properly stored, these onions can last all year.

Like onion sets, shallots are grown from bulbs. They are sold by volume, in pints or quarts, or by the pound. Thirty shallots planted in a 15 ft (4.5 m) row produce a crop of 4-5 lb (1.8-2.3 kg).

Plant shallots in late winter or early spring, as soon as the soil can be worked, in a sunny spot on land enriched for a previous crop.

If the soil is light, push the bulbs firmly into the soil until they are three-quarters buried. On firmer soil, make a hole with the tip of a trowel or draw a furrow with a hoe. Leave only the tips of the bulbs protruding. Set the bulbs 6 in (15 cm) apart with 9 in (23 cm) between rows.

After a couple of days, replant any bulbs that have become dislodged. Hoe and water regularly.

Harvesting and storing
When the foliage dies back in midsummer, lift the shallot clusters with a spading fork and lay

▲ **Shallots** Smaller than onions, these bulbs are desirable for pickling.

them out in single layers to dry for a few days.

Once the foliage has withered completely, split the clumps into single bulbs and leave them to dry for a few days longer. Store them in a cool, dry place, reserving some for planting the following season.

SCALLIONS
Scallions, or green onions, are among the easiest vegetables to grow. The stems can be used in recipes as a substitute for chives. These quick-growing onions are often out of the ground before onion fly strikes. They take up little room and need no special care.

Scallions do well in any fertile, well-drained soil. Choose a sunny site, and dig the soil over in the fall before sowing.

Just before sowing, rake in 1 lb (450 g) of 10-10-10 fertilizer per 20 sq ft (1.8 sq m) of bed. Sow the seeds thinly, ½ in (1.25 cm) deep, in rows about 8 in (20 cm) apart. Start sowing the seeds in early spring. You can repeat the process at intervals of four weeks until midsummer.

Cover the rows gently with soil after sowing, taking care not to disturb the seeds. Water lightly.

For early-spring crops you can make a first sowing in early fall, with a second sowing in late winter in a cold frame or under hot caps for pulling in early summer.

GROWING ONIONS FROM SEED

1 Sow seeds thinly, ½ in (1.25 cm) deep, in rows 9-10 in (23-25 cm) apart. For larger bulbs, start sweet onions indoors, two to three months before the last frost.

3 After danger of frost passes, set out transplants started indoors 4 in (10 cm) apart in rows 9-10 in (23-25 cm) apart.

2 When onions (except scallions) sown outdoors in spring and late summer are approximately 2 in (5 cm) high, thin them to 4 in (10 cm) apart.

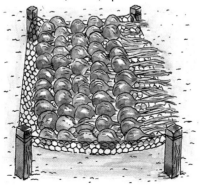

4 After digging onions, spread them to dry on a raised platform of chicken wire. In rainy weather, dry indoors.

CULTIVARS TO CHOOSE

Long-day cultivars
'Gringo': 105 days from sowing to harvest; "Spanish"-type; sweet, white-fleshed, medium-size bulb; copper-colored skin; resists splitting.

'White Sweet Spanish': 120 days; large white bulb, 5½ in (14 cm) in diameter; mild flavor.

Storage onions
'Red Baron': 115 days; red-skinned bulb; good flavor; excellent storage.

'Southport Red Globe': 110 days; globe-shaped red bulb; mild flavor.

'Spartan Banner': 120 days; medium-size globe with yellow skin; pungent flavor; excellent storage.

'Yellow Globe': 102 days; yellow skin, white flesh; 3½ in (9 cm) in diameter; early-maturing cultivar; high yield.

Pickling onions
'Barletta': 70 days; small, round bulb flattened at top and bottom; uniform in size and shape; crisp, mild flavor.

'Crystal Wax': 75 days; small, thin-skinned, pearly white bulb; resistant to pink root.

Shallots
Often sold simply as "French" shallots; 'Atlantic' and 'Success' are two good cultivars.

Short-day cultivars
'Colossal': 165 days; large, mild, yellow-skinned bulb; high yield; resistant to pink root.

'New Mexico White Grano': 185 days; large, mild-flavored white bulb.

'Red Creole': 187 days; medium-size, very hot, red-skinned bulb; red-purple flesh; stores well.

Onion 'Red Baron'

Onion 'Red Creole'

Onion 'Yellow Globe'

If space is at a premium, sow scallions between rows of slower-growing vegetables, such as carrots. This arrangement has an extra bonus; the onions will help fend off carrot rust fly.

Scallions should need no thinning. Water the plants well in dry weather, and weed carefully.

Harvest scallions when they are about 6 in (15 cm) high and the stems are pencil-thick.

BUNCHING ONIONS

Also called Welsh onions, bunching onions are a perennial species that send up multiple shoots from a single seed to form a tuft that grows up to 1 ft (30 cm) high. Use the stems in the same way as scallions and the leaves as chives.

Bunching onions do best on organically enriched, well-drained deep loam. Dig over the plot the previous fall. Sow in early spring where the plants are to grow, and thin until 10 in (25 cm) apart. In areas with severe winters, replant bunching onions annually.

Scallion 'White Lisbon'

CULTIVARS OF SCALLIONS

'Ishikura': 66 days from sowing to harvest; single stem; excellent for spring and late-summer harvests; not hardy enough to overwinter.

'White Lisbon': 70 days; mild, sweet flavor; crisp texture; quick-growing and cold-hardy cultivar; good if sown in fall for spring harvest.

PARSNIPS

Parsnips are easy to grow — and they taste much better fresh from the garden than from a store. Root parsley, salsify, and scorzonera can add variety and zest to your meals.

Mild-tasting parsnips are excellent for roasting, baking, or boiling, and they last into seasons when other root vegetables have already been harvested.

Often planted in early spring if the weather is favorable, parsnips are the earliest vegetable seeds to be sown outdoors. They occupy the ground for almost a year and are harvested in winter.

To get more out of the parsnip bed, sow lettuce or radishes between rows when parsnips are young; both can be harvested before the parsnips need the space.

Growing parsnips

Parsnips grow in most soils but do best in a deep, rich, loamy, and stone-free soil. Choose an open, sunny spot and a bed that has been well enriched with manure or fertilizer for a previous crop.

Do not enrich the soil with fresh manure before planting parsnips, or the roots may fork or split. Dig in 2-3 in (5-7.5 cm) of compost if the soil is poor. A 15 ft (4.5 m) row supplies 30 parsnips.

In the North sow the seeds in early spring, but in the South sow the seeds in late summer. Soak the seeds overnight, then plant them approximately ½ in (1.25 cm) deep, two seeds per 1 in (2.5 cm), in rows spaced 1 ft (30 cm) apart. The seeds will normally germinate at a slow pace. It's important that you keep the seeds moist during this period.

Thin the seedlings for the first time when they reach 1 in (2.5 cm) high, and continue to thin the seedlings until they are eventually spaced about 6 in (15 cm) apart. Alternatively, sow groups of three or four seeds 6 in (15 cm) apart; remove the weakest seedlings, leaving a single strong one growing in each group.

Mulch around the seedlings to control weeds. Water regularly to ensure healthy root development.

Long-rooted parsnip

Short-rooted parsnip

◀ **Harvesting parsnips** Long-rooted cultivars can snap off in the ground during harvesting. To avoid this, dig deep with a fork to loosen the soil around the roots; gently ease them out.

Harvesting

Harvest parsnips when the leaves die down in fall; a hard frost will improve their flavor. Carefully use a garden fork to avoid damaging the roots.

Leave parsnips in the ground and dig them up as required. Lift the last roots in late winter or before the roots start to produce new leaves. Store them in a cool place, covered with soil.

Pests and diseases

The pests likely to attack parsnips are the carrot rust fly and the onion maggot; floating row covers will exclude them. Parsnip canker is the most common disease. Because there is no treatment, grow short-rooted cultivars or those resistant to the disease.

CULTIVARS TO CHOOSE

Parsnip
'All-America': 110 days from sowing to harvest; early and vigorous; tender, wedge-shaped white roots.

'Cobham Improved Marrow': 120 days; white, smooth-skinned, medium roots; resistant to canker.

'Gladiator': 110 days; big crops; white roots; resistant to canker.

'Harris Model': 120 days; smooth white roots, 1 ft (30 cm) long, 1½-2 in (3.75-5 cm) wide at top.

'Hollow Crown Improved': 105 days; long, well-shaped roots for deep soil.

'Lancer': 120 days; long, slender, smooth roots; resistant to canker.

Root parsley
'Early Sugar': 78 days; small, sweet white roots like Chantenay carrots; will grow in soil too heavy for parsnips.

'Hamburg': 85 days; 6-8 in (15-20 cm) long, tapered, parsniplike roots.

Salsify
'Mammoth Sandwich Island': 120 days; off-white skin and white flesh; rich flavor.

Scorzonera
'Lange Jan': 120 days; long, cylindrical, black-skinned roots with white flesh; delicate flavor.

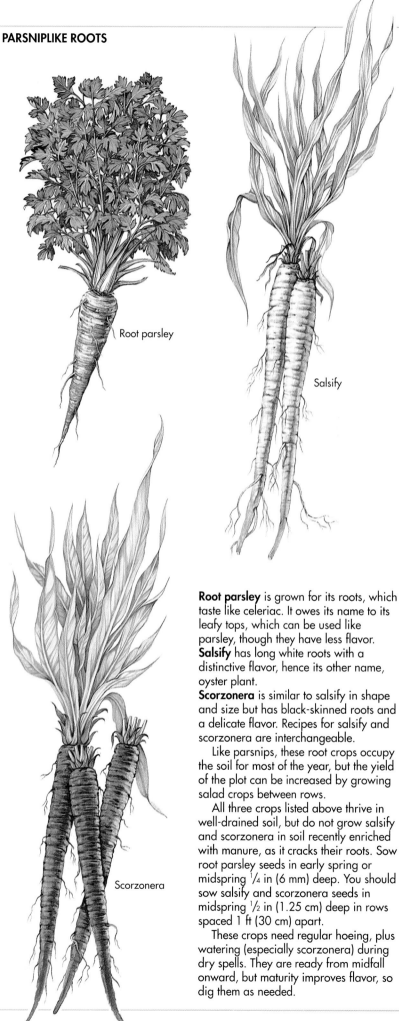

PARSNIPLIKE ROOTS

Root parsley

Salsify

Scorzonera

Root parsley is grown for its roots, which taste like celeriac. It owes its name to its leafy tops, which can be used like parsley, though they have less flavor.
Salsify has long white roots with a distinctive flavor, hence its other name, oyster plant.
Scorzonera is similar to salsify in shape and size but has black-skinned roots and a delicate flavor. Recipes for salsify and scorzonera are interchangeable.

Like parsnips, these root crops occupy the soil for most of the year, but the yield of the plot can be increased by growing salad crops between rows.

All three crops listed above thrive in well-drained soil, but do not grow salsify and scorzonera in soil recently enriched with manure, as it cracks their roots. Sow root parsley seeds in early spring or midspring ¼ in (6 mm) deep. You should sow salsify and scorzonera seeds in midspring ½ in (1.25 cm) deep in rows spaced 1 ft (30 cm) apart.

These crops need regular hoeing, plus watering (especially scorzonera) during dry spells. They are ready from midfall onward, but maturity improves flavor, so dig them as needed.

PEAS

Freshly picked garden peas have a superb flavor. They need a fair amount of attention and take up a lot of space but are well worth the effort.

There are two main types of garden pea: round-seed and edible-pod. Peas that have round seeds, known as green or English peas, must be shelled before cooking. Edible-pod peas may be eaten whole, just as they come from the vine; this group includes both snow peas and snap peas.

Both groups of peas have dwarf and vining cultivars. The vining cultivars must be provided with twigs or trellises on which to climb, while the dwarf peas grow unsupported. Depending on the cultivar, peas grow to heights of 1½-8 ft (45-240 cm). The taller, vining types involve more work for the gardener, but they produce roughly two or three times as many peas as the smaller, dwarf types.

Finally, peas are often classified as early, midseason, or late cultivars, depending on how quickly they bear pods.

Peas are a cool-weather crop sown early in the spring or sometimes, where winters are mild, in the late fall. Depending on the sowing date and the local climate, pea pods are ready for picking from midspring to early summer. Where summers are not too hot and dry, a late-summer sowing may also yield a fall crop.

Peas are prone to a number of pests and diseases and yield a comparatively small crop, considering the amount of space they take up. Yet they are well worth growing, since the flavor of freshly picked garden peas is so much finer than that of any peas you can buy, even at a farm stand. This is because the sugar in peas begins turning into starch the moment the pod is picked; just a couple of days on the shelf robs them of their special sweetness.

GREEN PEAS

Possibly the oldest of the cultivars, green peas were first grown in the Middle East. The peas are best fresh, but some cultivars can be dried. While the pods are usually discarded, you can use them in pea soup.

Planning the crop

Peas grow best in rich, well-drained but moisture-retentive soil. Because the seeds will rot in cold, wet soil, good drainage is especially important when planting seeds of early cultivars.

Dig the plot at least three or four weeks before sowing, working in two buckets of well-rotted manure or compost per sq yd/m. A week before sowing, rake in a topdressing of 5-10-10 fertilizer at a rate of 1-1½ lb (450-680 g) per 100 sq ft (9 sq m).

Growing green peas

If you plan to grow a number of rows, make the distance between the rows the same as the full-grown height of the plants. Early-maturing cultivars and dwarf cultivars reach a height of 1½-2 ft (45-60 cm); however, the later-maturing green pea cultivars can grow as high as 6 ft (1.8 m).

The earlier you plant in spring, within reason, the bigger the harvest will be. Generally, peas will stop bearing pods when the temperature rises above 75°F (24°C). But planting too early, while the soil is still soggy and cooler than 40°F (4.5°C), may cause the seeds in the soil to rot. Typically, four to six weeks before the last frost date is an ideal time for sowing. You can plant a week or two earlier if you are growing the peas in a raised bed.

Use a swan-neck hoe or a short-handled onion hoe to dig flat-bottomed planting drills (shallow trenches) 4 in (10 cm) wide and 1½-2 in (3.75-5 cm) deep. In spring and summer sow the seeds 2-3 in (5-7.5 cm) deep in three staggered rows in the drills. Sow overwintering cultivars a little more thickly to compensate for losses due to rotting seeds.

Pea seeds sometimes germinate poorly, or they may be dug up by mice. To fill any subsequent gaps in the rows, sow extra seeds in peat pots or spaced in trays. Once these seedlings have fully developed, transplant them into the gaps.

Edible-pod pea 'Sugar Ann'

Green pea 'Knight'

▲ **Pea classification** Peas are divided into two types: round-seed and edible-pod. Although they look similar, the cultivar 'Sugar Ann' bears pods that may be eaten whole, while 'Knight' bears peas that must be shelled from the pods before cooking.

Peas depend on a partnership with beneficial soil. If you are planting peas in a spot where they have never grown before, dust the seeds with a legume inoculant (available at garden centers) before planting them.

After sowing the seeds, you should level the surface by drawing the soil over the drills with the back of a rake; then firm the soil lightly.

Right after sowing, protect the seeds from birds by covering the rows with netting, black thread crisscrossed from sticks close to the ground, or clusters of twigs.

When the seedlings emerge, hoe on each side of the rows to get rid of weeds. When the seedlings are 3 in (7.5 cm) high, push in small twiggy sticks to encourage the plants to climb. Do not delay in giving this support because plants left to straggle on the ground are vulnerable to attacks by slugs and snails.

Once the plants are growing strongly, it's time to put in the final supports. These should be at least as high as the ultimate height of the plants. For final supports, use long twiggy branches; or stretch chicken wire or netting between stakes inserted into the ground 6 ft (1.8 m) apart.

Make sure the peas receive a constant supply of moisture. Water them regularly during dry spells, and give the rows a mulch of shredded leaves, straw, or even black plastic.

Harvesting and storing
When the pods seem to have reached their full length, check them daily by feeling the swelling peas inside the pods.

Aim to pick the pods when the seeds are well developed but before they are fully mature — about four weeks after the main flowering display. The pods at the base of the plants will be the first to ripen.

To harvest the pods, pull them upward with one hand while holding the stem with the other. With regular picking, more pods are likely to develop.

As soon as the plants stop bearing pods, cut the top growth down, and either put the roots on the compost pile or dig them into the soil. They are rich in nitrogen and will help to improve fertility.

Surplus green peas are excellent for freezing.

Pests and diseases
Aphids often infest growing vines. Pea weevils (tiny brown, black- and white-spotted beetles) chew holes in leaves, and their larvae tunnel into pods. Severe infestations may require a pyrethrin spray. Slugs also attack young vines and leaves; control them with traps or bait.

Diseases likely to affect peas include powdery mildew, root-rot fungi, and fusarium wilt. Crop rotation and good cultural practices are the best prevention.

SOWING AND SUPPORTING PEAS

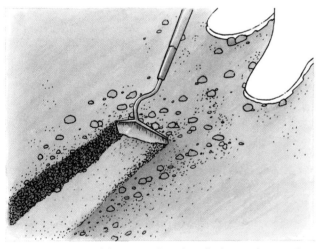

1 Using a swan-neck hoe or a short-handled onion hoe, make straight and fairly shallow drills, 1½-2 in (3.75-5 cm) deep and 4 in (10 cm) wide. Use short, smooth motions and keep the depth even. Allow 2-4 ft (60-120 cm) between rows.

2 Sow the seeds 2-3 in (5-7.5 cm) apart in three staggered rows. Sow peas for winter crops somewhat more thickly to compensate for any possible losses. After sowing, gently draw the soil over the drills with a rake and tamp it lightly.

3 Short twiggy sticks will start the peas climbing. Insert the twigs when the young plants are about 3 in (7.5 cm) high. Don't delay in providing support — plants sprawling over the ground may be attacked by slugs.

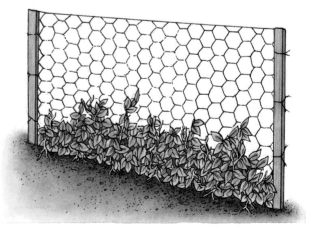

4 The final supports should be at least as high as the ultimate height of the plants. Use wire or plastic mesh tied to posts or long twiggy branches stuck upright and interwoven in a row. Water regularly during dry spells.

CULTIVARS TO CHOOSE

Green peas

'Alaska': 55 days from sowing to harvest; 2½ in (6.25 cm) long pods with six to eight small peas; 3-4 ft (90-120 cm) tall vines suitable for trellising; popular cultivar for drying peas.

'Burpeeana Early': 63 days; 3 in (7.5 cm) long pods with 8 to 10 medium to large peas; 2 ft (60 cm) tall vines.

'Daybreak': 52 days; 3 in (7.5 cm) long pods, six to eight medium peas; 2 ft (60 cm) tall vines need no support; early-maturing cultivar; easy to shell.

'Knight': 56 days; large, 4 in (10 cm) long pods, up to 10 peas; 2 ft (60 cm) tall vines.

'Little Marvel': 59 days; wrinkled; sweet and juicy; pods produced in pairs; 20 in (50 cm) tall vines.

'Multistar': 70 days; paired, 2½-3½ in (6.25-9 cm) long pods filled with sweet, slightly small peas; 3½-4½ ft (1.1-1.4 m) tall vines require trellising; tolerates heat; late-maturing cultivar.

'Tall Telephone' ('Alderman'): 68 days; 4 in (10 cm) long pods with eight large peas; 40 in (100 cm) tall vines, suitable for trellising.

'Wando': 68 days; pods hold seven to eight medium peas; heat-tolerant cultivar, suitable for late crops or warm-weather regions.

Edible-pod peas

'Oregon Giant': 60 days; early snow pea type; 4½ in (11.5 cm) flat pods; 2½ ft (75 cm) vines can be grown without support.

'Oregon Sugar Pod': 68 days; fleshy pods of snow pea type, 4-4½ in (10-11.5 cm) long; pick young; 3½-4 ft (105-120 cm) tall vines need support.

'Sugar Ann': 52 days; sweet, crisp pods; early-maturing cultivar; 2½ ft (75 cm) tall vines can be grown without support.

'Sugar Snap': 70 days; fleshy pods that are stringless when young; eat whole pods or allow seeds to mature and shell them; 5-6 ft (1.5-1.8 m) tall vines will require support.

Green pea 'Knight'   **Snow pea** 'Oregon Sugar Pod'

Green pea 'Daybreak'

Edible-pod pea 'Sugar Snap'

EDIBLE-POD PEAS

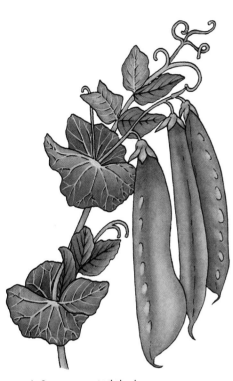

▲ **Snow peas** While these peas are grown in much the same way as green peas, snow peas are eaten whole, with the peas still in the pods. Pick the pods young, before the seeds start to swell.

Edible-pod peas are known as snow peas and snap peas (or sugar peas). They are similar to green peas, but the pods are bright green, more tender, thin-skinned, and often stringless. The whole pod is eaten, cooked or raw.

Edible-pod peas are available from supermarkets and produce stores, but as with green peas, homegrown ones are superior.

Pick snow peas while they are still young and cook them whole. Snap peas are grown and used in the same way, but you can leave their pods on the vine for the peas to swell without any loss of the sweet flavor.

Planning the crop

These peas like rich, well-drained soil. Dig the plot over several weeks before sowing; work in two buckets of well-rotted manure or compost to the sq yd/m. A week before sowing, rake in a topdressing of 5-10-10 fertilizer, 1-1½ lb (450-680 g) per 100 sq ft (9 sq m).

Growing edible-pod peas

Dig trenches 2 in (5 cm) deep, 2 ft (60 cm) wide, and spaced as far apart as the height of the grown plants. Sow the seeds in double rows, 2-3 in (5-7.5 cm) apart, in the trenches.

A first sowing produces pods about two months later. Sow at the same time as green peas, when the soil just starts to warm up. Typically, four to six weeks before the last frost date is a good time. You can plant a week or two earlier if you are growing the peas in a raised bed. If you are planting in a spot where peas have not grown before, first dust the seeds with legume inoculant.

To protect seeds from birds, cover the rows with netting, black thread, or twigs. When the seedlings are growing strongly, insert tall twiggy branches for support.

Water the crop well in dry weather, and mulch with shredded leaves or straw.

Harvesting

Harvest snow peas while they are still young and before the peas in the pods begin to swell. Leave snap peas on the vine until they develop a full, rounded shape.

Pick the pods in the same way as ordinary peas, pulling upward while holding the stem secure.

WINGED PEAS

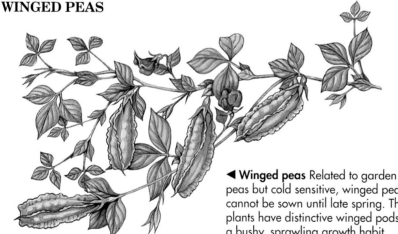

◀ **Winged peas** Related to garden peas but cold sensitive, winged peas cannot be sown until late spring. The plants have distinctive winged pods and a bushy, sprawling growth habit.

The winged pea takes its name from flattened ribs that run from end to end on the pods. The pods are cooked whole. They have an asparagus-like flavor, which is why the plant is sometimes called asparagus pea. The plant itself looks different from other peas, having a bushy, sprawling habit.

Planning the crop

Winged peas grow best in well-drained, fertile soil in a sunny spot. In the fall or winter before sowing, prepare the bed by digging in some well-rotted manure or compost. Before planting, rake in a topdressing of 5-10-10 fertilizer at a rate of about 1-1½ lb (450-680 g) per 100 sq ft (9 sq m).

A 20 ft (6 m) row will provide regular pickings for a family of four during late summer.

Growing winged peas

Winged peas are not cold hardy. In mild climates, sow the seeds directly into the garden after all danger of frost has passed. Plant the seeds 2 in (5 cm) deep, putting two seeds together in groups 8 in (20 cm) apart. Space rows 1½ ft (45 cm) apart. After the seedlings emerge, remove the weaker one of each pair.

In the North start the peas indoors in peat pots filled with sterilized potting mix a month before the last frost date. Plant the seeds 1 in (2.5 cm) deep, moisten the pots, and set them on a sunny windowsill. Plant the seedlings out 8 in (20 cm) apart in late spring, when the danger of frost has passed.

A second sowing can be made a few weeks later to give a succession of peas. Support the plants with twiggy sticks.

Harvesting and storing

Pick the pods when they reach 1-1½ in (2.5-3.75 cm) long. Longer pods are stringy and lose their flavor. To pick the pods, pull them up with one hand while supporting the stem with the other hand.

Go over the plants daily, because regular picking will help to prolong the production of pods.

Pests and diseases

Winged peas can suffer from the same pests as other peas, though they are generally disease free.

PEPPERS

**Brilliantly colored sweet and hot peppers
flourish in the South, and with a little extra attention
they will bear well in the North.**

Both sweet peppers and hot peppers, or chilies, are good performers in our hotter, sunnier regions. With a bit of care, they can do well in northern states, too.

Gardeners with greenhouses will find that peppers make a highly ornamental winter crop and that even a small harvest provides a great deal of flavor.

Planning the crop

Grown outside, sweet peppers need fertile, moist but well-drained soil and a sunny, sheltered site. In the North choose a warm microclimate, such as a bed at the foot of a south-facing wall.

Enrich the soil with well-rotted manure or compost during winter digging; keep it well watered. Before planting, rake in 2 oz (57 g) of a general fertilizer per sq yd/m.

For greenhouse cultivation, prepare 9 in (23 cm) pots with potting mix, or use commercially available soil-filled grow bags.

Sowing and planting

Because the seeds take a long time to germinate, peppers are often started indoors. Purchase transplants at a garden center, or sow seeds yourself for a greater selection of cultivars.

Two months before the last frost date, sow seeds indoors in peat pots filled with sterilized seed-starting mix. Sow three seeds to a pot, and keep the pots at a temperature of 75°F (24°C).

In three to four weeks, when the seeds sprout, move the pots to a warm, sunny windowsill. When the seedlings are 2-3 in (5-7.5 cm) tall, thin to one seedling per pot, leaving the strongest plant.

Harden the seedlings off and transplant them when the soil warms to 60°F (15.5°C), two to three weeks after the last frost. Plant them 1½ ft (45 cm) apart in rows 2 ft (60 cm) apart. Dig planting holes with a trowel. Mix 1 teaspoon of 5-10-10 fertilizer into the soil below each hole; cover this with 1 in (2.5 cm) of unfertilized soil. Drop in the seedlings; if exposed to wind, stake them.

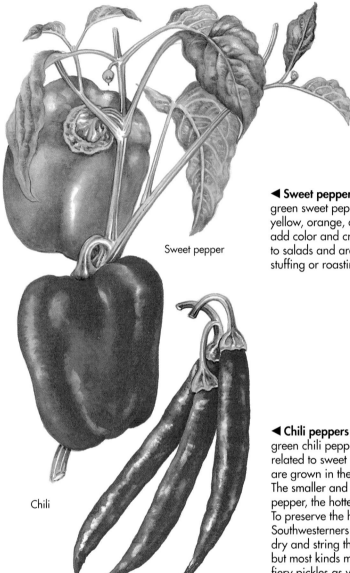

Sweet pepper

Chili

◄ **Sweet peppers** Glossy green sweet peppers ripen to yellow, orange, or red. They add color and crunchy texture to salads and are good for stuffing or roasting.

◄ **Chili peppers** Red and green chili peppers are related to sweet peppers and are grown in the same way. The smaller and redder the pepper, the hotter it will be. To preserve the harvest, Southwesterners commonly dry and string their chilies, but most kinds make excellent fiery pickles as well.

GROWING GREENHOUSE PEPPERS

1 When the plants are 6 in (15 cm) high, pinch off the growing points. Support each plant with a stake inserted in the pot, bag, or the soil.

2 Mist the plants daily when in flower to help distribute pollen and to discourage spider mites. After the fruits appear, apply a liquid fertilizer every 10 days.

If the weather is dry, water the plants weekly, soaking the soil deeply. At the onset of hot weather, spread an organic mulch, such as shredded leaves or straw.

Two months after setting out the seedlings, side-dress them with 5-10-10 fertilizer. Broadcast it over the bed at a rate of 5 cups (1.2 L) per 100 sq ft (9 sq m).

Greenhouse peppers
Start seedlings from midsummer to early fall. When they are 4 in (10 cm) tall, transfer them to individual grow bags or 9 in (23 cm) pots of sterilized potting mix.

To support the plants, insert 3 ft (90 cm) tall stakes in the pot or bag and tie the plants to them. Spray the flowers daily with water to help spread the pollen and discourage spider mite attacks. When the plants are 6 in (15 cm) high, pinch back the growing points to encourage branching.

After the first fruits appear, apply liquid fertilizer every 10 days. Keep the plants well watered.

Harvesting and storing
Early in the season, pick sweet peppers while young. If they ripen, the plant may stop bearing. Later in the summer let peppers ripen from green to red, yellow, or orange. The riper the pepper, the sweeter or hotter it will be.

Pests and diseases
Cutworms, flea beetles, and European corn borers are the most common insect pests. Diseases include anthracnose, mosaic virus, and tomato spotted wilt.

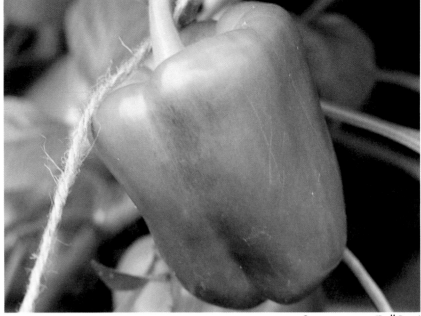

Sweet pepper 'Bell Boy'

Sweet pepper 'Gypsy'

Chili pepper 'Serrano'

CULTIVARS TO CHOOSE

Sweet peppers
'Ace': 60 days from transplanting to harvest; early, prolific; suitable for greenhouse or outdoors.

'Bell Boy': 70 days; prolific; suitable for greenhouse and outdoors; thick-walled fruits maturing to red.

'Chocolate Beauty': 88 days; sweet fruits mature from green to brown; resistant to mosaic virus.

'Corno di Toro': 68 days; curved, red-and-yellow "bull's-horn" fruits.

'Cubanelle': 65 days; yellow-green frying peppers.

'Gypsy': 60 days; early; yellow-green fruits ripen to deep red.

'Redskin': 65 days; dwarf plant for greenhouses or containers; green bell fruits mature to bright red.

Chili peppers
'Jalapeno': 70 days; thick, dark green fruits ripen to red; 3½ in (9 cm) long; medium hot.

'Long Red Cayenne': 75 days; thin green fruits ripen to crimson-red; 2-3 in (5-7.5 cm) long; very hot.

'Serrano': 105 days; red fruits; very hot; ideal for drying.

POTATOES

Few vegetables are as versatile as potatoes — and these popular tubers don't have to take up a lot of space in the garden.

Homegrown potatoes offer a couple of significant advantages over those from supermarkets. To begin with, the supermarket offers only a few types, but the home gardener can select from dozens of cultivars: yellow potatoes, russets, blue potatoes, pink potatoes, purple potatoes, fingerlings, and giants. Besides, if harvested at the peak of their flavor, homegrown potatoes offer a treat no store-bought tuber can match.

Potatoes are easy to grow. They can be expansive when grown in a field, but they provide one of the most productive crops. New styles of cultivation make potatoes a practical choice for small gardens, too.

In general, potatoes are classified by the length of time they require to reach maturity from the planting out of seed potatoes. There are early-season cultivars, which require 65 or more days; midseason potatoes need 80 or more days; and late potatoes need 90 or more days. Though traditionally potatoes are started from pieces of tubers — so-called seed potatoes — some newer cultivars allow the gardener to start the plants from true seeds.

Soil and site preparation

Potatoes grow reasonably well in most soils, although heavy clay soil may stunt the tubers. If your soil is heavy, dig in plenty of well-rotted manure or compost. This is a good prescription for almost any soil on which potatoes are to be grown — several weeks before planting, work in compost or well-rotted manure at the rate of a bucketful per sq yd/m. At planting time, broadcast 5-10-10 fertilizer over the prepared soil at a rate of 1½ lb (680 g) per 100 sq ft (9 sq m).

Test the soil's pH before planting. A slightly acid soil with a pH of 6.0-6.5 supports the best growth. Alkaline soils should be treated with sulfur or sphagnum peat to bring them down to an acceptable pH.

Potatoes need an open site with full sun. To prevent the buildup of soil-borne pests and diseases, rotate the crops to avoid growing potatoes on the same site in consecutive years.

▲ **New potatoes** The unique flavor and firm texture of these young potatoes depend on careful hilling up of the soil to protect developing tubers from all light. Dig the potatoes when the tubers are the size of a golf ball — they are ready when the plants blossom.

Ordering seed potatoes

For the majority of potato cultivars, it is necessary to start from pieces of tubers (seed potatoes). It is best to buy these from a reputable nursery, which certifies that its stock is free of viral diseases. The local garden center may offer seed potatoes in spring, but a far greater selection may be had from mail-order nurseries.

A couple of days before planting, examine the seed potatoes and cut the larger ones into pieces. Each piece should have at least one "eye" (a dormant bud) and should be about the size of a large ice cube. Cutting the seed potatoes into many small pieces will result in more plants but a smaller harvest of tubers.

◀ **Homegrown potatoes** The variety of cultivars available to the gardener makes growing (and eating) potatoes a treat. The cultivars shown (clockwise, from top left) are 'Red Pontiac,' 'Green Mountain,' 'Caribe,' and 'Purple Peruvian.'

GROWING POTATOES

1 Some gardeners prefer to sprout seed potatoes before planting because it may hasten the crop. To do this, set seed-potato pieces (with eyes upward) in egg cartons four to six weeks before planting. Keep them in a cool, light place until the sprouts are ½-1 in (1.25-2.5 cm) tall.

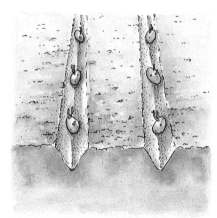

2 Plant the sprouting potatoes in furrows 6 in (15 cm) deep in rows 2 ft (60 cm) apart for early cultivars, 2½ ft (75 cm) apart for mid- and late-season ones. Set early potatoes 1 ft (30 cm) apart and main-crop cultivars 15 in (38 cm) apart. Cover with a shallow ridge of soil.

3 Begin hilling up potatoes when the top growth of the plants reaches 9 in (23 cm) high. Break up the soil between the rows with a garden fork, then use a hoe to draw the soil up around the stems of the plants, making a ridge about 6 in (15 cm) high. Hill the soil up again two to three weeks later.

After cutting, let the pieces of seed potato cure for a couple of days. Leave them in a humid place at a temperature of about 70°F (21°C). Then dust them with sulfur powder right before planting to protect against rot.

Planting

Plant early cultivars six to eight weeks before the last spring frost or as soon as the soil has dried enough to be worked. Midseason and late cultivars should go in the soil somewhat later — make sure late cultivars will have enough time to mature (90-100 days) before the first fall frost.

In the South begin spring planting as early as January in Florida, or February in Texas and Oklahoma; continue to the end of March in the upper South. There is also a late-summer planting season in this part of the country, from mid-August through September, which yields a fall crop.

To plant, use a hoe to make furrows 6 in (15 cm) deep and 2 ft (60 cm) apart for early cultivars or 2½ ft (75 cm) apart for midseason and late cultivars. Or plant potatoes in holes 6 in (15 cm) deep with a trowel.

Set the sprouted tubers in the furrows 1 ft (30 cm) apart for early cultivars and 15 in (38 cm) apart for midseason and late potatoes. Place them with the eyes uppermost. Pull the soil back over the furrow, taking care not to damage the eyes. Draw up enough soil to make a slight ridge over the line of planted potatoes.

Caring for the crop

As the first shoots appear, increase the height of the soil ridge as protection against late-spring frosts. Hill up again two to three weeks later, using a hoe to draw up the soil from between the rows. This increases the amount of soil over the roots and encourages them to spread and form tubers. It also reduces the risk of potatoes being exposed to light

▼ **Digging potatoes** Use a garden fork to lift plants out of the ground and dislodge all the tubers. The empty bed left by early potatoes can be replanted with a fall crop of some other vegetable.

and becoming green and poisonous (always cut off green portions of tubers before cooking).

When hilling up for the second time, fertilize with 5-10-10, applying about 1 lb (450 g) per 25 ft (7.5 m) of row.

You will have to hill up over mid- and late-season cultivars a couple of more times, doing this every few weeks until the foliage meets between the rows. The leaves will then shade the tubers.

Hilling up offers a bonus. The frequent moving of soil during the cultivation of potatoes helps rid the vegetable plot of weeds.

If the weather is dry, water potatoes regularly, especially as the tubers start to form 6 to 10 weeks after planting.

If pests and diseases trouble potatoes in your area, consider applying a potato spray or dust that mixes approved fungicides and insecticides. Another effective response is to plant disease-resistant cultivars. Crop rotation is especially important to producing healthy potato crops.

Harvesting

The first harvest comes when the plants flower. Pull aside the earth at the base of the plants, and pick off a few golf-ball-size tubers — these are "new potatoes." Push the soil back in place afterward so

that the remaining tubers will continue to grow and mature.

Early-season cultivars begin to mature 10 weeks after planting. Midseason cultivars will be ready for harvest about 12 weeks after planting, while late-season types mature in 13 to 14 weeks. In general, when the foliage begins to wither and die, it is a sign that the tubers are ready for digging.

When digging potatoes, insert the fork straight into the ground at least 6 in (15 cm) away from the stems to avoid spearing the tubers. Dig only as many tubers as you need at the time.

Storing potatoes

On a dry day, dig the potatoes, shake the soil off them, and leave the tubers on the ground to dry for a few hours. Check the tubers. Store only healthy ones in a cool, dry, frost-free place. Put them in lightproof but ventilated containers, such as boxes or paper bags, or pile them on a dry floor and cover with straw. They should keep until the following spring.

Never store damaged or diseased potatoes, as they will infect others nearby. Check stored potatoes every few weeks, and remove any that show signs of rotting. Use the potatoes before the eyes start growing white sprouts. Cut away and discard any green flesh.

▲ **Potatoes without hills** Eliminate the hilling-up process by growing potatoes under a black plastic mulch. Make slits in the plastic for the plants to grow through.

Other cultivation methods

Potatoes can be grown under a sheet of black plastic, which does away with the laborious hilling-up process. Plant the tubers as described before, and cover them with the plastic sheet. Anchor it at the edges with heavy stones. When the shoots start pushing against the plastic, cut holes in the plastic to allow the sprouts to grow through.

When the potatoes are ready, most of the tubers will be near the surface. Remove the plastic sheet and begin gathering potatoes of harvestable size. Replace the plastic sheet until the remaining tubers have matured.

Where space is limited, grow potatoes in plastic barrels. Drill holes in the barrel's bottom for drainage, and add 1 ft (30 cm) of loose, loamy soil heavily enriched with compost. Plant three or four seed potatoes in the barrel, and as the shoots grow, add more potting soil or enriched garden soil until the barrel is full. Then leave the tubers to grow to maturity. This growing method is more suitable for a small crop of early potatoes than for a crop of mid- and late-season types.

Finally, there are now a few potato cultivars, such as 'Homestead,' that may be grown from true seeds. Start these indoors in

◀ **Potato barrel** To grow potatoes in a plastic barrel, drill holes in the barrel's bottom for drainage. Pour 1 ft (30 cm) of compost-enriched soil into it, then plant three or four potatoes. Gradually fill the barrel with more soil as the plants grow.

peat pots eight weeks before the last frost date in spring. Keep the pots at 70°F (21°C) until the seeds germinate, then move them to a sunny but cool windowsill. Harden off the seedlings and plant them outdoors as soon as all danger of frost is past, spacing them as with seed potatoes.

Pests and diseases

The most common pests of the potato are aphids, flea beetles, Colorado potato beetles, leafhoppers, wireworms, and slugs. Chemical controls can be effective but must be applied regularly.

The diseases likely to occur are early and late potato blight, scab, and mosaic viruses. Crop rotation and good cultural practices can minimize these problems; plant seed potatoes certified as disease-free or disease-resistant cultivars.

CULTIVARS TO CHOOSE

From seed potatoes

'All Red': midseason; brilliant red-skinned tubers with pinkish flesh.

'Caribe': early; purple skin and white flesh; good for boiling, not baking or storage; high-yielding plants.

'Gold Rush': midseason; long russet-skinned tubers with white flesh.

'Green Mountain': late; heirloom cultivar; excellent for baking.

'Kennebec': late; large yields of buff-skinned, white-fleshed, flavorful, very big, oval tubers; disease- and drought-resistant plant.

'Purple Peruvian': midseason; fingerling type; long, thin tubers with purple skin and purple flesh.

'Red Pontiac': late; big, round tubers with deep red skin and white flesh; high-yielding plant; excellent for cooking fresh.

'Russian Banana': midseason; small, long, slender, yellow-skinned tubers; excellent harvested as new potatoes; good for storage at maturity; hardy, cold-tolerant, and disease-resistant plant produces huge yields.

'Yukon Gold': early; medium large, oval tubers with yellow skin and yellow flesh; stores well; large, disease-resistant plant.

From seeds

'Homestead': late; vigorous, high-yielding plant that produces 4 in (10 cm) tubers within 90 days of transplanting.

SWEET POTATOES

Because of its edible roots, the sweet potato plant is commonly classed as a potato, though it is more closely related to the morning-glory. Tropical in origin, the plant is extremely frost sensitive. Traditionally a southern crop, it flourishes in the long, hot growing season of the southeastern states, but northern gardeners have found that they can reap big harvests by planting the sweet potato in raised beds with soil warmed by a black plastic mulch.

Sweet potatoes require a sunny spot and well-drained, loose, fertile soil. When the soil warms to 60°F (15.5°C), till or dig a bed 8-10 in (20-25 cm) deep, working in a couple of inches of compost. In the North cover the soil with a sheet of black plastic, anchoring it in place by burying the edges.

Plant root sprouts (also called slips) purchased from a reputable nursery. Set these out two to three weeks after the last spring frost, making holes 6 in (15 cm) deep and 1 ft (30 cm) apart. Plant through slits cut into the black plastic mulch. Bury the sprouts up to the top leaves, firm in the soil around them, and water well.

If you prefer not to use black plastic, you can control weeds and encourage root development by spreading an organic mulch around the vines two weeks after planting. Periodically lift longer vines off the ground to discourage them from rooting at the nodes, which diverts energy from the formation of tubers.

Apply 1 in (2.5 cm) of water weekly in dry weather. Harvest roots any time after the leaves start to yellow but before the first frost, since that will rot tubers. Dig roots on a dry, sunny day, carefully turning the soil with a garden fork.

Northern gardeners typically find sweet potatoes a pest-free crop. Southerners may encounter sweet potato weevils, whose larvae tunnel into roots. Fungal diseases include black rot and stem rot. To minimize these problems, plant only disease-free sprouts, rotate crops, and avoid injury to the growing vines.

Popular cultivars include the bush-type 'Vardaman,' which bears large yields of orange-fleshed roots, and 'Centennial,' an early-maturing type good for northern gardens.

▶ **Harvesting sweet potatoes** Dig roots on a dry, sunny day, carefully turning the soil with a garden fork.

RADISHES

Quick-growing radishes mature in a few weeks and take up little space. Grow them among slow-growing vegetables.

Radishes are divided into two main categories: spring and winter. Spring radishes are usually small, red or white in color, and are used in salads. Winter radishes are larger (½ lb/230 g or more in weight) and black, white, or red in color; they are also good in salads and are a suitable addition to soups. Spring radishes are very quick to mature, making them a good choice for interplanting between rows of slow-maturing crops, such as cabbage and leeks.

Radishes are a cool-weather crop. Plant spring radishes as soon as the soil can be worked in spring, but wait until mid- to late summer to sow winter radishes for a fall harvest.

Preparing the site
As they are not in the ground for more than a few weeks, spring radishes do not need a deeply dug plot. However, they do grow better — especially as the weather becomes warmer — in fertile, moisture-retentive, well-drained soil. Dig well-rotted compost into the top 3-4 in (7.5-10 cm) of soil at the rate of a bucketful per sq yd/m. Winter radishes grow best in soil that was enriched for a previous crop.

Spring radishes
In spring make the first sowing as soon as the soil dries out enough

to be dug. Rake the soil to a fine tilth, then sow the radish seeds about ¼ in (6 mm) deep in rows spaced 6 in (15 cm) apart. Sow the seeds ½ in (1.25 cm) apart. Do not sow them thickly, or the plants will produce foliage at the expense of the roots.

Keep the soil moist to maintain growth. You should protect the seeds from birds by covering the bed with netting; alternatively, stretch black threads crisscross between stakes.

To ensure a continuous and manageable supply of tender radishes, sow only a couple of feet of row at a time and sow in weekly intervals until warm weather starts to set in with late spring. Don't sow too many seeds at one time, creating a larger than needed harvest. If the plants are left in the ground for more than a week or two after maturing, the roots

Long-rooted white spring radish

Globe-shaped spring radish

Long-rooted spring radish

Winter radish

▲ **Radish types** Globe-shaped or long-rooted spring radishes are eaten raw — they are often added to salads. The hot-flavored winter radishes may also be cooked in soups.

◄ **Sowing radishes** Radish seeds are fairly large and can easily be spread evenly in rows. The spring radishes shown here are being sown ¼ in (6 mm) deep. Firm down the soil over the seeds, and water lightly. Protect the seeds by covering the bed with netting or with black thread crisscrossed between stakes.

◀ **Interplanting** Quick-growing radishes are ideal for growing between slower-growing vegetables, such as cabbage. They will be out of the ground before they can crowd the other crop.

If radishes are attacked by flea beetles (look for small holes in the leaves), dust or spray with a recommended insecticide.

CULTIVARS TO CHOOSE

Spring radishes

'Cherry Belle': 24 days from sowing to harvest; round; bright scarlet root; remains crisp longer than most cultivars.

'Easter Egg': 30 days; red, pink, purple, or white root; crisp and mild, even when large.

'French Breakfast': 25 days; long-rooted type; red with white tip; crisp and mild.

'Scarlet Globe': 23 days; round; all-red root; matures quickly.

'Sparkler': 25 days; round; scarlet-tipped white root; crisp and sweet.

'White Icicle': 30 days; long-rooted type; white; crisp, nutty flavor.

Winter radishes

'Black Spanish': 70 days; long-rooted type; black skin and white flesh (must be peeled).

'Chinese Rose': 55 days; oval root; rose skin, crisp white flesh.

'Round Black Spanish': 55 days; round; black skin and white flesh (needs peeling).

---

will become woody and lose their crispness and flavor.

Winter radishes
Sow the large-rooted winter cultivars from midsummer to late summer. Sow seeds, one every few inches, ½ in (1.25 cm) deep in rows 1 ft (30 cm) apart. Thin the young plants to 8 in (20 cm) apart when large enough to handle. Always keep the soil well watered in dry weather, or the plants will not produce enough growth in fall.

Harvesting and storing
You can harvest spring radishes as needed while they are young and tender. Harvest the roots of winter radishes as they mature in the fall, or leave them in the ground into winter and dig them as needed. If you leave the roots in the ground into the cold weather, mulch over the bed with straw. Or dig the roots in midfall and store them in boxes of sand in a cool, airy place. Throughout winter check stored radishes regularly; discard any that show signs of either rot or mold.

Pests and diseases
Root maggots are the most serious pests. Protect the radishes with floating row covers, or dust the soil around the plants with wood ashes. Cutworms can be repelled by surrounding seedlings with cardboard or foil collars. Flea beetles eat the leaves of young plants, particularly during hot spells in late spring; spray with a recommended insecticide.

Spring radish 'French Breakfast'

Winter radish 'Round Black Spanish'

Spring radish 'Scarlet Globe'

RUTABAGAS AND TURNIPS

**Rutabagas are grown as fall or winter crops.
Turnips provide delicious spring and
fall harvests of roots and greens.**

Rutabagas and turnips are root crops and members of the brassica, or cabbage, family. Rutabagas have sweet yellow flesh and are especially flavorful if harvested young, before they develop woody cores. Turnips produce smaller, mainly white-fleshed roots. They too are sweet when young, and you can eat them raw when the size of golf balls. Each root has its advantages. Rutabagas store well but need a longer growing period; turnips produce greens that are delicious steamed or boiled.

Rutabagas and turnips will do best when grown in cool weather, flourishing in spring or fall. They need fertile, moisture-retentive, neutral to slightly alkaline soil. On hot, dry soil the foliage is susceptible to mildew and roots become tough and fibrous.

Sow rutabagas in late spring and early summer for a good fall crop; a mild frost will not harm them. In milder climates leave them in the soil through the winter and dig up as needed. In the North it is better to dig the crop all at once and store it indoors.

Sow turnips in midsummer for a fall crop. Early cultivars are available for sowing in spring and for harvesting in early summer, when they are small and tender.

You can leave a fall crop of turnips in the ground through the first frosts. Older roots are less tasty than younger ones, but they are good in casseroles and stews.

Cultivation

Sow both vegetables directly into the bed where they are to grow. Plant rutabagas in a bed vacated by a spring crop, such as peas. You can work quicker-growing turnips into the garden by planting them amid slower-developing crops, such as leeks or parsnips; the turnips are ready for digging six to eight weeks after sowing.

Turnips and rutabagas need full sun and an organically enriched soil loose enough for the roots to develop and expand without resistance. Avoid adding fresh manure; it makes the roots split.

Rutabaga

Globe
turnip

Flat-topped
turnip

Dig the soil well, and a week before sowing the seeds, work in 10-10-10 fertilizer at a rate of 4 lb (1.8 kg) per 100 sq ft (9 sq m). Test the soil. If it is acidic, add ground limestone to raise the pH to 6.5-7.0. Add about 5 lb (2.3 kg) of lime per 100 sq ft (9 sq m) for each point you wish to raise the pH (e.g., from 5.5 to 6.5).

Turnips should be sown three weeks before the last spring frost. They are cold tolerant and won't be damaged by a night or two of freezing temperatures. Sow fall crops in midsummer, two months before the first fall frost.

Sow the seeds ½ in (12 mm) deep in rows 1 ft (30 cm) apart.

Thin the seedlings to about 3-4 in (7.5-10 cm) apart when they are large enough to handle and again three weeks later. Or broadcast the seeds over a well-tilled bed; let the seeds fall ¼-½ in (6-12 mm) apart. Rake the bed to cover the seeds ½ in (12 mm) deep. When the seedlings are 4 in (10 cm) high, thin them so that they are 3-4 in (7.5-10 cm) apart.

Rutabagas are sown as for turnips, but 15 weeks before the first fall frost. When the seedlings emerge, thin them to 1 in (2.5 cm) apart. Two weeks later, thin them to 8 in (20 cm) apart.

For both crops, hoe regularly to control weeds. If the weather is

146

Rutabaga 'American Purple Top'

Turnip 'Purple Top White Globe'

Turnip 'Golden Ball'

CULTIVARS TO CHOOSE

Rutabagas
'American Purple Top': 90 days from sowing to harvest; purple top; sweet orange flesh; large globe; ready to dig from early fall.

'Laurentian': 90 days; purple top; yellow flesh; globe; hardy; good for overwintering and storing.

'Marian': 85 days; purple skin; yellow flesh; globe; bred for resistance to clubroot and mildew; good yields.

Turnips
'Gilfeather': 82 days; large root with green shoulders and white flesh; extra-sweet flavor improves with frost; good for fall crop.

'Golden Ball': 60 days; small top; tender yellow flesh; globe; keeps well; suitable for late sowing.

'Hakurei': 38 days; flat-topped root; delicate white flesh can be eaten raw; very early, matures just after radishes.

'Purple Top White Globe': 50 days; white flesh with purple top; traditional cultivar with traditional flavor.

'Shogoin': 30 days from sowing to harvestable greens; Asian cultivar grown for tender, mild greens; root matures to flat-topped white ball, 3-4 in (7.5-10 cm) diameter.

'Snowball': 40 days; white skin; mild-flavored, tender white flesh; globe; rapid grower.

'Tokyo Cross': 35 days; smooth white skin; globe; very quick to mature; can be sown as late as early fall.

---

dry, water deeply. Once a week apply 1 in (2.5 cm) of water, or the roots will grow tough and bitter.

Harvesting and storing
Pull spring turnips when they are the size of golf balls; if they grow larger, they become fibrous. Use them within a few days. Dig and store fall crops of turnips around the time of the first frost.

In milder climates, where the soil doesn't freeze, you can leave rutabagas in the ground over winter and dig them up as required — though the younger they are when harvested, the sweeter they taste.

Gently pry the roots out of the ground with a fork, and avoid bruising them.

To store rutabagas, twist the leaves off good unbruised roots and stack the roots on a bed of dry sand or soil in a box. Cover them with more sand or soil, and put the box in a cool, dry, frost-free garage, basement, or shed.

Pests and diseases
Army worms, flea beetles, cabbage root maggots, and leafhoppers can all be problems. To keep bugs out, use row covers of spun-bonded polypropylene. Spray or dust with recommended insecticides as necessary.

Clubroot, prevalent on poorly drained, acid soil, can ruin crops.

SPINACH

Leaf spinach is a cool-weather crop for spring and fall, but similar, spinachlike crops can provide tasty, nutritious harvests right through the hot weather.

Rich in iron and vitamins, spinach is quick and easy to grow in fertile, moisture-retentive but well-drained soil. New cultivars are less prone to bolting (running to flower prematurely); however, like the other cultivars, they are a cool-weather crop. You will have to restrict planting to early in the spring or after cool weather returns in the fall. In warm climates it helps to plant spinach in the shade of tall crops, such as corn or trellised beans. Or plant one of the similar-tasting greens that flourish in hot weather; these are the best plantings for northern summers, too.

Planning the crop

In order to produce large succulent leaves over an extended cropping period, grow spinach in rich, moist soil — ideally one that has recently been enriched with well-rotted manure or compost. Like radishes, fast-growing spinach is ideal for interplanting between other, slower-growing vegetables.

Growing summer cultivars

Plant spinach as soon as the soil can be worked in the spring and again in August for a fall crop. In areas where summers are cool, a second sowing may be made two weeks after the first to further prolong the harvest.

Before sowing, soak the seeds in water for 24 hours. Plant them about ½ in (1.25 cm) deep and 2 in (5 cm) apart all over the prepared bed. Because weak plants bolt more easily, sow the seeds thinly to encourage good-size plants. When they are 1 in (2.5 cm) tall, thin them to 4 in (10 cm) apart, then again to 6 in (15 cm) apart. (You can cook the last thinnings.)

Water liberally to reduce the risk of the plants going to seed. During dry spells, at least 1 in (2.5 cm) of water every week will be necessary.

Spinach doesn't grow well if the ground becomes too densely packed. Hoe carefully around the plants to break up the soil and remove any weeds.

Savoy-leaf spinach

Spinach is usually ready to pick eight weeks after sowing, though this varies with the cultivar. Pick up to half the outer leaves, but no more, from the plants just before they reach full size. Leave the rest for picking three or four days later. Continue to pick the plants every three or four days until they stop producing.

Growing a fall crop

Sowings for a fall crop may be made in late summer or early fall. To establish the latest safe date for sowing a fall crop of spinach, find out what the average date of the first fall frost is for your area, then count backward 45 days.

For the best fall harvest, sow seeds of a cultivar recommended for this purpose.

Harvesting

Break or cut the stalks — don't tear them off or you will damage the plants and prevent later leaves from growing.

Spinach deteriorates rapidly after picking. Use it as quickly as possible, while it is still crisp, or freeze it at once.

Pick the spinach just before cooking, cut off the stalks, and remove any coarse midribs. Wash thoroughly in several changes of water until all traces of sand and grit are gone. Drain well.

Pests and diseases

Spinach may be attacked by aphids, slugs, snails, flea beetles, and leafhoppers. Whitish tracks on the leaves mark the tunnels of leaf miner larvae; cut and dispose of marked leaves at once.

Downy mildew shows as grayish furry spots on the undersurfaces of leaves. Remove affected leaves and spray the remainder with a copper-based fungicide.

SPINACHLIKE LEAFY VEGETABLES

Several other leaf vegetables resemble spinach. Unlike spinach, some of them can tolerate hot weather — otherwise, they are grown, harvested, and used like true spinach cultivars.

SPINACH TYPES

▲ **New Zealand spinach** These plants produce spinachlike leaves on shoot tips. They are a good spinach substitute and tolerate drought without bolting. Strictly a summer crop, New Zealand spinach does well on moisture-retentive soil.

▲ **Perpetual spinach** (Spinach beet) This perennial vegetable bears spinachlike leaves. It is tolerant of frost and drought and can be harvested throughout the growing season. It stays in the ground a long time and needs well-enriched soil.

Malabar spinach flourishes in hot weather. It grows like a vine, producing long stems that run along the ground. You can grow it on a trellis, but because it does not twine or produce tendrils, you must tie it up.

Start the seeds indoors, six weeks ahead of planting time. Soak the seeds for two hours, then sow them ¼ in (6 mm) deep in flats of sterilized seed-starting mix. Water them well and set on a warm, sunny windowsill.

When the seedlings reach a height of 2 in (5 cm), transplant them to 4 in (10 cm) pots. Plant the seedlings outdoors when all danger of frost is past and the temperature, both night and day, averages 65°F (18.5°C). Set the seedlings 3 ft (90 cm) apart in a sunny spot on loose, rich soil. Pick leaves at random as they reach eating size.

New Zealand spinach is not hardy and you should not sow it until all danger of frost has passed. Soak the seeds overnight to aid germination. Sow the seeds 1 in (2.5 cm) deep in groups of two or three seeds; space them 12-15 in (30-38 cm) apart with 3 ft (90 cm) between rows.

Thin the seedlings to leave only the strongest in each group. These plants don't bolt but need conscientious irrigation. Pinch back growing tips to encourage more side shoots.

Harvest from early summer to early fall by picking young shoot tips with two to three leaves. Plants will produce more leaves if lightly but frequently picked.

Perpetual spinach, or spinach beet, is a perennial and does not begin to set seed until the second year. During the first year of growth it produces a succession of fresh leaves over a long period.

Plant the seeds 1 in (2.5 cm) deep and 9 in (23 cm) apart. Sow the seeds thinly in midspring for a summer and fall crop. Thin the seedlings to 8 in (20 cm) apart. Keep free of weeds, and water plants regularly during dry spells.

Pick the leaves regularly, before they grow big and coarse.

Swiss chard should be sown in midspring in good, moist soil. Thin the seedlings gradually until they stand 10 in (25 cm) apart. The plants produce large leaves, whose blades may be cooked like spinach. You can cook the midribs separately, like asparagus.

CULTIVARS TO CHOOSE

Spinach
'Bloomsdale Savoy': 50 days from sowing to harvest; thick, dark, savoyed (crumpled) leaves; excellent fresh in salads.

'Indian Summer': 39 days; thick, dark green, savoyed leaves with outstanding flavor; early-maturing plant but also slow to bolt; disease-resistant cultivar; spring or fall crops; good candidate for second sowing in spring.

'Olympia': 45 days; excellent for cooking or eating fresh; resistant to downy mildew; slow to bolt.

'Space': 39 days; smooth, upright leaves that are less likely to hold grit and mud, making them easier to clean before eating; compact, early-maturing, productive plant.

'Steadfast': 50 days; smooth green leaves with excellent flavor; exceptional resistance to downy mildew; very slow to bolt.

'Tyee': 45 days; semisavoyed leaves; very vigorous and disease-resistant cultivar; some resistance to bolting.

'Vienna': 40 days; long-lasting crops of dark green, thick, heavily savoyed leaves that resist downy mildew; outstandingly productive; good for early-spring or fall crops.

Malabar spinach
Heat loving, cold sensitive plant that is intolerant of frost; may be trained on trellis.

New Zealand spinach
There are no named cultivars; low, spreading plant with leafy shoot tips; easily killed by frost.

Perpetual spinach (spinach beet)
There are no named cultivars; hardy plant; good in dry soils where spinach might bolt.

Swiss chard
'Dorat': 60 days; pale green leaves; thick, mild-tasting stalks; cold- and drought-hardy plant.

'Fordhook Giant': 50 days; thick white stems for chards; 1½ft (45 cm) high; dark green leaves.

'Rhubarb Chard' ('Ruby Chard'): 59 days; productive; long, thick crimson stems; dark green leaves.

SPROUTING SEEDS

As a quick, cheap, and nutritious food crop, sprouting seeds are hard to beat, and they can be grown on a kitchen windowsill.

Alfalfa and mung bean sprouts are among the most familiar of edible sprouts, but there are many others, including azuki beans, buckwheat, chickpeas, cress, fenugreek, lentils, mustard, and sunflower, as well as various grains, such as rye and wheat.

Some sprouting seeds are available in seed packets from nurseries and large garden centers, while others can be bought from health food shops. If you buy seeds to eat directly, get ones that are intended for eating, as those sold for sowing in the ground may have been treated with fungicides or pesticides.

There are a couple of quick and easy ways to grow sprouting seeds. Besides the seeds, they require only canning jars, muslin or cheesecloth, and rubber bands or

string; or flats, paper towels, and brown paper or black plastic film.

Most seeds will germinate at room temperature, and you can usually grow them in the kitchen on a windowsill. Some may need a few days in a warm spot to germinate, and some require exposure to light to achieve their full flavor. You can eat them when they have ¼-½ in (6-12 mm) tall sprouts or when they grow into small seedlings with one or more pairs of green leaves.

Whichever method you follow, first wash the seeds well and soak them overnight in lukewarm water. Then drain off the water, rinse the seeds thoroughly, and put them in the sprouting container. During the next few days rinse the seeds again, once or more often every day, depending

on the type and the dryness of the weather. Rinsing is essential to keep the seeds fresh and clean; otherwise they will deteriorate.

You can mix sprouts together. Some sprouts have a strong, spicy tang, such as cress and radish; use less of these in any mix — no more than a fourth of the total.

Sprouting in flats
This is the traditional method for growing mustard and cress. Put a thick layer of paper towels or a folded absorbent cloth, such as flannel, in a seed flat or wide, flat plastic container. Spread the seeds thickly and evenly on top, then press down lightly. Sprinkle thoroughly with lukewarm water, and cover with brown paper or black plastic film.

Keep the tray at a temperature of 50°-61°F (10°-16°C). Remove the cover when the seedlings are 1½ in (3.75 cm) high. Put the tray on a windowsill. Wait a few days for the seedlings to turn green and expand fully, keeping them moist at all times. Use scissors to cut the crop when the stems are about 2 in (5 cm) long, 11 to 14 days after sowing. Mustard and cress do not need daily rinsing.

Sprouting in canning jars
Growing seeds in a canning jar is a better choice when the seeds must be rinsed at least once a day.

You will need a 1 qt (1 L) canning jar, a square of muslin or a double layer of cheesecloth, and a rubber band or string. Put soaked and rinsed seeds into the jar, then cover the opening with the cloth, holding it in place with the rubber band or string. Lay the jar on its side in a bowl with the covered end pointing slightly downward to help drainage. Place the bowl in a dark but warm corner.

Rinse the seeds at least once daily by removing the cloth and

◄ **Mung beans** These easy-to-sprout beans have a nutty flavor and are rich in vitamins and amino acids. They are ready for use after three to five days.

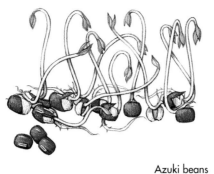

Azuki beans

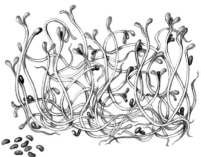

Alfalfa

▲ **Seeds for sprouting** Easy-sprouting seeds include (from top to bottom) fenugreek, sunflower, mung, alfalfa, soy, and azuki beans.

half-filling the jar with clean water. Replace the cloth, swill the seeds around gently in the water, then pour the water through the cloth cover. Another method is to empty the seeds into a sieve and rinse them under cold running water, allowing them to drain thoroughly before putting them back into the jar.

Repeat the rinsing regularly until the seedlings grow to a suitable length. If you want greener sprouts, leave the jar on a shady windowsill for a day or two. Keeping the seeds in the dark will produce whiter, crisper sprouts, while those kept in the light will be softer and greener. Empty the jar into a colander and rinse well before eating the sprouts.

It is nearly always best to grow small quantities of seeds and use them regularly. Growing little and often will ensure that the sprouts are always fresh. However, you can keep sprouts in the refrigerator for a few days. Put them in a bowl of water or in a plastic bag, and rinse them every day. Check for mold before eating.

What can go wrong
Seeds need heat and moisture if they are to germinate, but if conditions are too hot and humid, they can easily get moldy. Always use clean containers, and don't neglect regular rinsing. Seeds that become moldy or diseased will be discolored and quickly develop a sour smell.

SPROUTING SEEDS

Azuki beans
Grow in jars or flats. Rinse four times daily. Harvest after three to four days or when the crisp, sweet sprouts are 1 in (2.5 cm) long.

Alfalfa
Grow in jars. Rinse twice daily. Harvest after three to six days or when 1-2 in (2.5-5 cm) long.

Buckwheat
Grow in jars or flats. Rinse once daily. Harvest after two to three days or when the sprouts are ½ in (1.25 cm) long.

Chickpeas
Grow in jars. Rinse four to five times daily. Use after three to four days or when ½ in (1.25 cm) long.

Cress
Grow in flats. Moisten as needed. Harvest after 11 to 14 days or when 2 in (5 cm) long. Peppery.

Fenugreek
Grow in jars. Rinse once or twice daily. Use after four to seven days or when 3 in (7.5 cm) long. Spicy.

Lentils
Grow in jars. Rinse two or three times daily. Use after three or four days or when 1 in (2.5 cm) long.

Mung beans
Grow in jars or flats. Rinse three times daily. Harvest after four or five days or when they are 2-3 in (5-7.5 cm) long.

Mustard
Grow in flats. Moisten as needed. Ready in 8 to 10 days or when they are 2 in (5 cm) long. (Start three days later than cress.) Spicy.

Radish sprouts
Grow in jars. Rinse two or three times daily. Ready in three to five days. Hot and spicy.

Sunflower
Grow in jars. Rinse twice daily. Ready in two to three days or when they are ½ in (1.25 cm) long.

Wheat
Grow in jars. Rinse two or three times daily. Pick after two to five days or when ½ in (1.25 cm) long.

Mustard   Cress

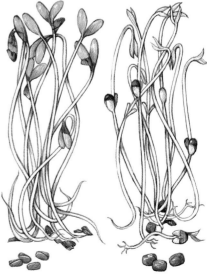

Fenugreek   Mung beans

SQUASH AND ZUCCHINI

**Zucchini, squash, and pumpkin
all belong to the cucumber family, with both
bush and vining cultivars available.**

Zucchinis are the most familiar members of this family and are known for producing huge crops. Summer squashes, such as yellow crooknecks and patty pans, are just as reliable and almost as prolific. All of these are excellent choices for a small garden.

Winter squashes and pumpkins are more expansive and require a larger plot (but some compact, bush-type cultivars are available). Bred to store well, they will keep for months in a cool, dry place.

SUMMER SQUASH AND ZUCCHINI

Virtually all of the summer squashes and zucchinis available are bush types, which are popular because the plants are very productive and need less space than old-fashioned vining cultivars.

Fans of heirloom vegetables, however, insist that there is no substitute for the flavor of some older cultivars, and they try to find space for these vining types.

In any case, both bush and vining cultivars have similar cultural requirements. Like all squashes, these heat-loving plants flourish in warm weather and on rich soil. In warm-weather regions, seed these plants directly into the garden in springtime as soon as all danger of frost passes and the soil is warm. Even in the North it is possible to sow seeds directly, though gardeners may want to secure an earlier harvest by starting seeds early indoors.

Preparing and planting

Summer squashes and zucchinis need a sunny spot and deep, rich soil. These conditions can be easily met in most gardens, though some gardeners like to sow the plants in an old pile of thoroughly rotted manure or compost. In general, two or three summer squash plants and four to six zucchini plants should be sufficient for the needs of most families.

Prepare the bed by digging a hole 10 in (25 cm) deep for each plant; set these planting holes 2 ft (60 cm) apart for bush cultivars

and 3-4 ft (90-120 cm) apart for vining ones.

Mix a bucketful of manure or well-rotted compost in with the soil in the bottom of the hole. Return the topsoil to the hole, and heap it into a ridge 2 in (5 cm) high for each plant. This will help to retain moisture around the young plants.

If you use a compost pile, mix in a little soil around each planting position (space these as for planting holes). You will have to pay extra attention to watering; compost piles tend to dry out faster than ordinary garden beds. Bush cultivars are better suited to growing in this way than vining cultivars.

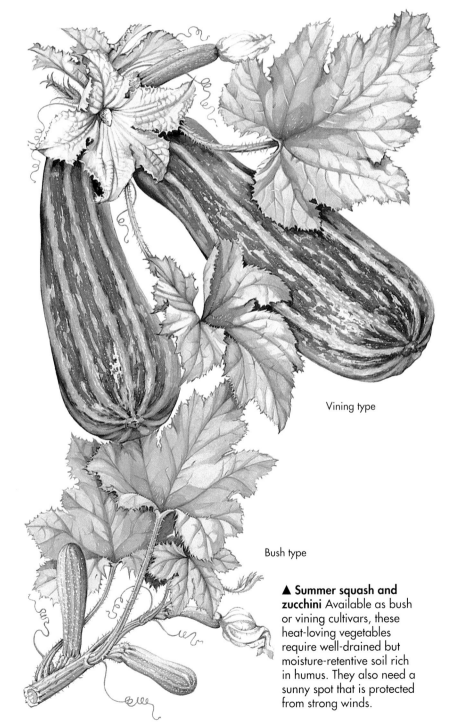

Vining type

Bush type

▲ **Summer squash and zucchini** Available as bush or vining cultivars, these heat-loving vegetables require well-drained but moisture-retentive soil rich in humus. They also need a sunny spot that is protected from strong winds.

To sow seeds directly, wait until a week after the last spring frost date, when the soil has warmed to 60°F (15.5°C), and sow two to three seeds per planting site, 1 in (2.5 cm) deep. After the seedlings emerge from the soil, snip off all but the strongest one.

In cold-climate areas with short growing seasons, sow the seeds indoors in peat pots filled with sterilized seed-starting mix a month before the last frost. Sow two seeds in each pot; snip off the weaker of the seedlings.

Keep the peat pots in a warm, sunny window. Harden them off and plant them out into the prepared sites a week after the last spring frost date, when the soil warms to 60°F (15.5°C). Space them as for direct-sown plants. Be sure to bury the rim of each pot just below the soil surface; otherwise the exposed rim will work like a wick, drawing moisture up out of the pot and causing the seedlings' roots to dehydrate.

A trick for northern gardeners is to cover the garden beds with a black plastic mulch right after preparing the planting holes. Anchor the plastic in place by burying its edges. The plastic traps solar energy and helps warm the soil. Sow seeds or plant seedlings through holes cut into the plastic.

Cultivation

When the first five leaves appear on each plant, spread a blanket of organic mulch around them (unless you have already covered the beds with black plastic). The mulch helps to control weeds and conserve the moisture in the soil.

If you added plenty of manure or organic mulch to the soil when preparing the beds, no further fertilization will be required. Otherwise, feed the plants when they reach a height of 6 in (15 cm) and again when they start flowering, sprinkling about 1 tablespoon of 5-10-10 fertilizer around the base of each plant.

Beware of overfertilizing, since that will encourage leaf growth at the expense of fruit production.

Keep the soil moist, but do not pour water over young plants; apply water directly to the soil with

▼ **Vining summer squash** Support is necessary for vining cultivars. Train them up tripods made of strong stakes lashed together at the top. Tie up the shoots as the heavy fruits develop.

▲ Pumpkin and winter squash
Available in a range of cultivars and shapes, these vegetables need lots of space.

a soaker hose or a drip irrigation system. Wetting the foliage encourages diseases such as mildew.

Squashes produce both male and female flowers on the same plant. The female flower has a swelling, an embryonic fruit, behind the bloom; the male has no swelling. Pollination is normally carried out by insects, which carry pollen between the male and the female flowers. In cold or wet weather, however, insects may fail to do the job, and the gardener must pollinate the flowers by hand to ensure the development of fruits. Each male flower will pollinate three female flowers.

Harvesting and storing
Harvest summer squashes and zucchinis while they are small and tender. Zucchinis, for example, are best under 4 in (10 cm) long. A good rule of thumb is to gently squeeze the squash; when ripe, you will feel the skin yield slightly. Always cut off squash and zucchini rather than pulling them off the vines.

Pests and diseases
Cucumber beetles may attack young plants and will continue to nibble on developing vines and fruits throughout the season. Use floating row covers to keep the beetles off the plants.

Squash bugs may attack the plants. Squash vine borers are a problem everywhere east of the Rocky Mountains. Wilting leaves and vines are a symptom of their

attack. Cut a slit along the affected vine until you locate the wormlike larva; destroy it and heap soil over the vine to allow it to reroot.

Squashes are susceptible to powdery mildew, mosiac virus, bacterial wilt, and downy mildew. Planting resistant cultivars and practicing crop rotation will help keep these diseases at bay.

WINTER SQUASH AND PUMPKIN
These come as bushy or vining cultivars in a range of colors and shapes. They have the same cultural requirements as summer squash but need a great deal of space. Two or three plants are adequate for most families.

Planning the crop
Winter squashes and pumpkins will flourish in a sunny spot if

sheltered from winds. They need rich, well-drained soil; the top of an old compost pile is ideal. Alternatively, dig planting holes 15 in (38 cm) square, spacing them 6 ft (1.8 m) apart. Fill them with well-rotted manure or with compost mixed with a handful of 5-10-10 fertilizer, then top them off with a couple of inches of topsoil.

Cultivation
In the South direct-sow outdoors after all danger of frost passes and the soil is warm. Plant six seeds in a circle 1 ft (30 cm) in diameter at each planting group, setting them 1 in (2.5 cm) deep. Thin to two or three plants per group after the seedlings emerge.

In the North start seeds indoors as for summer squash. After the danger of frost passes and the soil is warm, harden off and plant out the seedlings, two to three per planting group.

Pinch off the growing point of each vine after a few fruits begin to form to contain the growth of these sprawling plants.

Harvesting and storing
Harvest cultivars with small fruits as they mature during summer. Leave large-fruited cultivars on the stems until late fall; be sure to harvest them before the first frost. Store them in a cool (but frost-free), dry place.

Winter squashes have considerably more nutritional value and flavor than summer squashes and zucchinis. As a bonus, they are often highly decorative, in both their vining and bush cultivars.

Pest and diseases
These are the same as for summer squash and zucchini.

POLLINATING SQUASH

In cold or rainy weather, pollinate squash by hand. Detach a male flower (with no swelling behind the blossom); pick off the petals. Brush it against the open center of several female flowers.

HARVESTING SUMMER SQUASH

To harvest summer squash, cut the fruits when they are 10 in (25 cm) long; cut zucchini fruits when 4 in (10 cm) long. Do not pull the fruits from the stems.

CULTIVARS TO CHOOSE

Summer squash and zucchini

'Burpee's Golden Zucchini':
54 days from sowing to harvest;
bush type; golden yellow fruits.

'Gold Rush': 52 days; bush type;
shiny golden fruits; big, early crop.

'Long Green Striped': 55 days;
compact bush zucchini; dark green
fruits with pale green stripes.

'Peter Pan': 50 days; bush type;
light green patty-pan fruits.

'Yellow Crookneck': 65 days; large
bushy plant; bright yellow,
crooked-neck, warted fruits.

'Zucchini Select': 47 days; bush
type; slim green fruits; early crop.

Winter squash and pumpkin

'Atlantic Giant': 115 days; huge
orange-fleshed pumpkins.

'Blue Hubbard': 100 days; hard-
shell blue-gray fruits, sweet yellow
flesh; exceptional for storage.

'Butternut': 105 days; winter fruits
with firm flesh; sweet flavor.

'Chestnut': 105 days; dark green
fruits, thick deep orange flesh.

'Sweet Dumpling': 100 days;
small, round, green-striped fruits,
orange-yellow flesh.

'Table Ace': 85 days; semibush
plant; acorn-type fruits; black skin.

Zucchini 'Long Green Striped'

Squash 'Sweet Dumpling'

Zucchini 'Zucchini Select'

Zucchini 'Burpee's Golden Zucchini'

Squash 'Chestnut'

Pumpkin 'Atlantic Giant'

TOMATOES

The sweet, juicy flavor of homegrown tomatoes is incomparable. They bear from early summer until frost and even longer indoors.

Anyone disappointed by a tomato from a supermarket will find that this is a different vegetable when tasting one harvested from a backyard plot, picked ripe and at the peak of its flavor. No doubt that is why the tomato is the home gardener's favorite crop. Tomatoes are also easy to cultivate — given a sunny scrap of earth, almost anyone can grow tomatoes. You can choose from a fascinating diversity of fruits, ranging in size from tiny currant-size ones to huge beefsteak tomatoes that weigh 1 lb (450 kg) apiece. Tomatoes also vary in form, from pear-shaped plum tomatoes to stuffing tomatoes, which look like ripe bell peppers.

Most nurseries divide tomatoes into two basic groups: determinate and indeterminate. Determinate tomatoes grow only to a certain height, then their fruits ripen at approximately the same time. Indeterminate tomatoes produce their fruits a couple at a time throughout the season; they continue to grow until cut down by fall's cold weather.

Tomatoes are cold-sensitive plants. They may survive the cold weather of spring but can be stunted by the chilling and never develop properly in the following summer. They flourish in warm weather but may suffer from the heat of a Deep South midsummer.

Soil and site preparation
Tomatoes are greedy feeders and need rich, moisture-retentive soil. Deeply dig the soil where they are to be planted; add well-rotted manure or compost, one bucketful per sq yd/m. A week before planting, rake in a general-purpose fertilizer, such as 5-10-10, at a rate of 1-1¾ lb (450-800 g) for every 100 sq ft (9 sq m).

In general, plant tomatoes in a spot that receives full sun six to eight hours per day. In regions where summers are very hot, such as the Deep South or central southern states, light shade will benefit the plants and increase their yield. In the extreme South,

in southern Florida and the warmest parts of the Southwest, tomatoes do well if planted in fall and cultivated as a winter crop.

In areas of short or cool summers, cover the bed with a sheet of black plastic; bury the edges to anchor it. Later, plant through slits cut into the plastic mulch.

Sowing
Tomatoes are usually started indoors or in a greenhouse, then moved to the garden. You can buy young plants at the garden center, but you will have a greater range of cultivars at your disposal if you start the seeds yourself.

To do this, sow the seeds six to eight weeks before the last frost date. Plant them ¼ in (6 mm) deep and ½ in (12 mm) apart in flats filled with sterilized seed-starting mix, or sow the seeds in peat pots of the same mix, planting two or three per container.

▼ **Tomato cultivars** Numerous seed selections are available offering fruits that range from a large beefsteak size to miniature cherry tomatoes. Some are perfectly round, others squat or plum-shaped. Colors vary from yellow through gold and orange to bright scarlet; some are even striped.

'Celebrity'

'Yellow Canary'

'Burpee's Big Boy'

Moisten the flats or peat pots, and move them to a warm spot where the soil stays at 75°-85°F (24°-29.5°C); a shelf lit by low-hanging 4 ft (1.2 m) long fluorescent bulbs is ideal. The seedlings should emerge within a week.

Keep the seedlings in a bright spot where the temperature is no more than 70°F (21°C); either raise the fluorescent lights away from the seedlings or move the seedlings to a sunny windowsill.

When two true leaves form, prick out (or transfer) seedlings in flats into 3 in (7.5 cm) pots of potting soil. For those already in peat pots, snip off all but the strongest seedling in each pot.

Feed the plants once a week with a soluble fertilizer diluted to one-quarter strength. Harden off the seedlings and plant them out after all danger of frost is past. If tying the plants to stakes, set the seedlings 1½ ft (45 cm) apart in rows 2½ ft (75 cm) apart. If letting the vines sprawl, set them 3-4 ft (90-120 cm) apart all around. Mix 1 teaspoon of Epsom salts into the bottom of each hole, and plant the seedlings slightly deeper than when in the pot.

PRICKING AND PLANTING OUT

1 As soon as two true leaves fully develop, prick out the seedlings into 3 in (7.5 cm) pots of potting soil. Hold the seedlings gently by the leaves, and firm the potting soil around the stem.

2 When the plants are 6-8 in (15-20 cm) high and the danger of frost is past, plant them out in a prepared bed. Set them 1½ ft (45 cm) apart with the soil ball ½ in (12 mm) below ground level.

To tie up tomato vines, drive in sturdy, 6 ft (1.8 m) tall stakes at each planting position before you plant the seedlings.

Cultivation
Tomato vines sprawled over the ground produce a larger crop, but the fruits may be smaller, less perfect, and blemished where they touch the ground.

Most gardeners prefer to use some sort of support to keep the vines off the ground. One contraption is a "cage," a cylinder of coarse wire mesh set around the tomato plant at planting time and held in place with stakes. The vine can then climb the cage without needing to be tied.

In northern climates, where sun is at a premium, staking the tomatoes works better, since it allows more light to penetrate into the center of the plant. The key to success with stakes is to limit the tomato plant to one or two leaders (upright shoots) by pinching off the side shoots that sprout from the bases of the leaves. The leaders are tied in to the stake early on and secured again every 1 ft (30 cm) or so as they continue to grow upward.

Some gardeners also practice a system of trellising, tying the tomato vines up to horizontal lines of garden twine stretched between sturdy stakes. Two or three leaders are allowed to grow on each trellised plant.

Water tomato plants deeply during periods of dry weather, applying 1 in (2.5 cm) per week. Four or five weeks after planting out the seedlings, surround them with a thick blanket of organic mulch, such as straw or shredded

◄ **Grow bag cultivation** Tomatoes can be grown successfully in grow bags indoors or outside. If you want large fruits, grow two plants in each bag. For heavier yields of smaller fruits, grow four in each bag. It is important to water and feed the plants frequently.

TYING UP AND PINCHING

1 Tie each plant to a stake at intervals of 1 ft (30 cm). Wrap string twice around the stake, then loop it around the stem, allowing room for the stem to thicken.

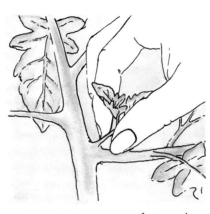

2 To concentrate energy on fruit production, remove all side shoots that appear on the leaf axils. Pinch them off or cut them off with a clean, sharp knife.

3 When greenhouse tomatoes form six trusses of fruits, pinch back the growing tips of the leaders; leave two leaves above the top truss.

leaves. Feed the vines when the first cluster of fruits forms and every three weeks thereafter. For each feeding, apply 1½ table-spoons of 5-10-10 to each plant, sprinkling the fertilizer around the base of the vines.

Greenhouse tomatoes

In cool-climate regions, you can greatly extend the tomato harvest by planting seedlings in a green-house in early spring; such a planting will produce fruits weeks earlier than an outdoor one. You can also start a second crop in midsummer to yield a harvest that continues on after the ar-rival of cold weather in the fall.

If you have a greenhouse with an open bed, you can plant the tomatoes right into the ground. However, tomato plants are vul-nerable to a number of soilborne diseases, and these can build up to a serious level in a greenhouse bed that is reused year after year. It is better to use large pots or bags of potting medium sold as "grow bags" (available from a garden center). Set the grow bags on the greenhouse floor, and plant the seedlings into them through a hole cut in the side of the bag.

Space greenhouse plants about 15-18 in (38-45 cm) apart in stag-gered rows 2 ft (60 cm) apart.

▶ **Greenhouse tomatoes** Grown in beds, bags, or pots, greenhouse tomatoes must be supported with stakes and the plants tied in loosely at 1 ft (30 cm) intervals.

Alternatively, tie string from the base of each plant to the greenhouse roof and twist the stem around it.

Cherry tomato 'Sweet 100'

Paste and sauce tomato 'Roma'

Early tomato 'Early Cascade'

For proper development of the plants and fruit set, it is essential to maintain warm temperatures in the greenhouse. Nighttime temperatures should not drop below 50°-55°F (10°-13°C).

Support greenhouse plants on stakes or trellises, training as for outdoor plants. To hasten ripening, pinch off the top of the stem when the plant forms six trusses, or clusters, of fruits. You can begin regular feedings with a dilute soluble fertilizer as soon as the first fruits appear.

Harvesting
For the best flavor, pick tomatoes when they are fully colored but still firm.

Pests and diseases
The most common pests of tomatoes are aphids, whiteflies, and spider mites. Biological control can be effective.

Tomatoes are also affected by various soilborne pests and diseases; the most common are verticillium wilt, fusarium wilt, and nematodes. When choosing cultivars, select those with the letters "V," "F," or "N" on the label; they indicate the cultivar is resistant to one (or more) of these pests.

CULTIVARS TO CHOOSE

Early

'Early Cascade': 55 days from transplanting to harvest; indeterminate vine; bears clusters of 7-9 medium-size bright red fruits.

'Early Girl': 54 days; V; productive indeterminate vine; large crop of 5 oz (140 g) red fruits.

'Oregon Spring': 60 days; V; hardy vine; red, globular, 6-7oz (170-200 g) fruits; ideal for northern gardens.

'Pixie': 55 days; determinate vine; big crop of small fruits; dwarf, good for container cultivation.

Midseason
'Better Boy': 70 days; VFN; indeterminate vine; 12-16 oz (340-450 g) fruits; excellent flavor.

'Celebrity': 70 days; VFN; stocky determinate plant; large crop of good-flavored, 8 oz (230 g) fruits.

Late
'Beefmaster': 80 days; VFN; vigorous indeterminate vine; large fruits, up to 2 lb (900 g).

'Burpee's Big Boy': 80 days; indeterminate vine; 12 oz (340 g) fruits; ideal for greenhouse.

Cherry tomatoes
'Gardener's Delight': 65 days; indeterminate vine; small red fruits.

'Sweet 100': 70 days; productive indeterminate vine; small, exceptionally sweet fruits.

'Tumbler': 49 days; small, bright red fruits; compact vine, ideal for container cultivation.

'Yellow Canary': 63 days; determinate plant; small golden fruits; suitable for container cultivation.

'Yellow Pear': 70 days; indeterminate vine; pear-shaped golden fruits; good meaty flavor.

Paste and sauce tomatoes
'Bellstar': 70 days; compact determinate plant; large, plum-type fruits, to 4-5 oz (115-140 g).

'Roma': 75 days; VF; determinate vine; plum-type red fruits with outstanding flavor; large crop.

Late tomato 'Beefmaster'

Cherry tomato 'Gardener's Delight'

Late tomato 'Burpee's Big Boy'

WATERCRESS

Tasty and nutritious, watercress will thrive in the vegetable garden if the soil is kept constantly moist with fresh, clean water.

Watercress grows along streams and in ditches at the edges of fields, but waterborne parasites and pollutants make wild watercress unsafe for consumption. However, with frequent watering, a healthy crop of watercress is easy to grow in the garden. The leaves have a delicious, distinctive mustardlike flavor and contain both iron and vitamin C.

Planning the crop
Choose a damp, slightly shady patch of the vegetable garden within easy reach of a hose.

Prepare the ground by digging a trench 9 in (23 cm) wide and 2 ft (60 cm) long. Mix a bucketful of moisture-holding organic matter, such as well-rotted manure or compost, with the soil in the bottom of the trench, smoothing it down to 3 in (7.5 cm) below the surrounding soil level. Fill in with topsoil when the time comes for sowing or planting in spring.

Cultivation
Sow watercress by sprinkling the seeds in the prepared trench from mid- to late spring. Water the soil thoroughly, or the seeds will not germinate. When the plants are big enough to handle, thin them to 6 in (15 cm) apart. For a fall crop, sow again in late summer.

Watercress will grow only in soil that is always damp. Keep the trench well watered, but take care not to wash away the plants.

Remove flower heads as they appear, otherwise they will reduce the plants' leaf growth.

In well-prepared soil, watercress plants should need no extra feeding. However, if the leaves are smaller toward the end of the season, encourage sturdier growth by applying a liquid fertilizer with a high nitrogen content.

Harvesting
Start picking watercress as soon as the plants are established. Regular harvesting encourages plants to grow a fresh supply of new stems. Take care, however, not to remove too many leaves in

the first few months after sowing, as this can weaken the plants.

Use watercress in sandwiches and as a garnish. It is also delicious when made into soup.

Pests and diseases
Homegrown watercress is usually free from pests.

UPLAND CRESS
Upland cress is also known as American cress. Though native to Europe, it grows wild in many parts of North America. It is very similar in appearance to watercress, but the leaves are smaller and have a less delicate flavor.

As few as six to eight plants will provide a constant supply of salad leaves during the summer months, as well as during winter.

Preparing the ground
Upland cress prefers a moist, shady spot. Prepare the ground by adding well-rotted manure or compost to the soil at the rate of one bucketful per sq yd/m. Or grow the cress in 7 in (18 cm) pots filled with potting soil.

Cultivation
Upland cress is hardy and able to overwinter, so successive sowing will give year-round supplies.

Sow the seeds ¼ in (6 mm) deep and 9 in (23 cm) apart in early spring for summer use. Water the

▲ **Watercress** The leaves can be eaten raw or cooked. To grow watercress in the vegetable garden, choose a damp, shady spot within easy reach of a water source.

prepared bed thoroughly before sowing. Three weeks later, thin seedlings to 8 in (20 cm) apart. Make successive sowings to prolong the harvest.

Keep the ground well watered, and mulch with well-rotted manure or compost.

For a winter harvest, sow in early fall in a cold frame. To harvest in early spring, sow and overwinter in a garden bed.

To grow in pots, sow three or four seeds in each container. Remove all but the strongest seedling when they are large enough to handle. Keep in partial shade, and water regularly.

Harvesting
You can take the first pickings about eight weeks after sowing. Pick the outer leaves, leaving the center to produce more. As the plants age, discard tougher, outer leaves and pick new, tender leaves growing from the center. Remove flower heads as they appear.

Pests and diseases
The pests most likely to occur are slugs and snails, which can be handpicked or trapped.

A–Z OF HERBS

**Culinary herbs are easy to grow,
rich in vitamins, and full of flavor, making all
other garden crops taste better, too.**

ANGELICA

Angelica *(Angelica archangelica)* makes a majestic display at the back of an herb garden or flower bed, especially since it can reach a height of 7-10 ft (2.1-3 m). A short-lived perennial or biennial, it is hardy in zones 4-9 but dies after it has produced seeds. However, if the flower stalks are cut off every year before the flowers develop, it can be kept alive for four or five years.

Thriving in damp meadows and on river banks, angelica is easy to grow, though it needs plenty of space.

The young, slightly bitter leaves can be boiled like spinach or added fresh to salads. The roots can be cooked like a vegetable and the seeds used as a substitute for juniper berries or to flavor liqueurs. Most commonly, the young stems and leafstalks are harvested before flowering and candied for decorating cakes and other confections.

Cultivation

Angelica prefers deep, rich, moist soil in a sunny or lightly shaded spot. Dig the soil thoroughly during the winter before sowing.

In late summer sow seeds in the prepared ground as soon as the new crop of seeds are available; angelica seeds lose their viability rapidly in storage. Sow the seeds ½ in (1.25 cm) deep in groups of three or four and 3 ft (90 cm) apart. As the seedlings develop, remove all but the strongest one in each group.

Alternatively, sow the seeds in a seedbed, and transplant the seedlings to their final site in late fall, before the taproot has become established.

In the first year angelica produces leaves but no stems. In the second or third year it shoots up a tall flower stem bearing clusters of greenish-white flowers in early summer. If the flowers are allowed to go to seed, the plant dies, though it self-sows freely.

Few pests trouble angelica.

▲ **Angelica** Young stems are candied for cake decoration and to sweeten acidic fruit desserts. Chopped leaves are added to salads, and the seeds are used in making liqueurs.

BASIL

Sweet basil *(Ocimum basilicum)* is grown for its pale green, highly aromatic leaves. Because this tender plant cannot withstand frost, it is sown annually. There are many different cultivars of sweet basil, but in general they reach a height of 2 ft (60 cm).

The young leaves of sweet basil have a pleasant spicy scent. Harvest the leaves at frequent intervals and use them fresh, torn into pieces rather than chopped. They do not dry well and are better preserved, either packed with a little salt in jars of olive oil or ground up with pine nuts, Parmesan cheese, and olive oil to make the Italian sauce *pesto*.

The purple-leaved cultivar 'Dark Opal' is highly decorative and suitable as a culinary herb.

◄ **Sweet basil** Popular as a flavoring for tomato dishes, basil is the main ingredient in pesto, a green sauce for salads, vegetables, fish, and pasta.

Cultivation

Basil needs a warm, sheltered site with well-drained, fertile soil and full sun or light shade. For early-maturing plants, sow seeds in early spring indoors. When large enough to handle, prick the seedlings out into flats of potting soil.

Harden off the plants in late spring, then plant them out in their final site when the soil warms to 65°F (18.5°C), setting them 2 ft (60 cm) apart. Water well until the plants are established. Basil seedlings can also be potted up and grown on a sunny windowsill. Feed such plants with a liquid fertilizer once a month.

You can sow basil seeds outside in late spring in their growing position. Thin the seedlings to 2 ft (60 cm) apart. Water well in dry weather. Pinch off flower buds to encourage bushy growth. For a continuous supply of fresh leaves, sow at two-week intervals.

Slugs can be a problem in wet summers.

BAY

▲ **Bay leaves** Strongly aromatic, bay leaves are used fresh or dried to flavor savory and sweet dishes.

Sweet bay *(Laurus nobilis)*, or bay laurel, is an evergreen shrub or small tree grown for its aromatic leaves. A native of the Mediterranean region, it flourishes in Southern California and is hardy only through zone 8. In the North cultivate it in a tub and move it indoors for the winter.

Bay can reach 20 ft (6 m) tall or more, but you can keep it to the desired shape and size by annual pruning, an essential practice if the tree is growing in a tub.

Bay trees are highly ornamental — clipped and trained cone-shaped or mop-headed specimens are sometimes available from nurseries and garden centers. They are expensive but long-lived as decorative specimen plants. As a free-growing shrub, bay is ideal for a sheltered mixed border.

Bay leaves are used fresh or dried to flavor fish dishes, stews, and casseroles, and they are an essential ingredient in a traditional bouquet garni.

Cultivation
Bay grows in ordinary garden soil in a sunny, sheltered spot. A loam-based potting mix is suitable for container-grown specimens. Move them indoors or to a cold but frost-free greenhouse for the winter north of zone 8.

Plant in early spring or mid-spring, and water well until the shrub is established. Prune in summer to maintain shape. Pick the leaves at any time of year.

To propagate, take heel cuttings in late summer or early fall. Root the cuttings in pots of peat mixed with coarse sand, and keep them in a cold frame or other protected spot over winter and the following summer; they often take up to six months to root. Water them just enough to prevent them from drying out. Grow the rooted cuttings on in a sheltered nursery bed for a couple of years.

Bay is generally disease free.

◀ **Bay tree** Often trained as standards and grown as specimen tub plants, bays can be clipped into topiary shapes. Trim to shape during summer.

BORAGE

Borage *(Borago officinalis)* is a hardy annual herb that is grown for its leaves. They have the cool taste of cucumber when crushed or bruised. In addition, borage is grown for its bright blue starlike flowers, which are added to salads and summer drinks. Borne in drooping clusters, the blossoms are attractive to bees. The plant grows 1½-3 ft (45-90 cm) tall.

Cultivation
Although borage tolerates a range of conditions, it does best in light, porous soil in a sunny spot. Sow the seeds in midspring, and thin the seedlings to at least 1 ft (30 cm) apart.

The seeds will germinate readily, and the seedlings will grow rapidly. The leaves are ready for use about eight weeks after sowing. They become covered with fine woolly leaves as they age, so you should harvest them while

they are still young. Use the leaves fresh and roughly chopped as additions to salads or iced drinks. Borage seeds itself freely, and once it is introduced to the garden, it perpetuates itself from self-sown seedlings.

Borage is disease free, but aphids may sometimes attack it.

◀ **Borage** The young leaves are used to flavor salads and drinks.

▼ **Borage flowers** The bright blue starry flowers can be candied and used for cake decoration. They can also be floated fresh in chilled wine.

CARAWAY

Caraway *(Carum carvi)* is a hardy biennial that in its first year produces feathery leaves and grows 8 in (20 cm) high. In its second year it sends up slender, branched stems 2-3 ft (60-90 cm) high.

Airy clusters of white or pink flowers are borne in late spring and early summer of the second year, followed by seed heads. The plants die after flowering.

Caraway is grown for its seeds. Their strong, distinctive, licorice-like flavor is ideal in breads, cakes, and gingerbreads. They facilitate digestion and are popular in German and Austrian cheeses and in cabbage and coleslaw.

The young green leaves can also be eaten, either fresh in salads or cooked in soups. They have a less pungent flavor than the seeds.

The young taproots, too, are edible and much used in eastern European cooking.

Cultivation
Caraway flourishes in fertile, well-drained soil in a sunny spot.

Sow the seeds in early fall in the South and in early spring in the North. When the seedlings are about 2 in (5 cm) high, thin them to at least 8 in (20 cm) apart; they do not transplant easily. Fall-sown seedlings will flower and set seed by the following summer.

The seeds begin to ripen in early summer to midsummer. Harvest the seed heads before the seeds turn brown and begin to burst open — the plants seed themselves freely, and self-sown seedlings could soon be all over the herb garden.

Cut the seed heads and hang them upside down enclosed in paper bags to dry in a cool place. When the seeds are thoroughly dry, clean them of chaff and stalks and store them in an airtight container until needed. You can use them whole or ground.

▶ **Caraway seeds** Popular in eastern European and Scandinavian cooking, the pungent dried seeds of caraway are used whole or ground to flavor bread, cakes, and cheese.

CHERVIL

▲ **Chervil** Remove the small white flowers that appear from early to late summer. The leaves have a delicate anise flavor.

Chervil *(Anthriscus cerefolium)* is an annual grown for its bright green feathery leaves; harvest them while young. The plant grows 1-1½ ft (30-45 cm) high.

Cultivation
Chervil grows in well-drained soil. Choose a sunny site in a cool climate, a partially shaded site in the South and Southwest.

Make successive sowings in the open between early spring and late summer. Sow the seeds ¼ in (6 mm) deep, and thin the seedlings to 1 ft (30 cm) apart.

Remove the flowering stems as soon as they appear. Six to eight weeks after sowing, pick the leaves and use them fresh in soups, salads, and egg dishes or for garnishing.

CHIVES

Chives *(Allium schoenoprasum)* are perennial plants (hardy to zone 2). Their grasslike leaves have a delicate onion flavor.

Cultivation

Chives grow in good garden soil in a sunny or semishaded spot.

It is easiest to buy young plants and set them 1 ft (30 cm) apart.

You can also raise chives from seeds sown in spring and transplanted a year later. They spread rapidly. Divide and replant established clumps every three years in early spring. To maintain a supply of leaves, remove the flower heads as they appear.

For fresh chives in winter, lift a clump in early fall, set it in a 4 in (10 cm) pot of potting soil, and place on a sunny windowsill.

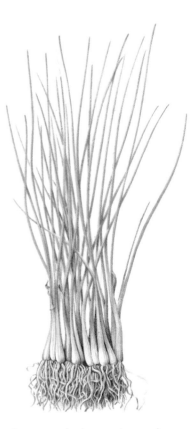

▲ **Chives** Cut the leaves close to the ground, and chop them into egg dishes, salads, and dressings.

◄ **Flowering chives** Remove these bright and cheerful flowers if you prefer a long harvest of leaves.

CORIANDER

Coriander *(Corinandrum sativum),* or cilantro, is a hardy annual grown for its parsleylike leaves and for its seeds. Use the leaves chopped and sprinkled over vegetables and salads, add them as flavoring to lamb and pork dishes, or use them as a garnish. The leaves do not dry well but will last if frozen.

Coriander seeds are sweetly aromatic and have a bittersweet flavor. They are commonly used in Indian dishes and are essential in curry spices. The seeds are also used in salsas, pickles, cakes, and cheese. Store seeds whole, then grind them as required.

Coriander will grow 1½-2 ft (45-60 cm) high as a slender, sparsely branched plant. It bears clusters of white or pale mauve flowers from early to late summer, followed by brown seeds.

◄ **Coriander** An ancient herb popular in a variety of cuisines, coriander is grown for its pleasantly aromatic leaves. Its flowers are followed by seeds, which are used dried in savory dishes and pickles.

Cultivation

Coriander grows in any good, well-drained soil and needs a sunny, sheltered spot.

Sow seeds outdoors ¼ in (6 mm) deep in early spring in the North and in late summer or fall where winters are mild. When large enough to handle, thin the seedlings to 4-6 in (10-15 cm) apart. About a dozen plants will provide enough leaves and seeds for the average household.

Begin to pick the leaves when the plants are 6 in (15 cm) high. The seeds are ready for harvesting when they become pale in color and smell pleasantly spicy.

Cut the plants at ground level, then hang them upside down to dry in a cool and airy place. Shake out the dry seeds and store them in an airtight container. The seeds can also be used for sowing the following spring; they remain viable and can be used for propagation for up to five years.

Coriander is easily grown in pots. Keep the plants staked, as they become top-heavy with the ripening seed heads.

DILL

Dill *(Anethum graveolens)*, a hardy annual that can reach 3 ft (90 cm) high, is grown for its delicate leaves and its seeds.

It thrives in any well-drained but moist soil in an open, sunny site. Sow seeds in early spring and again in late summer for a longer harvest. Thin the seedlings to 9 in (23 cm) apart.

Harvest the leaves fresh and use in sauces; with cucumbers, beets, and tomatoes; and as a garnish. You can freeze or dry the leaves, though they lose much of their aniseed flavor in drying.

The seed heads ripen in late summer and are used fresh or dry to flavor pickled cucumbers.

Avoid growing dill near fennel. The two cross-pollinate easily, and the resulting seedlings do not have the virtues of either parent.

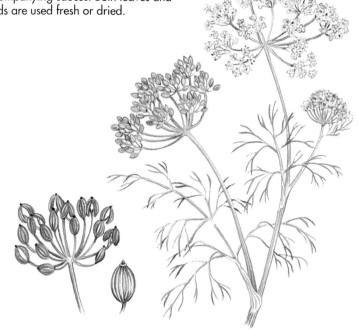

▶ **Dill** The pronounced anise flavor of dill goes particularly well with fish dishes and accompanying sauces. Both leaves and seeds are used fresh or dried.

FENNEL

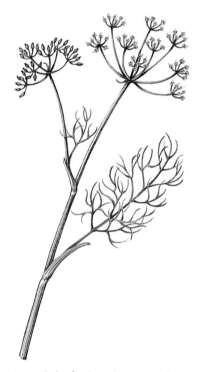

▲ **Fennel** The feathery leaves are best used fresh in fish and cheese dishes. Fennel seeds, much stronger in flavor, are used in pickles.

▶ **Decorative fennel** Bronze- and green-leaved fennels are highly ornamental. They are suitable for growing as foliage plants in borders. They may grow 5-8 ft (1.5-2.4 m) high. Both can be used for cooking, too.

Fennel *(Foeniculum vulgare)* is a tall, graceful perennial grown for the aniseed flavor of its leaves and seeds.

Cultivation

Fennel likes any well-drained soil in a sunny site.

Sow thinly in early spring for ripe seeds in early fall to midfall; if grown for leaves only, sow in mid- to late spring. Thin the seedlings to 1 ft (30 cm) apart.

Harvest the leaves from early summer onward, and deadhead unless seeds are wanted. Gather seed heads in early fall when they are pale brown; hang them upside down to dry in a cool, airy place. Store them in airtight containers.

Cut the tall stems back to ground level in late fall.

GARLIC

Garlic *(Allium sativum)* grows to 1-3 ft (30-90 cm) high and does well in temperate climates.

Garlic likes deep, rich, and moist but well-drained soil and full sun. In early spring or fall, plant cloves 6 in (15 cm) apart, pointed end upward and just covered by soil. Fall planting is best in northern gardens and in regions with very hot summers.

Remove flower stalks as they appear. Mulch fall-planted garlic with straw or hay for a northern winter. Dig the garlic at the end of summer. Leave it to dry thoroughly in a dry and shady site.

While usually pest free, garlic is sometimes affected by the same problems as onions (see p.130).

▲ **Garlic bulbs** Each bulb contains a dozen or so cloves (bulblets) with a papery covering. Fresh or cooked, they are used to flavor many dishes.

▶ **Harvesting garlic** Lift the bulbs carefully as the foliage dies down, easing them out with a fork. Dry the bulbs for a few days before storing them.

HORSERADISH

Horseradish *(Armoracia rusticana)*, a vigorous perennial, is easy to grow. Site it carefully; the taproot and branching side roots sucker freely and are difficult to eradicate. It is hardy to zone 5.

The sharp-tasting, fleshy white roots grow 1 ft (30 cm) long. The basal leaves are 2-3 ft (60-90 cm) high and die down in winter.

Cultivation

Horseradish prefers rich, moist soil in a sunny or partially shaded spot. Dig the plot deeply, and

◀ **Horseradish** A traditional accompaniment to roast beef, horseradish has the best flavor when freshly peeled and grated — to floods of tears by the cook.

work in plenty of compost the winter before planting.

Plant young root cuttings in early spring, spacing them 2 ft (60 cm) apart, with the thick upper part of each cutting 3-4 in (7.5-10 cm) below ground level. Leave the plants in the ground for at least two years before harvesting. Each year, in early summer, dig around the plants and rub out any side roots to ensure a single, well-formed taproot.

Dig up the roots in late summer, when they have the best flavor, or whenever required. You can store the roots over winter in damp sand in a dry and cool but frost-free place. If necessary, cut spare roots into 6 in (15 cm) pieces and plant out in spring.

Horseradish plants may be affected by leaf spot.

HYSSOP

Hyssop *(Hyssopus officinalis)*, an evergreen subshrub, is hardy to zone 3, growing 2 ft (60 cm) high and wide. From midsummer to fall it bears spikes of blue, pink, or white flowers. The foliage will release a pungent scent when bruised. Hyssop is often grown around herb beds and vegetable plots; it is said to discourage white cabbage butterflies.

Cultivation

Hyssop will grow best in any well-drained soil and in a warm, sunny location.

Plant in fall or spring, or sow seeds outdoors in late spring. When large enough to handle, thin the seedlings to 3 in (7.5 cm) apart. Transplant them to their permanent sites in fall or spring, setting them 1½ ft (45 cm) apart.

To encourage bushy growth in young plants, remove the tips of main shoots. Trim established plants back in early spring.

Pick hyssop leaves for use in salads in early summer.

▶ **Hyssop** This fragrant herb is now grown for decorative purposes. You can use its minty young leaves in salads.

LEMON BALM

▲ **Lemon balm** Traditionally used as a mild-flavored substitute for lemon, the leaves of lemon balm can also be floated on chilled drinks and used to flavor egg and chicken dishes.

▶ **Variegated lemon balm** Of limited culinary value, plants of this sort have mostly decorative appeal. Dried leaves can be added to potpourris.

Lemon balm *(Melissa officinalis),* a strongly aromatic perennial, is hardy to zone 5. It has a bushy habit with hairy, upright stems reaching 3 ft (90 cm) high. The lemon-scented leaves extend 3 in (7.5 cm) long and are pale green. Small flowers appear in midsummer. The golden-leaved cultivar 'Aurea' is particularly decorative.

Cultivation
Lemon balm seeds germinate slowly and irregularly. Sow them indoors in early spring. Or grow new plants from stem cuttings or from divisions in spring or fall.

Set the plants 1 ft (30 cm) apart in ordinary, even poor soil in a sunny spot. Keep them well watered in the first summer. In subsequent years cut the stems back to 6 in (15 cm) in early summer, encouraging new growth and a compact form. In severe winters cover with straw or evergreen boughs. Harvest throughout the summer for immediate use. Pick the leaves for drying before the plants begin to flower.

LEMON VERBENA

▲ **Lemon verbena** The leaves of this cold-sensitive shrub have a strong flavor and, used sparingly, add a pleasant flavor to fruit salads, jellies, and drinks. Use the young leaves only; the older ones tend to be tough.

Lemon verbena *(Aloysia triphylla,* syn. *Lippia citriodora)* is an aromatic shrub hardy to zone 8. It can grow 10 ft (3 m) high in ideal conditions but is rarely more than 5 ft (1.5 m) tall in the cooler parts of its range.

The woody, branching stems carry narrow, pointed leaves with a strong, persistent smell and flavor of lemon. Small white or pale mauve flowers appear from mid- to late summer but are not particularly decorative.

Cultivation
Plant in ordinary to poor, well-drained soil in late spring in a warm and sheltered site, ideally against a sunny wall.

Lemon verbena needs protection from strong winds and from hard freezes in zone 8. Cover the root area with a thick layer of straw to reduce the effects of frost. Alternatively, grow lemon verbena in a container and bring it indoors for the winter.

Container-grown plants need regular watering in summer but very little in winter. Prune in late winter to within 1 ft (30 cm) of the base, and pinch off the shoots during the growing season, thus preventing the shrub from becoming straggly.

Harvest the leaves as the flowers come into bloom, and store them in an airtight jar after drying. They keep their aroma for several years.

Propagate the plants by taking stem cuttings from half-mature wood before flowering. You can also grow plants from seeds sown indoors during early spring.

Lemon verbena has several uses. The leaves add flavor to salads, jellies, and iced drinks, but use them sparingly — they have a strong flavor.

Alternatively, dry the leaves quickly in a warm, dark place to retain the odor. Then use them in cushions and sachets to scent clothes and bed linen. A mixture of lemon verbena, lemon balm, and lemon-scented geranium imparts a fresh fragrance. Or use the dried leaves in herbal bath infusions. The essential oil extracted from lemon verbena is used in the manufacture of soaps, perfumes, and cosmetics.

Lemon verbena is attacked by spider mites and whiteflies.

LOVAGE

◀ **Lovage** A tall, aromatic herb, lovage is suitable for flavoring soups, salads, and stews. You can use young leaves as a vegetable or to add celery flavor to a dish. Dried seeds are good for adding flavor to soft cheeses and for sprinkling on rolls.

Lovage *(Levisticum officinale)*, a giant perennial, grows up to 7 ft (2.1 m) tall; it is hardy to zone 6. It has an erect stem with dark green, deeply divided leaves and bears small, pale green-yellow flowers between early summer and midsummer. The seeds are oblong and brown. All parts of the herb are edible and have a strong aroma and celerylike flavor.

One plant will provide ample fresh and dried leaves as well as seeds for culinary purposes. The stems can be candied and used like angelica.

Cultivation

Sow seeds in late summer in a seedbed or where the plants are to grow, preferably at the back of an herb border. For propagation, divide the fleshy roots in early spring; each piece should have a strong growth bud. The plants die down to the ground in winter.

Sow ripe seeds in rich, moist soil in sun or partial shade. When the seedlings are large enough to handle, thin them to 3 ft (90 cm) apart or transplant them to their permanent sites, leaving a similar space between the plants. In good soil lovage will last for many years. It is, however, invasive and self-seeds unless deadheaded.

During summer remove the early blooms, encouraging growth of young leaves. Use the leaves fresh or lightly blanched. They are excellent in vegetable soups or mixed salads and as flavoring for vinegars. In addition, they provide a celery flavor when added to meats and stews. When finely chopped, sprinkle them over young carrots and beans or add them to herb butters.

The dried leaves are used in potpourris. The seeds can be dried and sprinkled on rolls.

Lovage is generally free of pests and diseases but may occasionally be attacked by leaf miners or celery flies.

MARJORAM

Sweet marjoram *(Origanum majorana)* is a frost-sensitive perennial that is hardy only to zone 9 or 10; elsewhere it must be grown as an annual. It reaches a height of up to 1½ ft (45 cm) and produces sweetly scented gray-green leaves and tiny pink or white flowers in summer.

Wild marjoram *(Origanum vulgare)* is a perennial that is hardy to zone 3. Though native to Europe, it is can be found growing wild in North America. It is commonly called oregano — a name given to a number of herbs. Unlike sweet marjoram, the leaves of wild marjoram have little flavor and are not desirable for cooking.

▲ **Marjoram** Pinch off the flowers as soon as they develop to encourage the growth of fresh shoots and leaves.

Cultivation

Marjoram needs full sun and well-drained, fertile, preferably alkaline soil. Throughout most of the United States, sweet marjoram is treated as a half-hardy annual and sown indoors during early spring. Prick out the seedlings when they are large enough to handle into pots of potting soil. Harden off before planting out in late spring, and space 1 ft (30 cm) apart. To encourage the growth of shoots and leaves, pinch off the flowers as soon as they develop.

Begin harvesting leaves and stem tips when the plants are 4 in (10 cm) high. New stems and shoots will continue to grow. You can use leaves fresh, and they are suitable for drying or freezing.

▲ **Culinary marjoram** Sweet marjoram (left) is a small, ornamental plant. The aromatic leaves add flavor to meat, cheese, fish, pasta, egg, tomato, and potato dishes, and they are good in salad dressings. Pot marjoram *(Origanum onites,* right), a frost-sensitive perennial, has a similar, but sweeter, flavor.

MINT

Mints are hardy perennials, with a range of flavors and scents. Since antiquity, mint has been known and used as a flavoring. In European cooking it is often used to flavor jellies and candies, but it plays a much more important role in Middle Eastern and Indian cuisines. It is, of course, an essential ingredient of the mint julep, a cherished southern tradition.

Apple mint *(Mentha suaveolens,* often sold as *M. rotundifolia),* or round-leaved mint, is hardy to zone 4. It has the refreshing scent and flavor of apples and mint. It grows to 1½ ft (45 cm) tall with erect reddish stems. The toothed leaves are oblong or round, green above and white and velvety beneath. The flowers are white or pale mauve.

Bergamot mint *(Mentha × piperita* 'Citrata') smells like citrus. It grows 2 ft (60 cm) tall with dark green leaves, tinged with purple; the flowers are mauve.

Peppermint *(Mentha × piperita)* is hardy to zone 3. It, too, grows to a height of 2 ft (60 cm) but has green or black-green, oval, deeply indented leaves on green or reddish-purple stems. The small mauve or white flowers are sterile. It is used commercially to flavor candies and liqueurs.

Spearmint *(Mentha spicata)* is hardy to zone 3. This mint is used to flavor vegetables, cold sauces, chilled drinks, jellies, chutneys,

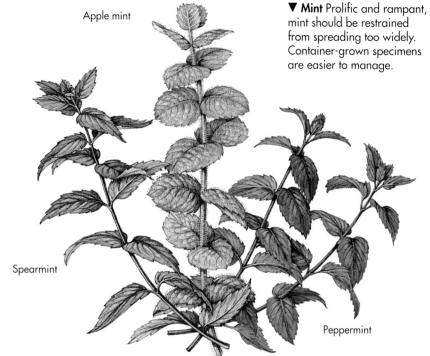

Apple mint

Spearmint

Peppermint

▼ **Mint** Prolific and rampant, mint should be restrained from spreading too widely. Container-grown specimens are easier to manage.

and tabbouleh. It grows up to 2 ft (60 cm) high, and it has bright green leaves with serrated edges. Mauve flowers are borne from late summer to early fall.

Another type is pineapple mint *(Mentha suaveolens* 'Variegata'). It has long stems and long, downy leaves, variegated with cream and apple green. Spicy ginger mint *(Mentha × gracilis)* has oval, pointed, shiny leaves, variegated with yellow and green.

Cultivation

Mint is all too easy to grow; it is difficult to keep it from spreading

through the garden. You can contain its underground runners with pieces of ceramic flue pipe sunken into the ground or by growing the plants in bottomless containers in the soil.

A deep, moist soil in a semi-shaded area is suitable, but mint grows almost anywhere, including damp, dark corners where few other plants survive.

Dig up the ground in late winter, adding a spadeful or two of well-rotted manure or compost.

Plant mint divisions in early spring, 2 in (5 cm) deep and 6 in (15 cm) apart. Three or four shoots will produce an ample supply for cooking and drying.

Mint requires little attention; simply water the soil thoroughly after planting. If necessary, divide the plants and replant in late fall. Mints die back each winter and reappear from early spring to midspring, producing leaves for picking any time from late spring until early fall. They can be dried but quickly lose their flavor.

For fresh supplies of mint throughout the winter, put young plants or pieces of root in pots of potting soil in midfall and keep them on a windowsill.

Mint may suffer from rust and powdery mildew.

◀ **Ginger mint** One of the more decorative forms, ginger mint bears pointed leaves, variegated yellow and green. Quick to spread, it makes an unusual ground cover.

PARSLEY

▲ **Parsley** This commonly grown herb is an essential ingredient in bouquet garni, and it adds flavor to a wide range of savory dishes.

Parsley *(Petroselinum crispum)* is a hardy biennial herb usually grown as an annual. This plant is rich in vitamins A and C. The foliage has a distinctive, mildly spicy flavor and is widely used for garnishing and for flavoring stocks, soups, sauces, dressings, and stuffings.

The leaves are triangular and deeply incised, and those of some cultivars are curled. Flat-leaved parsley has a more intense flavor.

Cultivation

Parsley thrives in well-drained, fertile soil in a sunny or partly shaded spot. Sow the seeds about ¼ in (6 mm) deep. They are slow to germinate in spring, and can take up to five weeks. To speed germination, soak the seeds for 24 hours in lukewarm water before planting. Keep the soil moist by sprinkling gently as necessary.

Thin the seedlings 3 in (7.5 cm) apart, later to 9 in (23 cm). Provide partial shade for seeds and seedlings sown in midsummer. In cold regions cover late-sown parsley with hot caps to encourage winter growth. Parsley is easily

▲ **Parsley cultivars** Curled and flat-leaved cultivars are available. They thrive in well-drained, fertile soil in a sunny or partly shaded spot.

grown in clay or plastic pots indoors on a sunny windowsill.

Dried leaves lose much of their flavor. Coarsely-chopped parsley leaves are better stored frozen in ice-cube trays. You can add these leaves to soups and sauces.

Parsley is sometimes attacked by cabbage loopers and carrot rust flies. Leaf spot can also be troublesome.

ROSEMARY

A strongly aromatic shrub, rosemary *(Rosmarinus officinalis)* can grow 7 ft (2.1 m) tall in sunny, dry climates, but 4 ft (1.2 m) is common. It does well outdoors in zone 8 and in protected spots in zone 7; farther north, grow it in a pot and bring it indoors in winter.

Fresh or dried leaves are used to season roasted meat, especially lamb, and strong-flavored fish.

The leaves are tough and narrow, dark green above and white and downy underneath. Blue or white flowers borne in small clusters in the leaf axils appear from midspring to early summer.

Cultivation

Rosemary likes any well-drained soil and a sunny site sheltered from cold winds. Set out young plants in mid- or late spring.

Old shrubs grow leggy; prune them back hard in midspring.

To increase rosemary, take cuttings of half-mature nonflowering shoots, 6-8 in (15-20 cm) long, between early summer and early fall. Root them in a cold frame or other protected spot. Transfer the

▲ **Rosemary** One of the oldest herbs — the herb of remembrance — rosemary is a handsome evergreen shrub for sunny and sheltered borders.

cuttings to 3 in (7.5 cm) pots of potting soil. Keep the pots in a cool, frost-free, and sunny spot; plant out in late spring. Alternatively, root hardwood cuttings, 6-8 in (15-20 cm) long, taken in early fall or midfall.

You can dry sprigs, but because the plant is an evergreen, fresh supplies will always be available.

▶ **Flowering rosemary** The blue or white flowers of rosemary open from mid- to late spring, but mature plants may produce a few flowers at almost any time of year. The narrow, dark green leaves are heavily scented, most strongly just before flowering.

SAGE

An attractive evergreen shrub, sage *(Salvia officinalis)* grows 2 ft (60 cm) or more tall and is hardy to zone 3. It has wrinkled, slightly hairy gray-green leaves with a strong, rather bitter taste and aroma. It is excellent for flavoring rich, fatty meats and stuffings.

There are many types of sage, but the most useful for cooking is common sage, which has lilac, purple, or blue flowers in summer. Purple sage *(Salvia officinalis* 'Purpurascens'), with deep purple leaves, is a highly decorative foliage plant and also suitable as a culinary herb.

Harvest the leaves as required. Their flavor is at its best in midsummer, just before the flowers appear. They can also be dried, though this seems unnecessary.

The aromatic pineapple sage *(Salvia rutilans)*, with bright scarlet flowers, is hardy only to zone 9 and will not survive a northern winter. It can be grown as a potted plant indoors. Use the leaves in potpourris.

Clary *(Salvia sclarea)* is a biennial (hardy to zone 5) that is usually grown as an annual. Like common sage you can use it as a culinary herb — fresh, dried, or frozen — to flavor soups and stews. It is decorative enough to grow in flower borders. It bears hairy, pungently aromatic leaves and, in late summer, tubular

▼ **Decorative sage** Culinary salvias are evergreen and retain their leaves through a mild winter. Even when top growth is killed by severe frosts, the plants often shoot up again from the base.

blue-white flowers with striking purple-blue bracts.

Cultivation

Sage thrives in a sunny, sheltered spot and needs rich, well-drained, slightly alkaline soil. Dig over the ground in late winter, mixing in well-rotted manure or compost.

Small plants are available, or in early spring sow seeds in pots and set on a windowsill or under fluorescent lights. Prick out the seedlings into flats; pot on into 3 in (7.5 cm) pots. Plant out seedlings when the roots fill the pots and all danger of frost is past; set them 1½-2 ft (45-60 cm) apart.

Or sow seeds directly in open ground in mid to late spring. Transplant seedlings to a nursery bed; move to the final site in fall.

Keep the growing plants well watered in dry spells; weed carefully to avoid damaging the roots. On established plants, cut the

▼ **Sage** The distinctive pungent flavor of sage blends well with rich, strong-flavored meat. You can add finely chopped leaves sparingly to cream cheese, omelettes, and casseroles.

Purple sage

Common sage

Golden sage

previous year's growth back in midsummer to keep the plants from becoming straggly. In cold areas mulch the plants with straw before the first frost.

Propagation

Sage becomes woody with age; renew it every four or five years. Take semihardwood cuttings in summer, and root them in a cold frame or other protected spot. Pot the cuttings on into individual pots; overwinter them in a cool but frost-free and sunny spot. In early spring pinch off the growing tips. Plant out in midspring.

Or take 6-8 in (15-20 cm) long hardwood cuttings in late summer or early fall, and root them in an outdoor nursery bed.

Pests and diseases

Spittlebugs attack leaves and shoots. Botrytis may occur; root-rot fungi occurs in heavy soils.

SALAD BURNET

Salad burnet *(Poterium sanguisorba)* is a perennial that is hardy to zone 3. Its young leaves have a fresh cucumber taste, pleasant in salads, soups, sauces, and iced drinks or as a garnish. Use young leaves, as old ones are bitter.

This plant is a European native that has escaped from gardens to grow wild in the northeastern United States. It grows up to 2 ft (60 cm) tall and is almost evergreen, the leaves staying green throughout winter if the cold is not severe.

Salad burnet thrives on light, well-drained soil in a sunny spot. It prefers an alkaline pH and dryish conditions; heavy soils and excess moisture cause crown rot.

Set out pot-grown plants in spring, or sow seeds outdoors in a seedbed in early spring or midspring. When seedlings are large enough to handle, transplant them to their permanent sites.

Keep the soil moist until the plants are established, and hoe often until they are large enough to smother weeds.

Pick and use the leaves while they are young and tender, before the plants flower. They are suitable for freezing. To encourage the formation of more leaves, cut back the stems of greenish and purple-red flowers as they develop. If allowed to flower and set seed, salad burnet spreads widely through self-sown seedlings.

To increase the plants, lift and divide established plants in early spring or midspring, replanting the divisions immediately.

Salad burnet is generally free of pests and diseases.

▲ **Salad burnet** Add finely chopped fresh leaves to soups, sauces, dressings, and salads. The cucumberlike taste goes well with egg, fish, and vegetable dishes.

SORREL

There are several types of sorrel, including garden sorrel. Known botanically as *Rumex acetosa*, this sorrel has sharp-tasting leaves with a high oxalic acid content, which can be poisonous if eaten in large amounts.

French sorrel *(Rumex scutatus,* syn. buckler-leaved sorrel), however, is less acidic and altogether more delicate in flavor. It is traditionally used in sorrel soup and in the green sauces served with roast pork and goose.

The similarity in common names has led to some confusion of the two sorrels, but the two are different in appearance.

Garden sorrel in flower grows to 1-2 ft (30-60 cm) high. It has long, narrow, arrowhead-shaped leaves with downward-pointing lobes and branched stems with small green-and-red flowers in erect spikes.

French sorrel in flower reaches 1½ ft (45 cm) high. It has small, broad, and bright green arrowhead-shaped leaves, and its tiny green flowers with red tints are borne in loose spikes.

Sorrels are perennial, and can be left to grow in the same spot for several years. *Rumex acetosa* is hardy to zone 3; *R. scutatus* to zone 6. They do well in any well-drained soil, particularly if it is acid. Garden sorrel tolerates partial shade and likes a moist soil;

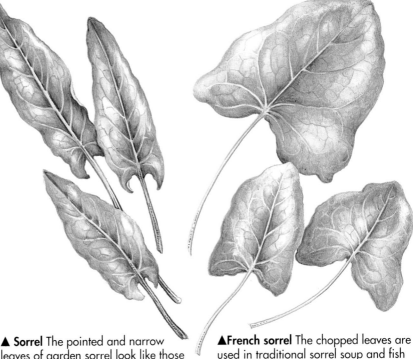

▲ **Sorrel** The pointed and narrow leaves of garden sorrel look like those of a small dock; they are one of the first green growths of spring.

▲**French sorrel** The chopped leaves are used in traditional sorrel soup and fish stuffings. As a purée, eat them like spinach or add to omelettes.

French sorrel is better in sun and prefers dryish soil.

To prepare a bed, dig thoroughly in late winter and add well-rotted compost. Sow seeds in midspring, and thin the seedlings to 1-2 in (2.5-5 cm) apart.

Set the plants out in permanent positions in mid- to late spring, 1-1½ ft (30-45 cm) apart.

Pick garden sorrel leaves when young, as old leaves are tough and acidic. If picked when no more than 3-4 in (7.5-10 cm) long, garden sorrel will have a pleasant lemony taste. French sorrel can be picked at any time. Cut flowering stems down to the base before they have developed to encourage the growth of leaves.

To increase stock, divide and replant mature plants every three to five years in spring or fall; both will self-seed if allowed to flower.

SUMMER AND WINTER SAVORY

Two types of savory are grown for their small, peppery, aromatic leaves, which are used in stuffings or with legumes, such as peas and beans. Summer savory *(Satureja hortensis)* is a bushy annual and has the sweeter flavor, reminiscent of thyme but more bitter. Winter savory *(Satureja montana)* is a perennial or evergreen subshrub (hardy to zone 6). The leaves of winter savory can be picked year-round and, like those of summer savory, are suitable for drying.

Cultivation
Both types grow well in a sunny spot in ordinary well-drained soil.

Sow summer savory seeds in midspring. When the seedlings are 2 in (5 cm) high, thin them to 6-9 in (15-23 cm) apart. Keep the plants watered in dry weather.

Pinch back the growing tips to encourage bushiness.

Winter savory is slow to germinate and is often started from rooted cuttings set 1 ft (30 cm) apart in early spring. Because it becomes woody with age, replace it every few years with new stock. Prune it back in spring.

Because old leaves often have a slightly bitter flavor, pick fresh young leaves and shoots as needed. Use them to flavor peas and beans in the same way as mint. Chopped, use the leaves to season sauces, meat stuffings, and bouquets garnis.

Savory is pungent — use it sparingly. The leaves dry well, losing little flavor. Pick the shoots of summer savory for drying in summer before flowers appear.

Savory is generally free of pests and diseases.

Winter savory

Summer savory

SWEET CICELY

Pleasantly scented and decorative, sweet cicely *(Myrrhis odorata)* is not an herb for the window box or small herb garden, as this long-lived perennial will in time reach 3-5 ft (90-150 cm) in height and spread. It is hardy to zone 5.

Also known as myrrh, sweet cicely has a sweet aniselike fragrance and taste in all its parts. In the past the long taproot was boiled and served sliced, dressed

▲ **Sweet cicely** Also known as myrrh, this plant has delicate fernlike leaves, which are used to temper the acidity of tart fruits. Ripe seeds can be included in fruit chutneys.

with vinegar, and the green seeds were used in salad dressings. Today, sweet cicely is often grown as an ornamental border plant, although the leaves are good for adding a sweet flavor to stewed fruits. If you add a chopped frond or two to stewed rhubarb or tart plums and apples, you won't need as much sugar. Unlike most other herbs, flowering does not impair the flavor of the leaves.

The seeds share the aniseed flavor of the leaves. They ripen to a glossy black color and are used to add flavor to fruit chutney.

Cultivation
Sweet cicely grows well in most conditions but does best in moist, acid soil and a shady spot. Set container-grown plants out in spring, 2 ft (60 cm) apart.

Alternatively, sow seeds in their permanent site in fall. For them to break dormancy and germinate, the seeds must be subjected to repeated freezing and thawing. You can also mix the seeds with moist peat moss and refrigerate them at 40°F (4.5°C) for 30 to 60 days before sowing in early spring.

Keep the plants well watered in hot weather, and pick leaves often to encourage more to appear.

The plant will die down in fall but it will start to grow again early in spring.

Sweet cicely

Sweet cicely plants will self-seed freely, so it is easy enough to use seedlings for increasing your stock. Alternatively, take root cuttings from the plants in fall and overwinter them in a cool but protected spot, such as a cold frame; or divide and replant the roots in spring or fall.

Sweet cicely is generally free of pests and diseases.

TARRAGON

Tarragon

Tarragon is a perennial that is hardy through zone 6. The sweetly aromatic leaves add flavor to fish and chicken dishes, sauces, salad dressings, and vinegars.

Easy to grow, tarragon needs little attention. For culinary use be sure to choose the right type.

French tarragon *(Artemisia dracunculus sativa)* has smooth, dark green leaves and a superior flavor to Russian tarragon *(Artemisia dracunculoides)*, which is a fresher green with rougher leaves. Not all garden centers distinguish between the two, so take care when buying. French tarragon has a strong, sweet smell; test by crushing a leaf between your fingers. Packaged seeds are usually Russian tarragon.

Cultivation

Tarragon thrives in a sunny spot in any well-drained soil. If your soil is heavy, dig in compost or manure at the rate of one bucket per sq yd/m in the fall before planting.

Tarragon grows 2 ft (60 cm) or more tall and quickly spreads to clumps from underground runners. The French type rarely flowers and does not set seed.

Buy container-grown plants and set out in permanent sites in fall or early spring. Keep them well watered during dry spells.

Once established, tarragon survives for years. The plants retain their flavor best if lifted and divided every three years. Lift in early spring or midspring; pull the underground runners apart. Replant the divisions immediately, setting them 15 in (38 cm) apart. In northern gardens protect tarragon through the winter with evergreen boughs laid down after the ground freezes.

Pick fresh leaves from summer until fall. Sprigs can be dried or frozen, but they have less flavor than fresh tarragon.

THYME

Though from the Mediterranean region, thyme has proved cold hardy and adaptable, escaping from gardens to thrive on poor and sandy soils up into New England (through zone 5). There are several species, and they vary in fragrance. In general they form hardy evergreen shrubs with tiny leaves that have a distinctive, slightly sweet, spicy flavor.

Both common thyme *(Thymus vulgaris)* and the citrus-scented lemon thyme *(Thymus × citriodorus)* grow 8 in (20 cm) high and 1 ft (30 cm) wide. The tiny flowers are lilac or purple in color. Lemon thyme has larger, more rounded leaves and comes into flower as ordinary thyme finishes. Bees love them both.

Thyme is an essential ingredient in bouquet garni, and its highly aromatic leaves are used to flavor soups, stews, sauces, salads, and baked, grilled, and roasted meat and fish. Commercially, thyme extracts can be found in antiseptics, soaps, and liqueurs. Lemon thyme is also used in custards and stewed fruits; dried, it goes into potpourris.

Cultivation

Thyme thrives in full sun in light, well-drained soil. Plants can be

Lemon thyme

Common thyme

grown from seeds, though germination is slow.

Sow seeds indoors in early spring. When the seedlings are large enough to handle, prick them out into 2 in (5 cm) pots, and grow on for one or two years before planting out.

It is quicker to start with purchased plants or to raise plants from cuttings of side shoots with a heel taken in midsummer. Root the cuttings in a shaded, cool spot. Pot up the rooted cuttings, then plant out in early fall.

Alternatively, divide and replant the roots of established plants in spring. Thyme roots naturally from layers where they touch the soil.

Pick sprigs of leaves as needed. Because thyme is an evergreen, there is little point in drying or freezing the leaves.

▲ **Aromatic thyme** One of the main herbs in a bouquet garni and much used in cooking, thyme is delightful as a carpeting plant or in between paving.

INDEX

Plant Hardiness Zone Map

Selecting plants suitable for your climate is half the secret to successful gardening. The U. S. Department of Agriculture (USDA) has created a plant hardiness zone map as a guide. Each zone is based on an average minimum winter temperature. Most nurseries and mail-order companies have adopted this map and indicate zones for their plants. Once you identify the zone you live in, buy only plants that are recommended for that zone. Local conditions, such as a garden near a pond or in a higher mountainous elevation, can affect the climate and the zone. In such cases, contact your county Cooperative Extension Service for assistance in adapting the map to your garden.

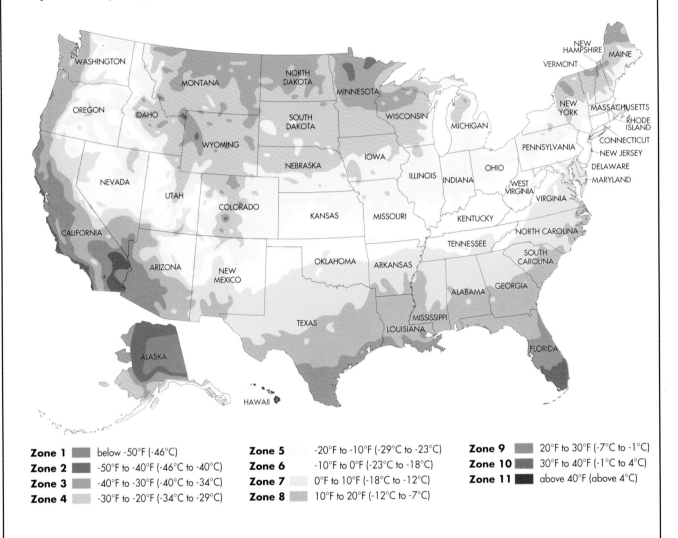

Zone 1 below -50°F (-46°C)
Zone 2 -50°F to -40°F (-46°C to -40°C)
Zone 3 -40°F to -30°F (-40°C to -34°C)
Zone 4 -30°F to -20°F (-34°C to -29°C)
Zone 5 -20°F to -10°F (-29°C to -23°C)
Zone 6 -10°F to 0°F (-23°C to -18°C)
Zone 7 0°F to 10°F (-18°C to -12°C)
Zone 8 10°F to 20°F (-12°C to -7°C)
Zone 9 20°F to 30°F (-7°C to -1°C)
Zone 10 30°F to 40°F (-1°C to 4°C)
Zone 11 above 40°F (above 4°C)

ACKNOWLEDGMENTS

Photo credits
A-Z Botanical Collection Ltd 36(br); Bernard Alfieri 127; Heather Angel 162(b); Biofotos 23, 126; Pat Brindley 79(br), 95(tr), 121, 125(bl); Brian Carter 164; Walter Chandoha 29(br), 33(tl,br), 57, 140, 147(tr), 159(tc,tr); Eric Crichton 26, 31, 90(c), 93(t), 97(t), 101(t,b), 131(b), 145(bc), 169, 171, 173, 174; Eaglemoss (Graham Rae), front cover; Thomas E. Eltzroth 29(bl), 33(tr,bl), 37(b), 71(b), 99(tl,bl); Derek Fell 19, 24, 37(c), 56, 62(t), 71(tr), 99(tr), 143, 159(bl); Mr Fothergill's Seeds Ltd 95(cr); Brian Furner Horticultural Pictures (Marion Furner) 78, 95(tl), 111(cl,b), 136(t), 147(tl,cl), 155(cr), 160; Garden Picture Library (Geoff Dann) 2-3, (Michael Howes) 131(cl); Rob Herwig 85(c), 109(r); Marijke Heuff 68(t), 162(t); Neil Holmes 8; Lamontagne 6, 20-21, 44, 72, 81, 155(br); 170; S & O Mathews 4-5, 131(c); James McInnis 155 (tr,bl); Ken Muir 68(b), 70(b); Natural Image (P Wilson) 49; Clive Nichols, back cover; Photos Horticultural 16, 30, 37(t), 38, 45, 46, 51 ,53, 59, 69, 70(t), 71(tl), 74, 77, 79(bl), 83, 85(br), 86-87, 88(bl), 90(b), 123(br), 125(t), 131(cr), 136(b), 150, 155(tl), 157, 158, 159(bc,br), 165, 167, 168;

Richard Shiell 25; Harry Smith Collection 18, 35, 40, 61, 63, 65, 67, 85(bl), 88(br), 93(c,b), 98, 99(br), 101(c), 104, 105, 107(tl), 109(l), 111(cr), 116, 122, 123(bl), 125(bc,br), 132, 136(c), 139(t), 141, 142, 145(bl,br), 151, 153, 155(cl), 159(tl); Suttons/Dobies Group, Hele Road, Torquay 84, 107(cl), 139(cr,bl); Michael Warren 163(b); Elizabeth Whiting Associates 144, 145(t).

Illustrators
David Ashby 48(b), 49; Elisabeth Dowle 12-15, 47, 48(t), 58(r), 64(t), 91-92, 94(t), 98, 114(b), 115(b), 119, 126-127, 138(t), 148, 163(t), 164(b), 165, 167(b), 171, 172, 173(b); Will Giles 69(tl,tr), 70; Christine Hart-Davies 9, 10-11, 27, 41-42, 43(tr,cr), 50(br), 82(tr), 100(bl), 118(b); Nigel Hawtin 23, 32, 43(bl,insets/r), 50(bl), 60-62, 66-67, 110(b), 135, 137(t); John Hutchinson 167(t); Dee Mclean 75-76; Reader's Digest 1, 36, 44, 46, 50, 54, 58(l), 71, 96(t), 97(b), 102(t), 107, 114(t), 117, 122, 132-133, 134, 137(b), 146, 149, 151, 160, 169, 170, (David Baxter) 52(t), 112, (Leonora Box) 89(t), 120, 144, (Paul Cox) 162(b), (Shirley Ellis) 108(tr), 110(t), 128, 130(tr), 161(b), 162(t), 163(b), 166(t), 168, (Colin Emberson) 20, 22, 26, 28(t), 34(t), 78, 100(r), 104, 115(t),

116, 118(r), 152, 156, 161(t), 166(c), (Donald Myall) 164(t), 166(b), (Basil Smith) 86, 154(t), (Kathleen Smith) 173(t), 174, (Norman Weaver) 124; Basil Smith 84; Claire Wright 17-18, 21, 28(b), 29, 34(b), 51, 52(b), 53, 55, 64(b), 80-81, 82(bl), 83, 87, 89(b), 94(b), 96(b), 102(b), 103, 105-106, 108(bl), 113, 121, 123, 129, 130(bl), 138(b), 140(t), 141, 154(b), 157-158.

Index compiled by Sidney Wolfe Cohen.

Reader's Digest Production
Assistant Production Supervisor: Mike Gallo
Electronic Prepress Support: Karen Goldsmith
Quality Control Manager: Ann Kennedy Harris
Assistant Production Manager: Dexter Street

Book Production Director: Ken Gillett
Prepress Manager: Garry Hansen
Book Production Manager: Joe Leeker
U.S. Prepress Manager: Mark P. Merritt